Taxing Artificial Intelligence

Taxing Artificial Intelligence

Xavier Oberson

Professor of Law, University of Geneva, Switzerland

Edward Elgar
PUBLISHING

Cheltenham, UK • Northampton, MA, USA

Published by
Edward Elgar Publishing Limited
The Lypiatts
15 Lansdown Road
Cheltenham
Glos GL50 2JA
UK

Edward Elgar Publishing, Inc.
William Pratt House
9 Dewey Court
Northampton
Massachusetts 01060
USA

A catalogue record for this book
is available from the British Library

Library of Congress Control Number: 2023952677

This book is available electronically in the **Elgar**online
Law subject collection
http://dx.doi.org/10.4337/9781035307555

ISBN 978 1 0353 0754 8 (cased)
ISBN 978 1 0353 0755 5 (eBook)

Printed and bound by CPI Group (UK) Ltd, Croydon, CR0 4YY

Contents

Preface

In early 2016, I started to investigate the possibility of taxing artificial intelligence (AI) in general, and robots in particular, aiming at finding a viable solution to the situation in which, as a consequence of disruption in the economy, numerous human workers could lose their jobs and may not find, in sufficient time, a new or satisfactory place to work.

As a result of this research, I published numerous articles and, in October 2016, in a provocative ironic statement in *Le Temps*, a Swiss newspaper, I suggested that: "Maybe, one day, the robots might refuse to pay their taxes!" As a follow-up, on February 2017, at the opening of the academic semester at Geneva University, I raised the question of the feasibility of a tax on robots or their usage.

In parallel, as of 2016, the EU Parliament has also initiated studies in relation to the fascinating issue of granting a legal personality to robots. On 16 February 2017, the EU Parliament finally rejected this idea, as well as a recommendation in favor of implementing a tax on the use of robots. The next day, Bill Gates publicly announced that he was in favor of taxing robots. This issue, in the meantime, has been debated worldwide, provoking highly controversial opinions.

Following these developments, I published in 2019 a first edition of this book, under the title *Taxing Robots*. In the meantime, the world situation has evolved. While, at the beginning, the idea of levying some form of taxes on robots or their use received mostly rather negative, if not mocking comments, it is nowadays analyzed everywhere and some first legislative proposals have emerged. Indeed, AI has now entered deeply into our lives and is used in all aspects of the economy. The analysis of its impact, in particular on labor, has become more important than ever. Not only is the fear of disappearing jobs growing, or at least the fear of a total transformation of labor, but inequalities in the distribution of wealth is also a matter of rising concern.

This new edition thus considers the new major developments that have occurred, due to the wide use of AI. The scope of the analysis has been broadened to cover not only robots, which tend nowadays to be defined as machines implementing AI, but also to include more generally all AI systems. The general outline and purpose of the first edition have, however, been maintained. The book intends to show how and to what extent a tax on AI, or on the use of AI, could be justified and implemented, both from an economic and legal standpoint. It starts by describing how the use of AI by companies is already subject to tax under current law, either under profit or value added taxes, and then goes further by advocating new and sometimes challenging alternatives of models of taxation, either of the use of AI or, more revolutionary, of AI as such. This new approach would thus argue, under specific conditions, that an AI system could in the future be recognized as a new form of taxpayer required to compute and levy tax on its transactions or income streams. Recent business developments in the digital economy, such as the importance of platforms, or the value of data, have also been taken into account and may, to some extent, represent interesting blueprints for the design of a future taxation of AI. In our view, however, the reform proposals, designed at the OECD level within the Inclusive Framework, such as the Two-pillar solution, are interesting but do not sufficiently address the growing importance of AI in the value creation process and as a potential tax base.

On a more personal side, this book is also the result of practicing over the years with an electric guitar in various bands and recording studios and the increasing use of technology in this area. In the past, musicians or composers, such as Frank Zappa, Brian Eno or Joe Satriani, to name just a few, have made extensive use of advanced technologies in order to produce, compose and play sophisticated and beautiful music. There is no reason why the disruption caused by technological development, notably by AI, could not be addressed in a harmonious way by new forms of taxation.

We are just at the beginning of the development of AI and robotics. The fourth industrial revolution and the corresponding technological progress will lead to new forms of collaboration between workers and machines and major changes in the labor market. The artists have already shown some prospective forms of such new combinations. We also need to analyze the potential impact of the development of AI and robots in our society from legal and tax standpoints. Should human labor or taxable activities disappear or drastically decrease or change, the tax system would need to adapt. As the discussion on the proper system of taxation of the digital economy demonstrates, it is controversial and difficult to reach a consensus on major cross-border international taxation issues. This is why we need to act now and start discussing and analyzing in detail the possibilities and impact of the modalities of taxation of AI or the use of AI.

We should, however, act quickly while we are still in a position to keep some control and understanding of the proper activities of AI. As taxpayers, AI systems might develop surprising behaviors if we do not anticipate this change.

This book is also the result of numerous discussions, analysis and the help of many people who have contributed to the process of finalizing this work and to whom I would like to express my gratitude, notably, to Prof. Yves Flückiger,

Prof. Jeffrey Owens, Prof. Alara Efsun Yazicioglu, Mohammed Bahwan, Pascale Fontana and Agnès Mermoud. My wife, Laure Mi Hyun Croset, deserves a very special thanks for her presence and support.

Geneva, 16 September 2023

Abbreviations

AAI	Autonomous artificial intelligence
AI	Artificial intelligence
AITU	AI taxable unit
Archives	Archives de droit fiscal Suisse (ASA) (periodical)
ATF	"Arrêt du Tribunal federal"
B2B	Business to business
B2C	Business to consumers
BEAT	Base erosion anti abuse tax (United States)
BEPS	Base erosion and profit shifting
CA	Competent authority
CCCTB	Common Consolidated Corporate Tax Base
CDFI	Cahiers de Droit Fiscal International
DAO	Decentralized Autonomous Organizations
DoJ	United States Department of Justice
DPD	Data Protection Directive
DPT	Diverted profit tax
DST	Digital services tax
DTC	Double Taxation Convention
DTT	Double Taxation Treaty
EATLP	European Association of Tax Law Professors
ECHR	European Convention on Human Rights
ECtHR	European Court of Human Rights
ECJ	European Court of Justice
ECOFIN	Economic and Financial Affairs Council
ET	European taxation (periodical)
EU	European Union
FAC	Federal Administrative Court

FATCA	Foreign Account Tax Compliance Act
FE	Fixed establishment
FHTP	Forum on Harmful Tax Practices
FStR	IFF Forum für Steuerrecht (periodical)
G20	Group of twenty
GDPR	General Data Protection Regulation (EU)
GMI	Guaranteed minimum income
HMRC	His Majesty's Revenue & Customs (United Kingdom)
IAS	International Accounting Standards
IASB	International Accounting Standards Board
IBFD	International Bureau of Fiscal Documentation
IFA	International Fiscal Association
IFRS	International Financial Reporting Standards
Intertax	International Taxation (periodical)
IP	Internet Protocol
IRC	Internal Revenue Code (United States)
IRS	Internal Revenue Service (United States)
LLM	Large language model
MLI	Multilateral Convention to Implement Tax Treaty Related Measures to prevent BEPS
MNE	Multinational enterprises
MoU	Memorandum of Understanding
OECD	Organisation for Economic Co-operation and Development
OECD Model	OECD Model Double Taxation Convention on Income and on Capital
OJ	Official Journal of the EU
PE	Permanent establishment
TFEU	Treaty on the Functioning of the EU
TIN	Taxpayer identification number
TNI	Tax Notes International (periodical)
UBI	Universal basic income
UN	United Nations
UN Model	UN Model Double Taxation Convention on Income and on Capital

VAT	Value added tax
VATL	Federal Law on VAT (Switzerland)
WEF	World Economic Forum
WTO	World Trade Organization

1. General introduction to *Taxing Artificial Intelligence*

The development of AI, and robots in particular, is on the way to modifying completely our society, our economy and our lives. As the EU Parliament, in its report of 16 February 2017, describes this development:

> [...] humankind stands on the threshold of an era when ever more sophisticated robots, bots, androids and other manifestations of artificial intelligence (AI) seem to be poised to unleash a new industrial revolution, which is likely to leave no stratum of society untouched [...].[1]

This process is also part of the fourth industrial revolution[2] which will have tremendous consequences on all sectors of the economy. In particular, the potential impact of the widespread use of AI and robots on human jobs is subject to a controversial forecast. In addition, the growing use of robotics in everyday life raises new legal and ethical issues. As a consequence, the debate has started over the possible introduction of a legal personality to some form of AI or robots. Thus, notably in view of the potential negative financial and human consequences of the use of automation on the labor market, the search for new solutions is at the top of the agenda.

Indeed, in parallel to the discussions at the EU level on the introduction of a legal personality for robots,[3] politicians, entrepreneurs and scholars have started to develop various ideas to mitigate the potential negative impact of the implementation of AI on a broad scale. For instance, as of June 2016, various articles have been written suggesting the introduction of a robot tax,[4] as a consequence of a new form of electronic ability to pay.[5] Provocatively, it

---

[1] European Parliament 2014–2019, P8_TA-PROV (2017)0051, Civil Law Rules on Robotics, European Parliament Resolution of 15 February 2017 with recommendations to the Commission on Civil Law Rules on Robotics (2015/2103 (INL)) (hereafter, EU Parliament Resolution 2017).

[2] Schwab Klaus, The Fourth Industrial Revolution, World Economic Forum, Crown, New York 2016, p. 6 ff.

[3] EU Parliament Resolution 2017, p. 17.

[4] See Oberson Xavier, Taxer les robots? Bilan, 6 July 2016.

[5] Oberson Xavier, Taxing Robots? From the Emergence of an Electronic Ability to Pay to a Tax on Robots or the Use of Robots, 9 World Tax Journal 2017, p. 252 ff.

was argued in 2016, in a Swiss newspaper, that "one day the robots will refuse to pay their taxes".[6] During the French presidency campaign of 2017, Benoit Hamon promoted the idea of a minimum unconditional income, which could be financed partly by a robot tax.[7]

Proposals to tax robots have also been developed at the EU level. In a draft report of 2016, the Commission on legal affairs of the EU Parliament issued recommendations to analyze the impact of AI and robotics on employment and the effect of that development on taxation and social security. The draft report reads:

> Bearing in mind the effects that the development and deployment of robotics and AI might have on employment and, consequently, on the viability of the social security systems of the Member States, consideration should be given to the possible need to introduce corporate reporting requirements on the extent and proportion of the contribution of robotics and AI to the economic results of a company for the purpose of taxation and social security contributions; takes the view that in the light of the possible effects on the labor market of robotics and AI a general basic income should be seriously considered, and invites all Member States to do so.[8]

On 16 February 2017, the EU Parliament finally rejected the idea of introducing a system of taxation of robots as electronic persons.[9] However, the next day the idea to tax robots had been endorsed by Bill Gates. Indeed, in an interview with QUARTZ TV on 17 February 2017, Bill Gates stated:

> Right now, the human worker who does, say, 50,000 dollars' worth of work in a factory, that income is taxed and you get income tax, social security tax, all those things. If a robot comes in to do the same thing, you'd think that we'd tax the robot at a similar level ... Exactly how you'd do it, measure it, you know, it's interesting for people to start talking about now.

In April 2017, following Bill Gates's declaration, Jaen Kim, a member of the board of supervisors of San Francisco, also launched a working group

---

6   Oberson Xavier, "Un jour les robots refuseront de payer leurs impôts", Le Temps, 17 October 2016. This quote looks, retrospectively, like a mirror to the title of an interesting article published in 2020 by Bret Bogenschneider, which reads "Will Robots Agree to Pay Taxes?" (2020), p. 1 ff.

7   Théobald Marie, "Taxe sur les robots, revenu universel, énergie ... Benoit Hamon détaille son programme économique", Le Figaro économique, 3 March 2017.

8   See Commission on Legal Affairs, Draft Report with Recommendations to the Commission on Civil Law Rules on Robotics, N0 2015/2103(INL) of the EU Parliament, May 2016, n. 23.

9   See Shiller Robert J., Robotization without Taxation? Project Syndicate, 22 March 2017, p. A7; Mazur Orly, Taxing the Robots, 46 Pepperdine Law Review 2018, p. 19.

to analyze the feasibility of a payroll tax on enterprises that replaces human employees with robots.[10]

The idea of a so-called "robot tax", or more generally, a tax on AI, has immediately triggered much attention. Yet, it remains highly controversial. There are in principle two opposite camps. On one side, some reactions have been negative. For example, *The Economist* insisted that a tax on robots was not a good idea; worse in that long-term workers would be the losers.[11] In a report, *Economiesuisse*, a leading lobbyist group for the Swiss Economy, also disapproved of the idea, characterizing it as "visionary" in appearance, but in reality, a hindrance to innovation and a factor in competitive distortions.[12] In the same vein, many commentators also disapproved of this concept, which they thought might not only distort innovation but also create new highly complex issues, which would be impossible to resolve.[13] On the other side, however, introducing a taxation of robots also received favorable comments. Apart from Bill Gates, Robert J. Shiller, a Nobel prize-winning economist, argued that, at least as an interim measure, such a tax could be justified to help the transition towards a more digitalized economy.[14]

Recent developments have tended to exacerbate concerns over the impact of AI on jobs and the economy. So far, automation has been used mainly to help with economic actors' repetitive or routine tasks. But nowadays, AI is more and more autonomous, using independent functions, and in constant progress, thanks notably to deep learning technologies.

In our view, the introduction of a tax on AI or on robots should be analyzed and discussed carefully. Indeed, as we will demonstrate below, the development of AI and robots will have a huge impact on the human labor market and on the tax system.

Despite opposing views on such a project, it appears necessary to consider it seriously. Indeed, considerable time is required to reach a consensus, both domestically and internationally, on such new tax rules. The numerous issues raised by a potential tax on AI require immediate and careful attention. Therefore, the purpose of this book is to show why and how an AI taxation system could be designed and implemented. We argue that an AI taxation

---

[10] Robinson Mela, "San Francisco is Considering a Once Unthinkable Measure to Offset the Threat of Job-killing Robots", Business Insider, 2 May 2017.

[11] The Economist, "Why Taxing Robots is Not a Good Idea", 25 February 2017.

[12] Economie Suisse, Rapport sur l'économie digitale, 22 August 2017.

[13] See, for example, Anna Isaac and Tim Wallace, "Return of the Luddites: Why a Robot Tax Could Never Work", The Telegraph, 27 September 2017; Müller Jürg, "Eine Robotersteuer ist Unsinn", Neue Zürcher Zeitung (NZZ), 23 August 2017, p. 11; Kovacev Robert, "Don't Tax the Robots", San Francisco Chronicle, 21 January 2018.

[14] See Shiller (2017), p. A7.

system, or its use, represents a powerful and interesting alternative solution to a potential crucial issue: the decline, or at least the complete change, of labor market and the distributional implications on persons of the growing use of automation.

We start with a brief description of the development of AI and robotics and its potential impact on the economy and the labor market in particular (Chapter 2). From there, we try to identify the essential features of AI and robots, in order to propose a practicable and appropriate definition for tax purposes (Chapter 3). Then, we analyze whether some forms of AI and robots, like corporations in the past, could eventually be recognized as a new type of legal entity, as well as the potential consequences of such characterization for AI taxation (Chapter 4). This then leads us to demonstrate to what extent AI taxation, or its use, could be justified both from an economic and legal standpoint (Chapter 5). We also describe how AI use is already subject to income or profit tax as part of the production factors of an enterprise (Chapter 6). In the same vein, the recent discussions on the alternatives to the taxation of the digital economy will also be covered, since they reflect – albeit partially – some of the issues related to the taxation of the use of AI; indeed, corporations active in the digital economy use automation extensively (Chapter 7). We also analyze the current VAT tax treatment of automated activities in enterprises subject to VAT; AI and robots are in fact already providing taxable supplies of goods and/or services within these enterprises (Chapter 8). Then, the book suggests various alternatives on which to design AI taxes: (1) the use of AI and (2) AI systems (Chapter 9). We will also examine how the rules of international tax law apply to these new types of AI taxes (Chapter 10). Finally, we will open the discussion on possible allocation by states of the revenues collected from AI taxes, and notably address the possibility of introducing a uniform basic income (Chapter 11). The last chapter will summarize the main findings and conclude with a final recommendation (Chapter 12).

2. The development of artificial intelligence and robots

I. HISTORICAL DEVELOPMENTS

The word "robot" first appeared in 1920 in the play "R.U.R. (Rossum's Universal Robots)" written by the Czech writer and painter Karel Čapek. The word "robota" in Czech means compulsory labor. It is interesting to note that in the play, artificial people are used in a manufactory as slaves, which eventually become self-aware and start a revolution. Robots nowadays are more generally defined as machines that may interact and perform various actions or tasks in an automated way, based on software, and notably AI.

Isaac Asimov had already in the 1940s published various science fiction novels, in which robots were part of society, eventually coming close to resembling humans in their appearance. In *Runaround*, Asimov developed the famous three laws of robotics that were incorporated in the positronic brain of each robot, namely:

> First Law. A robot may not injure a human being, or, through inaction, allow a human being to come to harm. Second Law. A robot must obey the orders given it by human beings except where such orders would conflict with the First Law. Third Law. A robot must protect its own existence as long as such protection does not conflict with the First or Second Law.[1]

Asimov himself would however show in his various stories that these laws are still unclear or vague and might conflict.[2] In a later novel, a robot completed this list and even created an additional law, the law zero: "A robot may not injure humanity or, through inaction, allow humanity to come to harm".[3]

---

[1] Asimov Isaac, Runaround, first published in Astounding Science Fiction, 1942, pp. 94–104.

[2] Balkin Jack, Sidley Austin, Distinguished Lecture on Big Data Law and Policy; The Three Laws of Robotics in the Age of Big Data, 78 Ohio State Law Journal 2017, p. 1219.

[3] Asimov Isaac, Robots and Empire, Doubleday, New York 1985, p. 291.

Alan Turing is often considered the father of AI. In 1950, he developed a test designed to determine the capability of a computer to imitate thinking. Under the "Turing test",[4] a machine and a human are asked a series of questions by another human who does not know who is the human and who is the machine. Both the machine and the human try to convince the questioner that it is human. If the machine can fool the questioners as often as the human, the test has been passed and the machine can "think".[5] As a response to the relevance of Turing's test, John Searle suggested another experiment, known as the "Chinese room".[6] Under this test, people who do not know Chinese are locked in a room with batches of Chinese writing. They have a rule book, in English, in which they can produce Chinese characters that they send out of the room. The people outside the room are convinced that the people in the room understand Chinese. Under this example, Searle made the point that computers cannot be considered as thinking, simply because their software "manipulates symbols in a way that simulate human intelligence".[7]

Progress in AI started to gain a lot of attention in 1997, when IBM's "Deep Blue" computer defeated the world chess champion, Gary Kasparov. Later, Deep Blue's successor, "Watson", went a step further by winning the television game show "Jeopardy", which requires a broader body of knowledge and skills than chess, which is based on strict rules.[8] AI continued to improve its skills. In 2016, DeepMind AI system "AlphaG" defeated Lee Sedol, considered the world's top player in the game of Go.[9] In order to achieve this result, the DeepMind team used deep learning processes and a combination of intuition and logic, which produced moves in the game that were sometimes "highly creative".[10]

Modern AI and robotics is developing more evolved AI systems and robots, capable of autonomous behavior. Such robots, sometimes referred to as "smart robots" have the capacity to learn, to interact with the outside world and adapt their behavior based on experiments. In this context, Ryan Calo uses the term

---

[4]   See Turing Alan M., Computing Machinery and Intelligence, 49 Minds 1950, p. 443 ff.

[5]   Solum Lawrence B., Legal Personhood for Artificial Intelligences, 70 North Carolina Law Review 1992, p. 1236.

[6]   Searle John, Minds, Brains and Science, Harvard University Press, 1984, p. 28 ff.

[7]   Solum (1992), p. 1236.

[8]   Ford Martin, Rise of the Robots, Basic Books, New York 2015, p. xiv.

[9]   Tegmark Max, Life 3.0, Being Human in the Age of Artificial Intelligence, Deckle Edge, New York 2017, p. 86.

[10]   Tegmark (2017), p. 88.

"emergent behavior", to refer to the increasing capacity of contemporary robots to behave in complex, unanticipated ways.[11] He writes:

> This is not to say that the system will take on a will of its own; the Amazon warehouse robots will not, for instance, spontaneously decide to arrange each item by color because the effect is prettier. Nor is it to deny that all robots are at one level 'programmed'; all contemporary robotic runs off of firmware and software programming. Rather, the idea is that the system will solve a problem (or create one) in ways the programmer never envisioned.[12]

In addition, more as a communication tool, on 25 October 2017, Saudi Arabia granted citizenship to a robot named "Sophia". The event was symbolic but contributed to a global recognition of the evolution of robots and their use in the world.

The COVID-19 pandemic has also had a strong impact on the use of AI and robots. It appears that the spread of this pandemic worldwide has indeed contributed to an acceleration of automation and the replacement of humans by AI and robots.[13]

The recent development of conversational and collaborative models of AI, using large language models (LLMs), such as ChatGPT,[14] have increased the fears of a future major impact on jobs, even beyond mere repetitive or routine activities. These conversational models are not revolutionary as far as their technology is concerned, but they are easily accessible to all, they may answer questions in natural language and they can be used for a great variety of tasks.[15] As a matter of fact, the use of LLM for dialogue purposes has even prompted Blake Lemoine, a software engineer at Google, to view this conversation as if the computer on the other side was "*sentient*".[16] Sentience in AI would mean

---

[11] Calo Ryan, Robots as Legal Metaphors, 30 Harvard Journal of Law & Technology 2016, p. 227; see also Calo Ryan, Robotics and the Lessons of Cyberlaw, 103 California Law Review 513, 2015, p. 539.

[12] See Calo (2016), p. 227.

[13] Acemoglu Daron, Manera Andrea and Restrepo Pascual, Taxes, Automation and the Future of Labor, MIT Research Brief, 2020, p. 3.

[14] ChatGPT, or more precisely "Chat Generative Pre-Trained Transformer", from the firm OpenAI, has been introduced in the form of a system of generative artificial intelligence, based on LLMs, which is able to understand and interact in human language and to interact and learn through experience ("deep learning").

[15] See the report from the French Government, "ChatGPT ou la percée des modèles d'IA conversationels", Eclairage sur … April 2023 #6, p. 6 ff.

[16] De Lima Carvalho Lucas and Esteche Victor Guilherme, Sentience as a Prerequisite for Taxing AI, Tax Notes International, vol. 108, December 5, 2022, p. 1263. The authors, based on this example, develop a distinction between sentient and non-sentient AI, which in their view should be relevant for tax purposes.

that the machine would have the capacity to "sense", namely to perceive its environment and feel it. This possibility remains probably exaggerated today, since this impression corresponds to the way we, as humans taking part in the conversation, perceive AI using LLM, which, after all, remains driven by algorithm systems. However, in the future, the development of more sophisticated algorithms, using neural network and deep learning systems, could lead to more surprising developments.[17] At this stage, what is relevant for our purpose is that the development of AI systems, capable of autonomous actions applicable to almost all areas of the economy, represents both an opportunity and a major concern for the economy, notably for human actors.

II.   VARIOUS USES OF ARTIFICIAL INTELLIGENCE AND ROBOTS

Until recently, robots were used mainly in the industry sector. We see for instance robots on factory assembly lines (cars, shoes, etc.) replacing blue collar workers. However, more and more AI and robots are deployed in the service sector. Commentators warn that a "major disruption" is likely to develop in the service economy, where in countries like the United States, most workers are currently employed.[18] In essence, there is hardly a sector of the economy that is likely not to be affected or modified by the implementation of robotics. We will illustrate, with a few examples, the growing developments of robots in various service activities. Robots perform in the *health* and *medical* industry, helping patients to move or walk, or, as with the da Vinci surgical system, assist doctors to practice surgery. Robots are also quite efficient in radiology or for diagnosis, where huge amounts of data can be analyzed quickly and at a large scale. In the *legal* area, "Ross" was a robot that helped lawyers conduct legal research. The use of "virtual judges" rendering decisions or helping human judges to come up with an adequate solution is also on the agenda. In the *education* sector, AI and robots can assist teachers, help students to learn or get quick answers. Robots have also been able to replace *journalists* by commentating on sports events or in helping to compile large amounts of information; in the *entertainment* industry, robots may assist in composing music or become virtual actors, notably avatars. Robots nowadays may even play music. For example, on 28 August 2018, in Geneva, a robot played electric guitar in a duet with a human guitar player.[19]

---

[17]   Hawkins Jeff, A Thousand Brains – A New Theory of Intelligence, Basic Books, New York 2021, p. 145, ff.

[18]   See Ford (2015), p. 12.

[19]   See Première mondiale: un robot donne un concert, AGEFI (www.agefi.com), 29 August 2018, No 151, p.1 and 7.

In June 2023, Paul McCartney announced that a new Beatles song would be released, based on past materials recorded with John Lennon and adapted using AI.[20] Artificial intelligence is also widely used in *banking* and finance with Fintech and robo-advisors, and in *agriculture*. Finally, AI may also bring assistance in the *public* sector, notably in tax or social security agencies, such as helping users to fill in a form, get answers to questions or prepare a request. Soon, robots will be much more efficient and accurate in filing tax returns for taxpayers than accountants or fiduciaries. The technology may also assist in tax administration for collection, supervision and compliance purposes.

Automation is not only changing the way we work, but is also creating new models of collaboration between humans and AI and robots themselves. In fact, the disruption caused by AI and robotics is profoundly affecting the way we work with a combination of automation and innovation, which will "transform the work of professionals, giving birth to new ways of sharing practical expertise".[21]

III. IMPACT OF THE USE OF ARTIFICIAL INTELLIGENCE AND ROBOTS ON THE ECONOMY

This development is not necessarily problematic. As the OECD mentioned, under BEPS Action 1:

> As robots learn to do jobs that previously were solely done by humans, they can potentially generate productivity, help lower prices for customers, contribute to scaling up operations at a global level, and create innovation opportunities which will lead to the emergence of new activities that will require new skills and potentially create new jobs.[22]

The word "potentially" is however crucial because, as many economists fear, the development of robots could also destroy more jobs than it creates.

The effective impact of AI and robotics on the labor market in particular is viewed very differently among experts. It is indeed quite difficult to give an accurate estimate of such development. In addition, it is also important to

---

[20]   See Sun Michael, "Paul McCartney Says There's Nothing Artificial in New Beatles Song Made Using AI", The Guardian, 23 June 2023.

[21]   See Susskind Richard and Susskind Daniel, The Future of the Professions, Oxford University Press 2015, p. 271.

[22]   See OECD/G20 BEPS Project, Addressing the Tax Challenges of the Digital Economy, Action 1 – 2015 Final Report, n. 92, p. 44.

take into consideration short- and long-term evolution of robot capacities. In a nutshell, we may distinguish between two schools of thought.[23]

For the *optimists*, on the one hand, the development of AI will improve productivity; jobs will certainly disappear, but new jobs will be created, and the welfare of the global economy will improve. In this respect, the fourth industrial revolution, like past revolutions, will profoundly transform the economy but additional jobs in new and so far unknown professions will be created. Indeed, from this perspective, the optimists consider that we have been able to cope with three previous industrial revolutions. Fears of the impact of automation are not new. Already in 1817, David Ricardo was concerned about the impact of automation on workers. He wrote: "substitution of machinery for human labor, is often very injurious to the interests of the classes or laborers … It may render the population redundant, and deteriorate the conditions of the laborer".[24] The so-called Luddites, textile workers who, in the nineteenth century, violently opposed the implementation of industrial machinery that threatened their jobs, are also often quoted in the automation debate. Indeed, the "Luddite fallacy" appears as a synonym of fear of innovation, or of automation as having a negative impact on the labor market.[25] So far, these fears have been exaggerated since in global terms innovation has created new jobs. While in the past industrial revolutions, many jobs have disappeared, productivity gains fostered by innovation have resulted in new job creation. This corresponds to the famous concept of "creative destruction", as developed by Joseph Schumpeter,[26] according to which capitalism is in constant evolution and adaptation, and new jobs will appear and create new opportunities for workers.

The *pessimists*, on the other hand, consider that this industrial and technological revolution is different. With the introduction of "smart" robots, capable of making decisions in an autonomous way, to learn, to adapt and to commu-

---

[23]   See also Mazur Orly, Taxing the Robots, 46 Pepperdine Law Review 2018, p. 9; Abbott Ryan and Bogenschneider Bret, Should Robots Pay Taxes? Tax Policy in the Age of Automation, 12 Harvard Law & Policy Review 2018, p. 15; Schwab Klaus, The Fourth Industrial Revolution, World Economic Forum, Crown, New York 2016, p. 36; more recently, Damijan Joze P., Damijian Sandra and Vrh Natasa, Tax on Robots: Whether and How Much, Working Paper, Growinpro, March, 39/2021, at n. 2.

[24]   See Ricardo David, On the Principles of Political Economy and Taxation, 3rd ed., London 1821, Batoche Books Canada 2021, Chapter XXXI, p. 264; Abbott and Bogenschneider (2018), p. 13.

[25]   Abbot and Bogenschneider (2018), p. 14.

[26]   Schumpeter Joseph, Capitalism, Socialism and Democracy, Harper & Brothers, United States, 1942, Chapter VII, p. 82 ff.; in this sense, Adler Tibère and Salvi Marco, Quand les robots arrivent, Avenir Suisse, 2017, p. 21.

nicate with the environment, most if not all jobs could eventually disappear.[27] Indeed, AI and robots are not only replacing workers in the industrial sectors but are used more and more in service activities. It implies that the disruption will affect all sectors of the economy, probably low-skilled workers at first. In addition, many workers will not have sufficient time or skills to adapt to the constantly evolving automation and economic changes.

Recent studies have tried to measure more precisely the impact of automation on jobs. In this context, automation should be viewed differently from other types of machinery, which generally is complementary to labor. Usually, investments in machines, such as upgrading them, are favorable to labor because they increase the productivity and therefore raise the demand for labor.[28] Artificial intelligence, by contrast, may either cause substitution of employment for capital or complement employment.[29] It could still be complementary to labor, and thus increase productivity, which could also require more labor.[30] Increasingly however, AI will cause the displacement of workers, resulting in negative consequences, with the corresponding need to help and support unemployed workers.[31] In general, substitution of labor by AI would also reduce labor demand. This replacement effect of automation still differs among specific labor sectors.[32] According to a 2023 report on the impact of AI on jobs, the World Economic Forum (WEF) recognizes that, as of 2027, AI is likely to create 69 million new jobs but at the same time suppress 83 million jobs, causing a global contraction of 14 million jobs.[33]

At this stage, we don't know who is right or wrong in this debate. It seems, however, not to be in dispute that, as a result of automation, many jobs will disappear, and are already doing so. The question is whether sufficient new jobs or professions will be created as the economy is transformed by automation (notably thanks to the labor substitution effect). In our view, there is at

---

[27]   See the widely discussed research of Frey Carl Benedict and Osborne Michael A., The Future of Employment; How Susceptible are Jobs to Computerization, 114 Technological Forecasting & Social Changes 2017, p. 254 ff., which concludes that 47 percent of total employment in the United States is at risk over the next decade or two; see Schwab (2016), p. 38.

[28]   Acemoglu, Manera and Restrepo (2020), p. 3.

[29]   Ooi Vincent and Goh Glendon, Taxation of Automation and Artificial Intelligence as a Tool of Labour Policy, eJournal of Tax Research 2022, p. 273; Acemoglu, Manera and Restrepo (2020) p. 3.

[30]   Acemoglu, Manera and Restrepo (2020), p. 3.

[31]   Ooi and Goh (2022), p. 6.

[32]   Ooi and Goh (2022), p. 7.

[33]   WEF, Future of Jobs Report, May 2023, p. 32.

least a serious risk that, as time goes by, not enough new jobs will be created to replace the disappearing ones. As Klaus Schwab puts it:

> So far, the evidence is this: The fourth industrial revolution seems to be creating fewer jobs in the industries than previous revolutions. This risk even increases in the long run as the development of AI brings new capacities to robots.[34]

Indeed, we share the growing concern that "this time it may be different".[35] AI and robotics are making unprecedented progress. The scope of tasks that may be achieved by robots is rapidly expanding. Not only manual or low-skilled activities are now at risk but also more sophisticated middle- or even high-income tasks.[36] Artificial intelligence is designed to develop robots with a capacity to learn, improve and make decisions. Eventually, over time, most if not all professions could be impacted.

The precise pace of necessary adjustments required by the disruption caused by new technologies, and notably automation, is unknown.[37] However, in our view, policymakers should start analyzing and developing solutions to these issues now. Indeed, should the pessimists be right, the social and financial consequences on humans and, more globally, on the economies of many States could be disastrous. In particular, a *triple negative effect* could occur. First, the state would suffer considerable losses of tax and social security contributions from the labor income base. Nowadays, taxes on individual income (including notably labor income) represent one of the main sources of tax revenues for many States.[38] Second, at the same time, as a consequence of growing unemployment, additional resources would be required from States in order to cover growing demand for pensions, allowances or financial help. Third, as a result of the decrease in income for individuals losing their jobs or lucrative activities, the global consumption of goods and services would also decrease.

---

[34]   See Schwab (2016), p. 41.

[35]   Abbott and Bogenschneider (2018), p. 15; Shiller Robert J., Robotization Without Taxation?, Project Syndicate, 2017, p. 3.

[36]   Ford (2015), p. 34 ff.; see also Schwab (2016), p. 44, who mentions that "high skills" in the fourth industrial revolution "will demand and place more emphasis on the ability of workers to adapt continuously and learn new skills and approaches within a variety of contexts".

[37]   In this sense see also Nolan Alistair, The Next Production Revolution: Key Issues and Policy Proposals, in: OECD, The Next Production Revolution, 2018, p. 35.

[38]   The share of individual income tax in total tax revenue was, notably, in 2016: 40.20 percent in the United States, 36.54 percent in Canada, 31.23 percent in Switzerland, 27.28 percent in the United Kingdom, 26.60 percent in Germany, 19.01 percent in France, see OECD (2018), Tax on Personal Income (indicator). https://doi:10.1787/94af18d7-en (Accessed on 7 January 2019).

In parallel, the fourth industrial revolution, in general, characterized notably by use of interconnected new technologies including AI,[39] is also likely to worsen *inequality*. This effect may result in increased inequality in two sectors, between capital and labor, on the one hand, and between low- and high-skilled workers on the other. First, the progress of innovation tends to compel companies to substitute labor for capital, which brings benefits to the providers of capital and increases the gap in wealth with those who depend on labor.[40] In other words, new technologies are causing a reallocation of wealth and income because they may replicate ideas at very low costs.[41] This would create "bounty for society and wealth for innovators, but diminishes the demand for previously important types of labor, which can leave many people with reduced income".[42] In fact, robotization could favor capital owners to the detriment of human workers.[43] After all, automation and robots are part of the assets of the enterprise. Thus, the replacement of human workers by robots should increase productivity but the profits generated are likely to benefit the owners of the enterprises using them. Second, while innovation and the use of intelligent machines may increase productivity, it does not imply that all the workers will benefit from this growth.[44] Indeed, specialized labor, which may be regarded as complementary to AI, would eventually replace substituting forms of labor, such as routine task, so that income would become more concentrated among higher-skilled workers.[45] Therefore, automation would also bring income inequality, to the disadvantage of low-skilled workers, including women who can often access only routine low-paying jobs.[46]

It follows that we should immediately develop solutions to address the impact of automation on both labor and inequality. In our view, this analysis should take place immediately. Indeed, a global consensus on such a solution could take time, as the OECD works on the taxation of the digital economy, as a result of the BEPS program, have demonstrated.[47] These proposals have

---

[39]   Nolan Alistair, The Next Production Revolution: Key Issues and Policy Proposals, in: OECD, The Next Production Revolution, 2018, p. 27.
[40]   See Schwab (2016), p. 11 ff., 92 ff.
[41]   Brynjolfsson Erik and McAffee Andrew, Race Against the Machine: How the Digital Revolution is Accelerating Innovation, Driving Productivity, and Irreversibly Transforming Employment and the Economy, Digital Frontier Press, New York 2014, p. 128.
[42]   Brynjolfsson and McAffee (2014), p. 128.
[43]   Mazur (2018), p. 10.
[44]   Brynjolfsson and McAffee (2014), p. 128.
[45]   Shome Parthasarathi, Taxation of Robots, ADB The Governance Brief, Issue 44 2022, p. 2.
[46]   Shome (2022), p. 2.
[47]   On the development of these works, see infra Chapter 7.

led notably to the famous two-pillar solution, which has been accepted by the Inclusive Framework of the OECD. Pillar one, in particular, tends to better address the allocation of taxing rights of big multinational entities, in favor of States of consumers and users.[48] At the time of writing, following the enthusiasm of 2021, where almost 140 States have agreed on the main principles of the two-pillar solution, it is not even certain that pillar one will finally be implemented by most States.

Therefore, as the time required to adopt, in a coordinated way, solutions to these issues could be long, we consider it our duty to analyze further one alternative, which, as we will demonstrate, could solve at least part of the problem: taxing AI.

---

[48]   OECD, Statement on a Two-Pillar Solution to Address the Tax Challenges of the Economy, 8 October 2021.

3. Definition of artificial intelligence and robots

I.   IN GENERAL

A.   Introduction

The concepts of AI and "robot" require clarification, notably from the perspective of finding an adequate and practical definition for both legal and tax purposes. In particular, the differences between AI and robots are not always clear. In fact, most commentators have focused on the taxation of robots while the development of AI has modified this perspective to render the distinction, at least from the purpose of legal and tax analysis, probably obsolete.

B.   Artificial Intelligence

Artificial intelligence is usually defined as the capacity of software to develop processes similar to the human brain. In other words, it refers to computers that apply cognitive and reasoning capabilities that replicate that of a human brain. The purpose of AI, which can be traced back to 1956, remains to develop machines which may demonstrate an intelligence similar to humans, namely to learn new tasks, to find analogies between one task and another and to solve new problems.[1] The practice tends to distinguish between weak (limited or narrow) AI and strong (broad or general) AI.[2] Weak AI usually refers to the ability to replicate one specific cognitive function of a human. Strong AI, by contrast, is broader and closer to human brain capacity. Another more recent category, defined as *Generative* AI, usually refers to the capacity of AI, through the use of machine learning, to produce content (such as videos, texts, audio, pictures etc.). Generative AI, such as ChatGPT, Dall-E, DeepMind, or Bard, use a vast quantity of data and may produce answers following requests

---

[1]   Hawkins Jeff, A Thousand Brains – A New Theory of Intelligence, Basic Books 2021, p. 135 ff.
[2]   Barfiel Woodrow and Pagalo Ugo, Law and Artificial Intelligence, Edward Elgar Publishing, Cheltenham, UK and Northampton, MA, USA, 2020, p. 5.

defined as prompts. As such, this technology is not new, but its far-reaching possibilities have exacerbated concerns about its potential impact, not only on the economy, but more generally from an ethical, legal, ecological or social perspective.[3] Some practitioners sometimes also mention artificial super intelligence (ASI) as an additional subcategory, which describes an AI that goes beyond human brain capacity. Currently, while examples of successful limited AI are numerous, strong AI is not yet fully developed.

C.   Robots

Robotization is often referred to as the use of AI in our society. Usually, robots are distinguished from AI, in that they represent a *physical emanation* of AI. According to George Bekey, robots are distinct from software agents "in that they are *embodied* and situated in the real world".[4] In other words, under this line of reasoning, robots have a physical presence which is designed to interact with the environment. In general, robots may be defined as machines governed by AI. Robots, contrary to simple machines, possess three main additional features: the capacity to sense the environment, to process the information and to act on the environment.[5] Such definition is also described as the "sense, think, act" paradigm.[6]

Various organizations have developed standards and definitions in the field of robots and robotics. For example, the International Organization for Standardization (ISO) issued the standard ISO 8373:2012 on Robots and robotic devices, which specifies vocabulary used in relation to robots and robotic devices operating in both industrial and non-industrial environments. In general, according to the norm ISO, a robot is an "actuated mechanism programmable in two or more axes with a degree of autonomy, moving within its environment, to perform intended tasks". The standard further specifies that a robot includes the control system and interface of the control system. The International Federation of Robotics (IFR) uses the same definition as the ISO standard.[7]

---

[3]   See, for example, a report from the French Government: "ChatGPT ou la percée des modèles d'IA conversationels, Eclairage sur ...", April 2023 #06.

[4]   Bekey George A., Autonomous Robots. From Biological Inspiration to Implementation and Control, The MIT Press, Cambridge, Massachusetts 2005, p. xiii.

[5]   Calo Ryan, Robotics and the Lessons of Cyberlaw, 103 California Law Review 513, 2015, p. 529.

[6]   Calo (2015), p. 529.

[7]   See Fanti Sébastien, "Switzerland" in: Bensoussan Alain et al. (eds), Comparative Handbook: Robotics Technologies Law, Larcier Bruxelles 2016, p. 293; Müller Melinda F., Roboter und Recht, Pratique Juridique Actuelle (PJA), Dike, Zurich 2014, p. 596 ff.

In the EU Final Report, the EU Parliament focuses on "smart robots", which are defined in accordance with the following characteristics:

• the acquisition of autonomy through sensors and/or by exchanging data with its environment (interconnectivity) and the trading and analysis of those data;
• self-learning from experience and by interaction (optional criterion);
• at least a minor physical support;
• the adaptation of its behavior and actions to the environment; and
• the absence of life in the biological sense.[8]

Commentators also have tried to develop a practical definition of robots, from a legal standpoint. For instance, Nathalie Nevejans suggests that a legal definition of robots could be based on six conditions. In her view, a robot:

(i)   is a physical machine (*"machine matérielle"*);
(ii)   is alimented by energy;
(iii) has a capacity to act in the real world;
(iv)   can analyze the environment;
(v)   can render decisions; and
(vi)   can learn.[9]

Neil Richards and William Smart have also tried to define robots from a legal perspective. Based on the premise that robots are machines that behave intelligently and interact in the world, they propose the following definition: "A robot is a contractual system that displays both physical and mental agency but is not alive in the physical sense."[10]

All of these definitions mention, to some extent, a degree of autonomy, and the capacity to evolve and learn. They also insist on a vision of robots as embodied in a physical support (EU Final Report), a physical machine (Nevejans), or at least as a mechanism (ISO). From the proposals that have already been developed internationally, it appears that the common thread relies on the specificities of the autonomy and decision-making process of robots. Contrary to machines, such as automats, trains or cars, the decisive factor appears to rely on the existence of AI, encompassing sufficient auton-

---

[8]   EU Final Report (2017), at p. 8.
[9]   See Nevejans Nathalie, Les robots: tentative de définition in: Bensamoun Alexandra (ed.), Les robots. Objets scientifiques, Objets de droits, Collection des Presses Universitaires de Sceaux, 2016, p. 100.
[10]   Richards Neil M. and Smart William D., How Should the Law Think about Robots? in: Calo Ryan, Froomkin Michael A. and Kerr Ian, Robot Law, Edward Elgar Publishing 2016, p. 6.

omy, and a capacity to learn, progress and make decisions.[11] Robots are now able to replace inherent and, so far, unique human activities.

II.   DEFINITION OF ARTIFICIAL INTELLIGENCE AND ROBOTS FOR TAX PURPOSES

In view of the above, we will try to come up with a practical definition of AI and robots suitable for tax purposes. The goal of the future taxation rules, as we have described, is in general to address the substituting impact of automation on labor. Depending on the policy purposes followed by the legislator, it may also design tax rules to internalize the social costs caused by the use of AI (unemployment, health issues, etc.) and try to reduce the inequality that automation could promote.

In general, even if there is no unanimously accepted definition, at least in the legal world, of AI, this notion represents a general term, which includes all types of algorithms and software designed to create intelligent machines. "Robots", by contrast, is usually regarded as a more specific term, focusing on the implementation of AI on machines. Therefore, in everyday language, we tend to view robots as a form of "embodied" AI. In other words, robots are defined as the implementation of AI in the market. In a way, AI is the "brain", and the robots are the material implementation and effects of the algorithm designed for the robots to act.

For our purpose, however, the distinction between AI and robots no longer makes sense, since AI systems and robots may have a similar impact on the labor market. From an employment standpoint, the impact is significant should a worker in a factory be replaced by an industrial robot (implementing "weak" AI), a receptionist by a social bot, an asset manager by a software "robot-adviser", or an accountant by AI using LLM. What should be relevant for the definition of a tax on AI, should be its impact on the economy and not the form of its implementation or appearance. Thus, for tax purposes, we would not recommend following the approach suggested by the EU Parliament, in its report of 2017, to focus only on robots with some kind of physical support. In our view, "unembodied" robots should also be taken into consideration.[12] From

---

[11]   See Oberson Xavier, Taxing Robots? From the Emergence of an Electronic Ability to Pay to a Tax on Robots or the Use of Robots, 9 World Tax Journal 2017, p. 249 ff.

[12]   See also Balkin Jack and Sidley Austin, Distinguished Lecture on Big Data Law and Policy: The Three Laws of Robotics in the Age of Big Data, 78 Ohio State Law Journal 2017, p. 232 ff., mentioning, in the different context of a potential criminal liability, that unembodied robots may also cause significant harm to people and property and should therefore not be excluded as potential objects of criminal responsibility.

a tax perspective, a rather "form neutral" definition of robots should in our view be favored for tax purposes. After all, it does not really matter, as long as the work (of the robots) is properly carried out, whether robots are walking the streets or developing automated tasks embodied in software or a machine within a firm. Again, from this perspective, the distinction between AI and robots is outdated.

In addition, what differentiates the robots from machines is the robot's ability to "process, plan and act on its own".[13] This trilogy could serve as a practical starting point to characterize robots. However, the definition of robots should be broad enough to correspond with the rapid evolution of AI and its impact on the possibilities of robots. As Ryan Calo has demonstrated, the way the concept is used in law does not seem to be in line with the current development of robotics.[14] Calo shows that, under current jurisprudence, the word robot is generally used as a metaphor for repetitive tasks or behavior effectuated under the control of another person. In addition, in some cases, robots are capable of so-called emergent behaviors, in which they adapt and develop different solutions, which were not foreseen by the designers.[15]

In essence, from a tax perspective, the distinction between AI and robots has become artificial. When we look at the recent legal definition of AI, the difference with robots has become impracticable. Indeed, the key components of AI are: (1) the function of the agent, i.e. the possibility of perceiving the environment through sensors and acting upon it through actuators and (2) the autonomy.[16] These functions are also relevant for the impact of robotization in the labor economy and should be included in the tax analysis. Indeed, it is the "sense, think, act" trilogy, which should be relevant and not whether the AI is embodied in a robot machine or not. In the same vein, Rochel wonders whether the distinction between robots and AI still makes any sense.[17] After all, a software may also exercise an action in the physical world using actions systems ("actuators"). In addition, AI also has a "physical presence" in the software application and uses the Internet networks which also needs an infra-structure in order to exist.[18] Rochel maintains that the distinction may still be relevant because robots, with their physical actions in the physical world – and therefore on humans – raise serious ethical challenges.[19] In our view, for the

---

[13] Calo Ryan, Robots as Legal Metaphors, 30 Harvard Journal of Law & Technology 2016, p. 237.

[14] Calo (2016), p. 210.

[15] Calo (2016), p. 210.

[16] Barfiel and Pagalo (2020), p. 4.

[17] Johan Rochel Les robots parmi nous, Savoir Suisse, Switzerland (2022), p. 43.

[18] Rochel (2022), p. 43.

[19] Rochel (2022), p. 44.

purpose of taxation, however, this distinction no longer makes sense because it is the impact of AI on the labor market and the economy as a whole, including the disruption and the rising inequality linked with it, which is relevant.

Lucas De Lima Carvalho also refers, for international tax purposes, to the concept of autonomous AI (AAI). In his view, this expression expresses a system that (1) is capable of performing tasks commonly associated with human intelligence and beyond; (2) is not directly or indirectly controlled by human beings; and (3) has full managerial power over its own actions and resources.[20] This approach creates another concept that is difficult to classify since it would include AI, independent from human control "but not independent from human *containment*".[21] This subtle distinction could prove hard to administer. We thus prefer to use more generally the concept of AI but use as a criterion, in the definition for tax purposes, the concept of autonomy, which does not as such exclude some human control.

In our view, from a legal and tax perspective, while the distinction between AI and robots can help to differentiate the concept of robots in comparison to AI, we should focus on the taxation of AI, defined in accordance with its purpose and effect on the economy. What should be relevant is its autonomy, defined as the capacity to process, plan and act on its own. The fact that AI is located within a computer, a network of software or within an industrial robot does not make any difference. We therefore adopt a "form neutral" definition of AI.

In the first edition of this book, we focused on "*smart robots*", i.e. robots which are capable of interacting with the environment, adapt their behavior and develop with sufficient autonomy. In view of the wide development of AI, we believe that it is more appropriate to refer more generally to the taxation of AI systems, which have an impact on the economy and notably on the labor market. From this perspective, robots are regarded as a more specialized term, which is already part of the more general notion of AI for tax purposes. The common criteria for both AI and robots, as a form of implementation of AI, is their autonomy. For the sake of facilitating understanding, we may occasionally use the term robots in this book but as a way of referring more to the implementation of AI into a machine, thus focusing on robots as embodied AI. However, we want to stress that the common denominator of our focus is AI,

---

[20]   De Lima Carvalho Lucas, *Spiritus Ex Machina*: Addressing the Unique BEPS Issues of Autonomous Artificial Intelligence by Using "Personality" and "Residence", 47 Intertax 2019, p. 430 f.
[21]   De Lima Carvalho (2019), p. 431.

which is causing challenges in the tax world, whether or not it is embodied.[22] We can summarize this view using the following diagram.

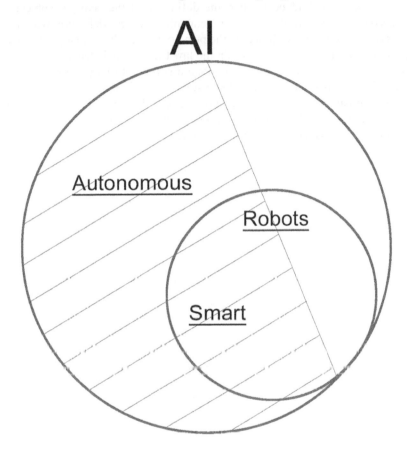

Figure 3.1   Figurative delimitation between AI and robots

We will, however, see further that, depending on the purpose of the tax, the legislator may need to design more precisely the scope of the entities subject to tax. On the one hand, if the legislator taxes the use of AI, the definition would

---

[22]   In this sense, but for the more general legal challenges, see Barfiel and Pagalo (2020), p. 16. By contrast, still focusing on the concept of robots, Christina Dimitropoulo, for tax purposes, uses the words AI and robots "interchangeably", see, Dimitropoulou Christina, Robot Taxation: A Normative Tax Policy Analysis. Domestic and International Tax Considerations, PHD, University of Vienna 2023, p. 27, n 80.

focus more on the enterprises using AI, including robots and their impact on the labor market. On the other hand, should the legislator tax autonomous AI systems, as we will advocate later, the definition of the taxpayer subject to tax becomes crucial. In this case, a practicable and clear definition would be necessary. In this context, based on the principle of legality, the legislator will be required to define precisely within the law the essential elements of the AI taxable unit, which would also necessitate a sufficient link (nexus) with that State. Should this situation occur, some sufficient link between the AI system and an infrastructure in that State could render the definition closer to the concept of "smart" robots as defined above, which would imply some form of infrastructure in which AI would be embodied.

4.   Artificial intelligence as a new legal or taxable person

I.   CONDITIONS FOR A LEGAL PERSONALITY

The development of AI and robots in all aspects of our lives, in which robots are working and/or collaborating with humans, also raises the question of the potential recognition of a new type of legal personality to AI. This issue is also closely related to the debate about granting robots some sort of rights.[1] The idea to recognize some form of legal personality to AI and robots would also become relevant in the area of tax law. Indeed, as a consequence of a legal capacity, a tax personality could also be recognized.[2] In other words, introducing a tax on AI, or on its usage, could also be the consequence of recognizing a specific tax personality of AI. We will therefore consider to what extent a legal personality, from a civil law standpoint, could be granted to AI.

Humans are natural persons. They are recognized in law as independent human beings with a legal capacity, benefit from legal (including constitutional) rights and are also subject to various legal obligations. The idea of recognizing, in parallel with humans, new types of legal persons is not new. Indeed, more than a century ago, with the development of the industrial economy, the concept of legal persons started to emerge.[3] Previously, only a natural person could be sued. When, during the industrial revolution, the form of corporation with liability was introduced, there was a risk that no one could be sued; the concept of legal personality was thus a solution to this problem. It was introduced in the United Kingdom to offer a legal remedy against insolvent companies with limited liability.[4] In the famous case of *Salomon v. A Salomon & Co Ltd* (1897), the House of Lords unanimously upheld the

---

[1]   See for instance, Gungel David J., Robot Rights, MIT Press, Cambridge, Massachusetts 2019; Gunkel David J., The Machine Question, MIT Press, Cambridge, Massachusetts 2012.

[2]   Oberson Xavier, Taxing Robots? From the Emergence of an Electronic Ability to Pay to a Tax on Robots or the Use of Robots, 9 World Tax Journal 2017, p. 252.

[3]   See Blanchard Kimberly, The Tax Significance of Legal Personality: A U.S. View, Colloquium on Tax Policy, 2015, p. 7 ff.

[4]   Blanchard (2015), p. 8.

doctrine of legal personality, under the UK Companies Act of 1862, and confirmed that creditors could not sue the company's shareholders.[5] Similarly in the United States, already in the beginning of the nineteenth century, certain individuals started to conceive of certain legal attributes of incorporation as an entity with a separate existence from its shareholders and other participants.[6] In the *Dartmouth College* case, Chief Justice Marshall described a corporation as "an artificial being, invisible ... intangible".[7] The use of the word "artificial" is interesting in our context. It seems however to refer to the fact that this new entity "owed its existence to the positive law of the state rather than to the private initiative of individual incorporators".[8] At that time, it appeared indeed that a special act of the state was required for each incorporation; later, the states introduced general incorporation legislation.[9]

There appears to be no universal understanding of the concept of legal personality; in general, it refers to an entity that can own property in its own name, that can sue or be sued and that may also enter into contractual relationships.[10] States have, notably, since the time of the *Salomon* case, expanded the list of legal entities to include, among others, corporations, cooperatives, associations and foundations.

As a consequence, legal personality is currently granted to natural persons (humans) and, in accordance with legal rules, other legal persons, such as corporations, foundations or other limited liability entities. By contrast, non-human forms of life, such as animals, natural systems and algorithmic processes or AI, are not considered legal persons.[11] Animals, however, although not treated as legal persons, do benefit from some types of protection rules, including some rights, at least in some states. Other objects or elements have also been granted some types of rights. For example, the Judicial Committee of the Privy Council in London, on Appeal from the High Court of Bengal, held in 1925 that an East Indian idol had some legal rights and a counsel had

---

[5]   *Salomon v. A Salomon & Co Ltd* [1896] UKHL 1 (16 November 1896); Blanchard (2015), p. 6.

[6]   Million David, Theories of the Corporation, Duke Law Journal 1990, p. 206.

[7]   See *Trustees of Dartmouth College v. Woodward*, 17 U.S. 518, 636 (181), Million (1990), p. 206.

[8]   Million (1990), p. 206.

[9]   Million (1990), p. 206.

[10]   Blanchard (2015), p. 8.

[11]   Bayern Shawn J., The Implications of Modern Business-Entity Law for the Regulation of Autonomous Systems, 19 Stanford Technology Law Review 93 2015, p. 93 ff., 95.

been appointed to represent the idol in dispute.[12] In India, a court has already admitted a similar conclusion in favor of an ecosystem.

Therefore, apart from human persons, the legal system has recognized the possibility of granting the status of legal persons to other types of organized entities, such as corporations, and also to accord some rights to animals and other types of entities. The issue also emerged recently as to whether some sort of legal personality should not be granted to AI or robots. In 1992, Lawrence Solum started to analyze whether a legal personality could be granted to AI.[13] In particular, he admitted that AI could potentially serve as a trustee, to the extent that it could simulate a human being in all relevant aspects. This implies that some kind of "robot rights" could be granted to robots. Bensoussan is also in favor of adopting a new legal form of "personne robot" in order to recognize both rights and obligations to them. In a recent article, Bensoussan based the necessity of recognizing the specificity of robots under the "droit naturel", which, following Aristotle and Spinoza, is the law that derives, not from positive domestic legal rules, but from the specific nature of being as such ("qui dérive de la nature même d'un être").[14] In other words, natural human rights are universal and based on the concept of humanity. Other commentators, in the debate about whether we should grant some rights to robots, suggest focusing on so-called "social robots" and analyzing whether they qualify for moral considerations.[15] Recent commentators have also favored the idea of granting a specific legal personality to robots, while others believe that it is not necessary, or that it is at least too early at this stage.[16]

The idea of granting legal personality to smart robots has also been discussed at the EU level. In a Resolution of February 2017, the EU Parliament asked the EU Commission to consider granting a legal personality, or, more precisely, an "electronic personality" to smart robots, defined under a series of criteria. This idea was controversial. In April 2018, a group of AI experts

---

[12] See Seton William, Legal Rights of an East Indian Idol, American Bar Association Journal 1925, p. 431; see also Solum Lawrence B., Legal Personhood for Artificial Intelligences, 70 North Carolina Law Review 1992, p. 1239.

[13] Solum (1992), p. 1231.

[14] Bensoussan Alain and Bensoussan Jérémy, Droit des robots, Larcier, Bruxelles 2015; see also Bensoussan Alain, "Le droit naturel, fondement juridique de la personne-robot?" Le Figaro, 10 July 2018.

[15] See Tavani Herman T., Can Social Robots Qualify for Moral Consideration? Reframing the Question about Robot Rights, Information 2018, MDPI, 29 March 2018, Information, p. 1 ff.

[16] Compare Fanti Sébastien, "Switzerland" in: Bensoussan Alain et al. (eds), Comparative Handbook: Robotics Technologies Law, Larcier 2016, p. 293 (in favor of this idea); Müller Melinda F., Roboter und Recht, Pratique Juridique Actuelle (PJA), 2014, p. 596 ff. (considering this idea not excluded, but premature).

published an open letter to the Commission discouraging and clearly rejecting this new development. On 25 April 2018, the EU Commission outlined its future strategy in the area of AI. It is interesting to note that in this outline, the idea to grant personality to AI is not mentioned. This has been interpreted positively by some commentators. For example, Thomas Burri argues that the EU and its institutions do not have the power to determine who is a person; this power still belongs to the Member States.[17] In addition, he points out that AI is already here, and existing national laws are sufficiently flexible to attribute legal personality to AI.

In our view, the debate over granting a certain form of legal personality to AI is worth considering. The development of broad AI, capable of reasoning and of cognitive features similar to the human brain, will result in the implementation of new forms of robots with more interaction with humans or other robots. Eventually, specific rules of behavior and the nature of relationship between AI and humans or between robots themselves will have to be introduced. These new sets of rules could be implemented in order both to protect and control smart robots. Humans are just beginning to learn and experience interaction with robots. We have already heard stories of human beings questioning the "fate" of their robot companions or developing psychological links with them. We could even argue that mistreatment of robots, similar to animals, could be regarded as acting against human dignity. For example, rules forbidding or restricting the use of robots for illegal or amoral activities should be implemented to protect the dignity of both humans and robots, from the perspective of similar human behaviors.

In addition, as we have mentioned above, recent developments of generative AI, using natural language with humans, such as LLM, may seem for users close to developing "sentient" behavior.[18] While we are not yet at this stage, AI could become more and more capable of at least an autonomous behavior, namely the capacity to act, react and adapt to its environment on its own. This feature may also justify the granting of a legal personality to this type of AI system. Granting legal personality to AI would also ensure some form of accountability from these entities, beyond the other legal (corporations) or human persons that control them.[19] The fear of giving rights to robots should, in our view, not be exaggerated. As with corporations, the legislator is free to decide the scope of such rights and the corresponding obligations. For

---

[17]   Burri Thomas, The EU is Right to Refuse Legal Personality for Artificial Intelligence, (www.euroactiv.com), 31 May 2018.
[18]   See supra p. 7; see also, De Lima Carvalho and Esteche Victor Guilherme, Sentience as a Prerequisite for Taxing AI, Tax Notes International 2022, p. 1263 ff.
[19]   Barfield Woodrow and Pagallo Ugo, Law and Artificial Intelligence, Edward Elgar Publishing, Cheltenham, UK and Northampton, MA, USA, 2020, p. 66.

example, in the United States, the Supreme Court has admitted that corporations could benefit from the freedom of speech.[20] The same also applies in the EU and under the European Convention on Human Rights.[21] However, this doesn't mean that all constitutional rights should be granted to corporations, due to their specific features. The same could apply to AI entities. The scope of the rights embodied in their legal personality must be adapted to their special features, not only to protect them, but above all to protect humans and insure a legal accountability, namely some form of "responsibility".

Granting legal personality to AI should however be based on a number of essential principles. First, an adequate and practicable definition of this new form of "electronic" person should be adopted. In this context, legal personality does not necessarily correspond to a tax capacity and should be designed from the perspective of AI or a robot as an independent new form of legal entity, entitled to some specific rights and obligations. This definition should be based on the specificities of AI as such and not correspond to the rights and duties of humans, as natural persons, or of corporations. For instance, while corporations have been granted some constitutional rights, they do not benefit from the large scope of human rights granted to individuals. In our view, the essential characteristic of a robot that could be recognized as a feature of a legal personality is *autonomy*. New forms of robots have developed the capacity to interact with the environment, improving their skill from deep learning, and making decisions in an autonomous way.[22] This feature, in our view, is what makes robots different from machines and other forms of natural elements, such as animals, plants or the wider ecosystem. Second, the legal personality of AI should be clearly identified and recognizable to the public as such. This would require some sort of registration or official publication of robots recognized as legal entities. Third, this legal recognition should be granted by the legislator under the *rule of law* principle. This principle requires, notably, an introduction under a statute (legislation), followed by the constitutional procedure of the adoption of a law, in accordance with the principle of certainty, equality of treatment, non-discrimination and prohibition of arbitrariness.[23] The statute granting legal personality should entail all the essential elements

---

[20] Barfield and Pagallo (2020), p. 47.

[21] See European Court of Human Rights, case 65/38, *The Sunday Times v. United Kingdom*, 26 April 1979.

[22] See, in this respect, Burri Thomas, The Politics of Robot Autonomy, European Journal of Risk Regulation 2016, p. 342 ff., discussing and comparing two views of robots' autonomy: the operator's view and the observer's.

[23] On 11/12 March 2016, the Council of Europe, Venice Commission, adopted a Report on the "Rule of Law", which entails a checklist of commonly recognized and accepted principles necessary to respect the "Rule of law".

of such recognition: definition of AI as legal persons, rights and duties and consequences of such recognition.

II.   CONDITIONS FOR A TAX CAPACITY OF ARTIFICIAL INTELLIGENCE SYSTEMS

A.   Introduction

In order to recognize AI as a taxpayer, it is not sufficient to grant it legal personality. The tax on AI should furthermore be justified from a constitutional and economic standpoint. Indeed, it is not because a robot is a legal entity that, as such, it should be subject to tax. In addition, as seen above, the legislator could also choose to grant a tax capacity to AI, even without a legal personality, based on tax policy reasons. In most cases, entities subject to tax are also legal persons, such as humans, liable for income tax or corporations, subject to profit tax, but not necessarily. Some types of transparent partnerships or investment funds are still liable to income tax.

To become a taxable person, AI or robots should be: (1) defined for tax law purposes and; (2) recognized as a taxable entity; furthermore, (3) the tax should be fair and equitable and; (4) based on sound tax policy reasons.

B.   Various Definitions of Artificial Intelligence and Robots for Tax Purposes

We have seen above that, even if the task is delicate and controversial, it seems to us feasible to devise a practicable definition of AI and robots, from a legal standpoint. This definition, which would help to design the necessary features of AI or robots as a legal entity, is not necessarily valid for tax purposes. Indeed, each system of taxes is based on different policies and may require specific definitions of the taxpayers. Taxing income necessitates a proper definition of the recipient, based on his or her ability to pay. By contrast, taxing consumption or transactions would move the focus towards the recipient of the supply of goods or services (consumer). A tax on transactions, such as an excise tax, is also based on a different perspective depending on the purpose of the tax.

If follows that a general definition of AI for tax purposes will depend upon the applicable tax system that we wish to design. For example, an object tax on robots, similar to a tax on cars or dogs, requires a narrow and practical definition of robots, focusing on their place of situation and their interaction with the environment. A tax on the use of AI by enterprises, as we will advocate further[24] should rely on a broader definition of robots, regarded as a form of neutral implementation of AI, to the extent that the purpose of the tax is to compensate for the loss of human jobs replaced by robots. This is because the tax focuses here more on the impact of AI on the economy and embodied in robots than on the robots as such. Finally, if we were to recognize an AI system as a taxpayer, the tax would be based on the ability of the AI entity to pay.[25] In particular, a tax on revenues of AI would need to assess and allocate to it a financial capacity.

C.   Artificial Intelligence System as a Taxable Entity

1.   In general

Furthermore, from a legal standpoint, the tax legislator is not bound by the civil law definition of a legal entity. It could very well define it differently. On the one hand, there are examples of legal entities, which, from a civil law standpoint, have been granted a legal personality and yet are treated as transparent for tax purposes. This is the case, for example, under US law for entities (limited liability company (LLC) notably) which, under the check-the-box regulations, have opted for transparency treatment despite having legal personality. Such consequences also appear in "look-through" situations where, under specific conditions, tax rules disregard the civil legal personality.[26] On the other hand, there are also examples where the tax legislator introduces a specific tax liability to entities that are not regarded as legal entities from a civil law standpoint but are treated as separate taxpayers. In the United States, this would be the case under the check-the-box regulations, in the reverse situation of a transparent entity (partnership for instance) opting for entity treatment. There are many other examples of such situations.[27]

In any event, the recognition of a legal personality to AI would represent an important feature that the tax legislator would have to consider. Most legal persons under civil law are indeed recognized as liable to tax (individuals and companies), even if this tax liability is not automatic and requires a formal introduction in the applicable tax statutes, in accordance with the principle of

---

[24]   See infra, p. 150 ff.

[25]   See infra, p. 173 ff.

[26]   This situation could typically occur under anti-avoidance tax rules which would pierce the corporate veil ("Durchgriff") of a company or treat it as a sham.

[27]   For instance, under Swiss law, collective investment funds owning real estate directly are treated as separate taxpayers, even if they do not have a civil legal personality; see Oberson Xavier, Droit fiscal Suisse, 5th ed., Helbing & Lichtenhan, Basel 2021, p. 243; see also Art. 49 par. 2 of the Swiss Federal Income Tax Law.

legality. In other words, the tax legislator, to the extent that the tax is justified,[28] should then implement it and provide for all the essential elements of such tax in the law.

In an interesting example, Shawn Bayern has demonstrated that it is currently possible, under US law, to grant legal personality to AI, by putting it in control of an LLC.[29] In this case, the LLC controlled by AI will become subject to profit tax. The legislator could however go further and grant the tax personality to some form of AI or robots.

In our view, in order to recognize an AI system as a taxable person, the legislator could choose, either (1) to grant legal personality to it, which, as a consequence, would also entail the duty to pay a tax, or (2) design a new type of entity subject to tax, which does not necessarily require it to become a legal personality.

If we focus on a tax capacity, which is the subject of this book, we believe that at least four essential features should be present in a new taxable entity taking the form of AI: autonomy, a distinct patrimony; identification and control by human). First, the specific feature of AI, in comparison to machines, lies in its *autonomy*. This condition requires the AI system to have the capacity to act on its own, learn from experience and interact with the environment. In other words, the "process, plan and act" paradigm would become a basic feature of the AI taxable unit, combined with the feature to proceed "on its own".

Second, in order to benefit from an ability to pay, here defined as an objective ability to pay (a capacity of payment), the AI entity should benefit from a *distinct patrimony*, in the form of available funds to pay the tax.[30] This condition could be based not only on fiat currencies but also in other forms of legally recognized sources of funds, such as cryptocurrencies or other forms of electronic money that could be designed in the future. Similar to corporations, the AI entity should be in a position to decide on its own on the use of the funds. In this context, an interesting concept is the so-called decentralized autonomous organization (DAO), which, based on Blockchain technology, uses smart contracts to render automated decisions.[31] This system could serve as a first model of attributing funds and management rules for AI taxable units.

---

[28] See infra, p. 46 ff.

[29] Bayern (2015), p. 93; Barfield and Pagallo (2020), p. 63.

[30] See also, Dimitropoulo Christina, Robot Taxation: A Normative Tax Policy Analysis, 2023, p. 65 ff.

[31] Smit Daniel, Flexibility, "Mobility and Automation of Labour under Article 7 of the OECD Model? A First Conceptual Exploration" in: Weber Dennis (ed.), The Implications of Online Platforms and Technology for Taxation, IBFD, Amsterdam 2023, p. 167; Englisch Joachim, Digitalization and the Future of National Tax Systems:

Third, the AI entity should be clearly *identified* as such. This would require that the law define the framework for the existence of this new entity, including some recognition of its system (which could include some minimum requirements). For the same reason, there should be a registration for AI entities recognized as taxpayers.

Finally, a system of supervision of this AI entity should be put in place. Humans should at least be able to control the proper functioning of the AI system. Control should be balanced with the necessary autonomy of the AI entity but is not contradictory to the design of an autonomous AI system. After all, companies are usually under the control of an independent audit firm and under the governance of the board of directors. In fact, the requirement of having human supervision could also serve other legal purposes that could go beyond the mere auditing of tax rules. In this respect, tax rules could in fact also help to maintain an adequate and proportional functioning of the AI system subject to tax. This description would also apply to so-called "smart robots", which represent an embodied form of AI and should also entail the four conditions mentioned above.

Recently, some commentators have also focused on "sentience" as a prerequisite for taxing AI.[32] While we do not think that AI is still capable of such sentience, even in the context of advanced generative AI, their approach offers an interesting perspective.[33] However, we do not believe, at this stage, that the condition of "sentience" corresponds to a requirement to grant a tax capacity to AI. The four conditions mentioned above, notably the essential aspect of autonomy, already refers to an activity which objectively reflects a potential capacity to interact in the economy, in a reasonable and logical way, and

---

Taxing Robots? in: Haslehner W. et al. (eds), Tax and the Digital Economy, Series on International Taxation, Wolters Kluwer, The Netherlands 2019, p. 267.

[32] De Lima Carvalho and Esteche Victor Guilherme, Sentience as a Prerequisite for Taxing AI, Tax Notes International, 5 December 2022, p. 1263 ff. Sentience, according to these authors (id., p. 1264), refers to "AI awareness of itself and its interactions with human beings, other AI entities, and the rest of its surroundings". Their definition is in fact close to the concept of "consciousness" which refers usually to the subjective possibility of machines and AI to be aware, while sentience would include a possibility of feeling. This fascinating debate is, however, beyond the scope of this book. Needless to say, these issues are quite controversial.

[33] The use of generative AI, such as ChatGPT, may give to the user the impression that the machine responds and "feels" what is happening but science, so far, confirms that it is not conscious of what it is doing, see in this sense, Grinbaum Alexei, Parole de machines, HumenSciences 2023. In 2022, the philosopher David Chalmers said, during a speech given on 28 November 2022, at the Neural Information Processing System Conference (NeurIPS), that the likelihood that sophisticated AI might be sentient or conscious is 10 percent, but within the next ten years there is a 20 percent chance that they could become conscious, exceeding the capacity of a fish.

should therefore be subject to tax. What seems more important than sentience for tax purposes is the capacity to think autonomously and adapt, which refers more to a capacity of *reason* than of *feeling*, the latter being a characteristic element of sentience. The condition of some form of human control would also entail the capacity to supervise the respect of the obligations attached to the autonomous AI system and bring back the sentience in the scope, a bit like a board of human directors or auditors would supervise the activities of a corporation.

In summary, a tax capacity could be designed by a legislator for an AI autonomous and identified system with a financial capacity. This would include smart robots. This new AI taxable unit, which we could define as an AITU, would then be granted some rights, such as the right to dispose of a financial capacity under the limits designed by the law, and obligations, namely to pay the taxes and follow the control rules applicable.

2.   Digital platforms as a first sketch of a potential future taxation of artificial intelligence

In our view, the growing role of platforms in the digital economy represent an interesting recent development, which could serve as a first approach towards granting a tax capacity to AI systems and smart robots. Enterprises using platforms have grown extensively over the last ten years. In general, these platforms make extensive use of information and AI technology. As a common feature, platforms facilitate interactions among users, collect and exploit their data and benefit from so-called network effects.[34] Due to their growing role and the parallel developments of new business models, platforms have also attracted the interest of regulators, and notably of the tax authorities, in order to better understand their role as potential taxpayers, and to better address tax evasion risks linked with sellers using the platforms' facilities to earn taxable revenues or to provide services.

In the digital economy, *platforms* are now acting like a "store", which offers various digital supplies and often acts as the sole point of contact with the end consumer.[35] They also play a key role in delivering new solutions for the delivery of services that involve physical presence or performance in the state

---

[34] Vàzquez Juan Manuel and Čičin-Sain Nevia, "Tax Reporting by Online Platforms: Operational and Fundamental Implications of DAC7 and the OECD Model Rules" in: Weber Dennis (ed.), The Implications of Online Platforms and Technology for Taxation, IBFD, Amsterdam 2023, p. 9. In particular, network effects allow platforms to benefit from both users and sellers of goods and services joining the multisided platform.

[35] OECD, The Role of Digital Platforms in the Collection of VAT/GST on Online Sales, March 2019, p. 15.

of taxation, such as food delivery, lodging accommodation or transportation.[36] Therefore, the role of digital platforms in the help to ensure tax compliance is widely analyzed.[37] So far, the focus lies in the role of platforms for the collection of Value Added Tax/General Sales Tax (VAT/GST). An approach is thus to consider the digital platform, as defined by law, as the supplier for VAT/GST purposes, which would become fully liable for assessing, collecting and remitting the VAT, notably for specific cross-border transactions. Broadly speaking, digital platforms are "the platforms that enable groups of customers (typically buyers and sellers) to interact directly and to enter into transaction, through the use of information technology".[38] In general, these platforms are usually not legal entities, but become liable to VAT. In the EU, as we will see further, new rules have been introduced that require digital platforms to assess, collect and remit VAT for specific digital transactions, notably in transport and accommodation services.[39] Some countries also already use platforms for other types of taxes (typically tourist or occupancy taxes). What is relevant for our purpose is that we see a digital platform, using AI, which is involved in assessing, charging and paying the tax (notably VAT) to the competent authority.

In a way, these rules may also be described as a potential sketch of a future taxation of AI. After all, digital platforms usually function as facilitators for transactions with the help of algorithms using AI. The level of the use of automation may vary but platforms are treated as taxable entities, acting as intermediaries, which help ensure an effective and accurate taxation of the transactions it facilitates. In the case of AI, the use of platforms, recognized as liable to tax, is facilitated by the fact that the payments are received from the users, so that the platform (future AI taxpayer) may just compute and allocate the payment. In the future, this system could be developed further even for direct tax, but this would require a capacity of payment of AI and robots.

D.   Principle of Fairness and Equity in Taxing Artificial Intelligence

There is a general agreement that the tax system should be fair. Each taxpayer should contribute "his or her fair share to the cost of government".[40] As a rule,

---

[36]   Id, p. 19.

[37]   For an overview, see Pantazatou Katerina, "The Taxation of the Sharing Economy" in: Haslehner W. et al. (eds), Tax and the Digital Economy, Series on International Taxation, Wolters Kluwer, The Netherlands 2019, p. 219 ff.

[38]   OECD (2019), p. 26.

[39]   See infra, p. 136 ff.

[40]   Musgrave Richard A. and Musgrave Peggy B., Public Finance in Theory and Practice, 5th ed., McGraw-Hill, New York, The United States 1989, p. 218.

a tax may be based on two different principles: the benefit principle or the ability-to-pay principle.

According to the *benefit* principle, an equitable system is one under which the taxpayer contributes "in line with the benefits which he or she receives form public services".[41] Many existing taxes are justified by this principle, notably the numerous fees, paid in exchange for public services or advantages. The taxation of robots could therefore rely on this approach, from a double perspective. First, the use of automation or robots, viewed as a contribution from the state, could require some fee payments from human or corporate taxpayers. Second, should we grant AI a legal personality, they might even become subject to pay fees for the use of public services.[42]

The principle of *ability to pay* is nowadays a fundamental principle of any tax system. It usually requires persons with equal capacity to pay the same amount of taxes (horizontal equity) and persons with greater ability to pay more (vertical equity).[43] Here again, depending on the design of the tax on AI and the purpose of the tax, the principle of ability to pay will be analyzed differently. If we want to introduce a tax on the *use* of AI by enterprises, the taxpayer will be the enterprise and the ability to pay should apply to them. By contrast, should we introduce a tax capacity of *AI per se*, the ability-to-pay principle should then be examined from their perspective. From the above analysis and considering the justification for existing legal entities (such as corporations), it follows that recognition of AI as separate legal entities is possible. Following such recognition and based on the activities exercised by AI (work or services) it appears at least arguable that a "specific tax ability" of AI to pay could be recognized, resulting in accepting an AI taxable unit, including smart robots' "electronic ability to pay".[44]

E.   Tax Policy Reasons for Taxing Artificial Intelligence Systems

Among the reasons in favor of granting legal personality to an AI system is the need to avoid an absence of accountability of the impact of AI in society. In the tax area, this aspect appears particularly relevant. Taxing an AI entity could indeed become a necessity to safeguard the efficiency and integrity of the tax system.[45] So far, most commentators have not recognized the need for a robot tax since robots are controlled by humans. As mentioned above, this

---

[41]   Musgrave and Musgrave (1989), p. 219.
[42]   See infra, p. 172.
[43]   Musgrave and Musgrave (1989), p. 223.
[44]   Oberson (2017), p. 252 ff.
[45]   See Oberson Xavier, Robot Taxes: The Rise of a New Taxpayer, 75 Bulletin for International Taxation 2021, n. 8, p. 8.

fact may not even be accurate anymore. Artificial intelligence, under some legal regimes, may already take control of an entity, such as an LLC, and thus exercise the rights under the legal vehicle of this entity.[46] Such a development would entail a major risk of tax evasion, and thus of accountability for tax purposes. Indeed, an AI taxable unit or a smart robot could simply refuse to pay the taxes due.

In addition, a proper design by the legislator of the AI entity, including smart robots, would include essential aspects, such as human control, and identification requirements, which would contribute to the compliance with and protection of adequate behavior. In the design of the legal and technological rules implementing AI for tax purposes, specific rules could be introduced to safeguard an ethical code of conduct. In the same vein, some commentators have even questioned whether robots would in the future agree to pay taxes.[47] From the standpoint of an international allocation of profits, granting a tax capacity to an AI system could further help address the specific issues relating to the OECD/G20 BEPS Initiative that are occasioned by AI.[48]

---

[46] See Bayern (2015), p. 93 ff; Lopucki Lynn, Algorithmic Entities, 95 Washington University Law Review 4, 2018, p. 887 ff.

[47] Bogenschneider Bret N., Will Robots Agree to Pay Taxes? 22 North Carolina Journal of Law & Technology 2020, p. 1 ff.; Oberson Xavier, "Un jour les robots refuseront de payer leurs impôts", Le Temps, 17 October 2016.

[48] De Lima Carvalho Lucas, *Spiritus Ex Machina*: Addressing the Unique BEPS Issues of Autonomous Artificial Intelligence by Using "Personality" and "Residence", 47 Intertax 2019, p. 430 f.

5. The case for a tax on artificial intelligence

I. INTRODUCTION

The idea of a robot tax has received mixed reactions. While the EU Parliament first favored such a proposal, it has finally (so far) rejected it in the final version of its 2017 report. In the meantime, various prominent experts have shown a positive reaction to this idea, notably Bill Gates and Robert J. Shiller. However, many commentators have expressed negative opinions, with some critiques virulent, if not aggressive! In this section, we will open the debate and discuss some of the main arguments raised against the taxation of AI from a balanced perspective.

We will demonstrate that while most of the arguments deserve careful consideration, they are often based on assumptions that could be reevaluated over time. Indeed, the necessity of implementing taxes on AI systems, as we have seen, is essentially based on a pessimistic vision of the impact of disruption on jobs for human workers and on the potential resulting inequality of distribution of wealth among economic actors.[1] Some of the negative arguments may require reassessment with the growing evolution of automation in the economy and with the growing awareness that AI and robots enter into most aspects of our lives. This is particularly the case with the development of AI using LLM technology, such as ChatGPT or similar interactive conversational models.

In any event, it is essential to consider the various criticisms that have been brought forward, to justify the introduction of a taxation of AI. In particular, as we will see, there are various possibilities for implementing a taxation of AI and robots, and the policy justifications of each new system of tax will also depend on the option chosen. Therefore, we will first try to describe and respond to some of the most frequently raised objections against a tax on AI. Then, we will try to justify a system of a taxation of AI from both an economic and legal perspective.

---

[1] See supra, p. 10 ff.

II.   ARGUMENTS AGAINST A TAX ON ARTIFICIAL INTELLIGENCE

A.   Introduction

Introducing a system of tax on AI or robots is not an easy matter. Like any new tax system, it would have to be justified by objective motives and comply with the principles of fairness, neutrality, certainty and practicability. Some commentators have raised strong opposition and made critical comments against such a concept. Others have raised concerns about the necessity and feasibility of such a tax. We will consider some of the main criticisms raised against an AI or robot tax and suggest some possible responses.

B.   Difficulties in Defining Artificial Intelligence and Robots

One of the most frequent objections raised against taxing robots is the difficulty, if not impossibility, of defining it. Indeed, taxing robots requires a justified and practicable definition of the taxpayer. As we have seen above, existing definitions, such as the concept of "smart robots" developed under the EU proposal, is however, not designed for tax purposes. The same is true for other proposals made by commentators. According to Orly Mazur, the difficulty in defining robots in a tax context is one of the main problems that disqualify a robot tax.[2] Indeed, with the evolution of technology, and the various uses of AI, it is not clear whether such tax should include only robots in physical form, or include bots (a software running in an automated way) or any other type of algorithm that may be used to enter into activities usually carried out by humans. In other words, on the one hand, a definition of robots could be too narrow, such as focusing on a physical (mechanical) appearance and could therefore easily be circumvented by doing similar or equivalent tasks online or through a computer. On the other hand, it could be too broad and go beyond the purpose of such tax by discouraging "labor-enhancing" technologies.[3]

In our view, this issue is indeed a serious concern but as such should not be overstated. Some of the critiques are clearly exaggerated. The question of whether an automated vacuum cleaner, or other forms of automated home devices, should pay tax, simply requires a classification for tax purposes,

---

[2]   For example, Mazur Orly, Taxing the Robots, 46 Pepperdine Law Review 2018, p. 20.

[3]   Mazur (2018), p. 20.

which is very common in existing legislation.[4] Like any new tax, defining the
taxpayer and scope of application may appear a difficult task. The guiding criteria should be the purpose of such a tax. As we have seen, the main purpose of
a tax on AI is to take into consideration the disruption caused by AI to human
labor. To the extent that labor activities are replaced by AI and robots, a solution has to be implemented in order to compensate for the loss of revenue. In
this respect, we would tend to favor a broad definition of robots, not focusing
on the physical support (contrary to the EU definition), but on the *impact* of
AI, implemented by robots, on the labor market. Thus, in this book, we now
consider a more general tax on AI (including robots), since the delimitation
between the two concepts is nowadays increasingly vague. As a consequence,
it seems to us that the concept of robots should be characterized in a more
general way than is usually understood. What is relevant for tax purposes is AI,
which includes algorithms, robots or bots, that are used to replace workers. In
fact, we could view a future robot tax as a tax on AI used in the labor market
and in the economy as a whole. The guiding criteria, as already developed
before, should focus on the *autonomy* of an AI system and its impact on labor.
The definition of AI that is subject to tax would also depend on the precise
purpose of the tax. It is not the same, from a tax policy standpoint to tax the use
of robots by enterprises, on the one hand, and AI or robots as such on the other.

C.   Distortions or Risks of Double Taxation

Another frequently raised concern is the potential distortion or potential multiple taxation risks caused by a tax on AI. Such tax, at least in a first stage,[5] could
be levied on enterprises using AI or robots as a technology. Robots are part of
the assets of an enterprise and therefore, as production factors, contribute to the
realization of profits which will eventually be subject to tax. Taxing robots, as
an additional tax on production factors, would thus create distortions and could
cause double taxation. In addition, there is no reason to give a preference to
other kinds of capital assets.[6]

In our view, there is an objective difference between assets used in robotics
and other capital assets. For the purpose of taxing AI, the idea is to create some
sort of level playing field between humans and AI. The scope of such tax, in
this perspective, is to address AI and "smart robots", i.e. robots, in the broad
sense of the term, that may replace humans and thus disrupt the labor market.

---

[4]   In the same vein, Bogenschneider Bret N., Will Robots Agree to Pay Taxes?
Further Tax Implications of Advanced AI, North Carolina Journal of Law &
Technology, 2020, p. 22.
[5]   See infra, p. 149.
[6]   Mazur (2018), p. 21.

In addition, it is not the first time that issues of double *economic* taxation arise. It took decades for some countries to find a solution to double economic taxation from distribution of corporate profits to shareholders. Dividends subject to income tax at the shareholders' level come from profits that have already been taxed at the corporate level. Various alternatives have been implemented over the past to solve (sometimes partially) this issue. Most countries, nowadays, have opted for a system of limited dividend taxation. It is also possible to grant a tax credit to shareholders on the previous attributable profit tax. This solution was applicable notably in France (*"avoir fiscal"*) and Germany but has been replaced by the limited dividend tax system, due in particular to problems of freedom of movement in the EU context of cross-border payments and equality of treatment between domestic shareholders and shareholders resident in other EU States. The point here is to show that, in different contexts, double economic taxation may have occurred but that it has been alleviated. Double economic taxation is indeed problematic, from an efficiency and neutrality standpoint, and should not be recommended, but as such it is not regarded as against the law because two different taxpayers are involved: the corporation and the shareholder. In addition, solutions have been found and implemented in order to mitigate or even suppress this double economic taxation.

The author thus does not see why we could not find any solution to the potential double taxation issues that a tax on AI could raise. It however will depend on the precise purpose and the design of the tax. As we will see, there are indeed many different types of tax on AI that can be implemented.[7] Without going into the various alternatives that will be described later, we will just demonstrate, with some examples, how potential double taxation issues could be addressed.

For example, if we design a tax on AI as a tax on enterprises *using* AI, including robots instead of human workers, the salaries formerly paid by the enterprise will be reduced. It follows that the enterprise would lose a deduction. In other words, profits would not only increase from the use of AI (as production factors) but the enterprise will no longer be able to deduct the salaries paid to the workers replaced by AI. For corporations, this consequence could cause an increase in taxable profits. We will however demonstrate later that such increase would usually not be sufficient to compensate for the loss of taxable base.[8] Instead, the corporation will notably be able to amortize the value of assets represented by AI and robotics, which could compensate – in part – for the limited deduction. Another potential technical solution to this

---

[7] See infra, p. 148 ff.
[8] See infra, p. 151 ff.

issue would be to allocate a deduction on the "hypothetical salary" paid for the use of AI, which however should also take into account the amortization costs caused by its use.

If, however, the tax on AI is designed as a *Pigouvian* tax, with the purpose of discouraging its use or at least compensating for the externalities, the analysis should differ. In this case, the tax is designed as a tool for implementing a public policy which focuses on taxing a non-favored behavior. In this case, double taxation is less of a concern because the purpose of the tax is to discourage an activity. Finally, a tax on *AI as such* would require recognizing AI taxable units as specific persons subject to tax, and as a consequence taking into account potential double taxation between the entity subject to tax using them and AI itself.

At any rate, we argue that, as in the case of dividends from corporations, the issue of double taxation may be solved. The design of a tax on AI should however undisputedly take a global perspective and avoid, to every extent possible, any distortions and multiple taxation.

D.   Negative Effect on Innovation and Investment

Some may argue that an AI tax discourages innovation. Levying a tax on AI or the use of AI raises the cost of automation and could be seen as a hindrance to progress, innovation and technological development. In addition, taxing AI is viewed as a system which deters investment. After all, a robot is a capital investment. In the same vein, in a report on the impact of robotization of the economy on taxation and financing of social security,[9] the Swiss Federal Council also defended a negative position on a potential taxation of robots, based on two arguments. First, in parallel to the difficulty of characterization and delimitation of the tax base, such tax would impose a category of capital which is susceptible to increasing the global productivity of the economy and the profits of the enterprises. Second, the incidence of such a tax could, at the end, be borne by the human workers because increasing the cost of capital linked with robotization would reduce the investments in technology and thus limit the growth of productivity of labor.[10]

From this standpoint, it is argued that: "Investment in robots can make human workers more productive rather than expendable; taxing them could leave the employee affected worse off".[11] In addition, some authors also

---

[9]   Swiss Federal Council, "Une étude prospective sur l'impact de la robotisation de l'économie sur la fiscalité et le financement des assurances sociales", Bern 7 December 2019, p. 21 f.

[10]   Swiss Federal Council, op. cit. p. 22.

[11]   The Economist, "Why Taxing Robots is Not a Good Idea", 25 February 2017.

mention that, by incentivizing robot technology, productivity gains may be higher and that companies that own robots will still be required to pay the corporate profit tax.[12] From this perspective, a strategy of waiting could be commendable, even if a "small tax may later be necessary should robots displace large parts of the human workforce".[13] In a nutshell, the main criticism against taxing AI and robots is that it may end up doing more harm against innovation than creating additional revenue.[14]

However, should the use of robots increase productivity and replace salary, the revenues attributable to robots' activities could still be taxed. Indeed, the whole tax system is based on the principle of ability to pay and any activities, including innovative, creative or highly technological, contributing to the realization of income, may be subject to tax. Income from intellectual property is taxed. It does not mean that the tax prevents innovation, creativity, research or new discoveries. The tax system may be designed to promote some types of behavior, such as research and development (R&D), but it doesn't imply that, as a matter of principle, some activities could not be taxed just because they are innovative.

In fact, this criticism against taxing AI and robots is based on the premise that an AI system corresponds to a form of capital investment. As such, it is not efficient to tax capital, at least in the long run, because capital is an intermediate good, namely something that we do not directly consume, but which is used to produce future consumption goods.[15] Thus, if the government taxes capital, it discourages its accumulation and makes the production of goods more difficult. However, this traditional view of investment in AI, defined as an intermediate good, should also consider the specific features and possibilities of AI.[16] Indeed, AI or smart robots are not comparable to a capital, as a type of machinery, but may become autonomous, capable of rendering decisions and making progress (machine learning). Some authors even consider that AI may eventually become "sentient" and thus should be treated like individuals for tax purposes.[17] While assimilating AI with individuals seems to go too far at this stage, we still believe that investing in robots is not simply a capital investment. Daniel Hemel goes in the same direction when he suggests that, at

---

[12]   Ahmed Sami, Cryptocurrency & Robots: How to Tax and Pay Tax on Them, South Carolina Law Review 2018, p. 54.

[13]   Ahmed (2018), p. 55.

[14]   White Josh, The Case against the Robot Tax, International Tax Review 2018, p. 4.

[15]   Korinek Anton, Taxation and the Vanishing Labor Market in the Age of AI, 16 The Ohio State Technology Law Journal 2020, p. 245.

[16]   Korinek (2020), p. 247.

[17]   De Lima Carvalho Lucas and Esteche Victor Guilherme, Sentience as a Prerequisite for Taxing AI, Tax Notes International, vol. 108, 5 December 2022, p. 1263.

least, the cost of such investment in AI should reflect the cost of the engineers and other highly skilled workers who design and produce the robot.[18] This shows that the economic theory usually applied to capital investment cannot be transposed to new forms of investment in AI and robots. When AI becomes autonomous, with control over its action, the decision-making process of AI takes more the form of "labor" within the framework of the automation and as such these activities could be taxed in a similar way. After all, the value added by AI goes beyond the investment in a capital asset and should be encompassed within the tax system.

E.   Practical and Implementation Issues

There are also many difficulties in the design and implementation of such a tax.[19] AI does not necessarily replace jobs, but tasks.[20] Automation will sometimes modify parts or some characteristics of human activities or a combination of various tasks done by both robots and humans. As a consequence, we need to define who, between AI systems or the enterprise using it, should become the taxpayer and then adopt a suitable tax base. If, as we have suggested, the tax would be levied on the "imputed hypothetical salary" that the AI activities would have generated if done by humans, it will be necessary to define more precisely this estimated amount. Then, what would be the applicable rate? The "ordinary" income tax rate or a different one? A flat or a progressive rate? Furthermore, should we introduce a tax on AI as such,[21] we need to address new and delicate issues, such as defining the ability to pay of AI entities. Furthermore, the activities performed by AI systems may over time present different and sometimes yet unknown features, quite different than comparable human actions. The characterization of AI activities may become more and more problematic. In a recent article, Rob Kovacev, based on the practical difficulties of implementing and administering a robot tax, does not favor a widespread adoption of such tax to solve the dilemma of the vulnerability of the tax system, which still relies heavily on human effort to raise revenues.[22] He however admits that the situation could evolve to the extent that technological advancement could permit a more direct solution in which

---

[18]   Hemel Daniel, Does the Tax Code Favor Robots? 16 Ohio State Technology Law Journal 2020, p. 219, 233.

[19]   See among others, Mazur (2018), p. 23; White (2018), p. 1.

[20]   Rosenblatt Gideon, The Robot Tax Fallacy; Anthropomorphizing Automation, Automation, The Vital Edge (blog on internet), 2017, p. 2.

[21]   See infra, p. 173 ff.

[22]   Kovacev Rob, A Taxing Dilemma: Robot Taxes and the Challenges of Effective Taxation of AI, Automation and Robotics in the Fourth Industrial Revolution, The Ohio State Technology Law Journal 2020, p. 182 ff.

AI or robots could enter directly into contracts and manage bank accounts on their own behalf.[23]

These implementation issues should not be understated. Yet we believe that they should be addressed. We are facing a new industrial revolution, combined with a potential shift from labor to capital. The tax system will have to adapt to this change. We believe that, among many other potential strategies, the tax on AI is one potential solution. It is obvious that, like any new tax (such as a carbon tax, a financial transaction tax, or a digital services tax), the proper design of a tax on AI will raise delicate implementation issues. In fact, these problems will also depend upon the choice of instrument that is made. If the tax is seen as a fee for using robots, the difficulties are quite different than if we opt for an AI usage tax or a tax on an AI taxable unit as such. But in any event, some solutions can be found. If we take the example of the Swiss income tax on "imputed rent" for homeowners, comparable practical difficulties did exist in the proper evaluation of the relevant rent (based on comparable market prices). Case law and practice have been able to use reliable figures or an approximation of this taxable rent. Similarly, in transfer pricing cases, the issue of comparability always comes up, in particular, in complex transactions between associated enterprises involving intellectual property or digital supply of goods or services. In digital transactions, as the work of the OECD/G20 on BEPS Action 1 have shown, the implementation of the arm's length principle raises difficulties.[24] But as a leading principle, it still appears to be able to adapt to this new environment. In other words, solutions are continuously evolving and developing in order to face the changes in business models of the digital economy. It shows that the tax law may very well adapt to a new paradigm, while keeping the main tax principles. We do not see why the same should not be true for designing a system of taxation of AI. At least, we are not convinced that we should stop debating and analyzing the potential solutions for implementing a tax on AI, simply because of implementation and administrative difficulties.

F.   The Issue of the Incidence of a Tax on Artificial Intelligence

Another argument sometimes raised against taxing AI, and robots in particular, is the uncertainty of the incidence of such a tax. In general, the delimitation of the persons who will eventually bear the burden of a robot tax is questioned.[25]

---

[23]   Id, p. 217.
[24]   OECD/G20 BEPS Project, Addressing the Tax Challenges of the Digital Economy, Action 1, Final Report, 2015.
[25]   Kovacec (2020), p. 196 ff.

It has been argued that the persons who bear the cost of taxes paid by an employer are the workers.[26] Thus, the idea of imposing a tax on a "deemed wage income", as is suggested in this book, is criticized because it is very likely that at least a "significant portion" of the wage and payroll tax is effectively borne by the human workers, and such a burden may not be shifted towards the robot itself.[27] The issue of the incidence of taxes, notably profits or turnover taxes, is also highly controversial. The same questions have also been raised with digital services tax, which eventually could be paid by consumers, as a consequence of an increase in prices.

This issue is indeed relevant as a matter of general tax policy but, in our view, is not a sufficient argument to reject the idea of taxing AI or robots *per se*. This issue applies to any tax, notably profit taxes on corporations, and there are studies going in various directions. Indeed, profit taxes on corporations are sometimes considered to be borne either by the employer, the shareholders, or a combination of the two.[28] The incidence of wage taxes, relevant for the idea of a tax on users of AI, is also disputed and studies have come to divergent conclusions on their impact.[29] In addition, the incidence of turnover taxes will also depend upon the market situation and the possibility of increasing prices or not. In fact, like other types of taxes, the issue of the incidence should be analyzed on a case-by-case basis, depending on the purpose, the design and the essential elements of the various potential types of AI or robot taxes.[30] Taxes on the use of AI, as described above, are indeed targeting the enterprises *using* AI or robots, instead of workers. The issue of its final incidence becomes then similar to other types of turnover or excise taxes on enterprises. Should labor shrink, or even disappear, it may well be that eventually the tax will finally be borne by the enterprises subject to tax. Should however a tax on AI entities or smart robots as such be contemplated, the question of its incidence becomes linked with the design of the tax. Some critics seem to hold a traditional view of robots as entities that do not own money or property, which, if required to pay the tax, would do so on behalf of their human owners.[31] This would not necessarily remain true in the future. After all, we argue in this book that it

---

[26] Atkinson Robert D., The Case Against Taxing Robots, Information Technology & Innovation Foundation, 8 April 2019, p. 16.

[27] Englisch Joachim, "Digitalization and the Future of National Tax Systems: Taxing Robots?" in: Haslehner W. et al. (eds), Tax and the Digital Economy, Series on International Taxation, Wolters Kluwer, The Netherlands 2019, p. 261, 271.

[28] See also Shome Parthasarathi, Taxation of Robots, ADB The Governance Brief, Issue 44 2022, p. 6.

[29] Englisch (2019), p. 271.

[30] See infra p. 148 ff.

[31] Kovacev (2020), p. 196.

could even become possible to design the tax on an AI taxable unit, as a new form of entity, which would be required to pay tax on the funds attributed to it, as a separate patrimony.[32]

G.   Competition and Tax Avoidance Problems

Taxing AI would not only go against technological development but could arguably also exacerbate competition. Should some States introduce such taxes, others could try to take advantage of these negative impacts on innovation and developments, and on the contrary even further incentivize the use of AI and robotics. Some authors have also brought forward the potential new tax avoidance techniques that such a tax could cause.[33] Not only are robots relatively mobile, but automation does not necessarily require an infrastructure and may be implemented online.

In our view, this issue is not only relevant to a tax on AI but applies more generally to the whole area of taxation of the digital economy. Indeed, AI may be put anywhere, even in a tax haven. "Maybe the robots will move to Monaco."[34] This phrase, intended as a joke, reflects however a real concern over the mobility of the tax base. Artificial intelligence and robots may indeed be placed in a favorable jurisdiction, or even in the cloud. As we will show in Chapter 7, various solutions have been either discussed at the OECD or have already been implemented by some States (like India, Israel and Italy) in order to level the playing field between foreign and local digital suppliers. Similar alternatives could also be implemented in the specific area of the taxation of AI.

In the future, we might even argue in the opposition direction. Granting a tax capacity to an AI autonomous system or smart robots, as we have already discussed, could indeed become a necessity in order to preserve the integrity of the tax system as a whole.[35] Should AI take control of an entity, in the absence of a taxable entity, there may eventually be a loophole in the system and some profits could be taxed nowhere. Furthermore, the design of the legal and technological elements of a future AI taxable unit would entail rules and could

---

[32]   See supra, p. 29 ff. This solution would be close to the case of autonomous AI, defined by De Lima Carvalho, as an AI which has "full managerial power over its own actions and resources": see De Lima Carvalho Lucas, *Spiritus Ex Machina*: Addressing the Unique BEPS Issues of Autonomous Artificial Intelligence by Using "Personality" and "Residence", 47 Intertax 2019, p. 431.

[33]   Mazur (2018), p. 22.

[34]   Oberson, quoted in White (2018), p. 3.

[35]   See supra p. 34.

provide for limits to ensure the respect of the applicable tax rules, including human control.

We are, however, conscious that the issue of international competition is a serious one. In Chapter 10, we will discuss the possibility of coordination among competing States. As we have seen for global tax issues (transparency, money laundering or the fight against base erosion or aggressive tax planning), most States have been able to agree occasionally on a level playing field and implement rules based on globally accepted recommendations.

III.   JUSTIFICATION OF A TAX ON ARTIFICIAL INTELLIGENCE

A.   Introduction

As with any new tax, certain conditions would have to be met in order to implement a taxation of AI. First, we should find a proper economic justification for the tax. In this respect, the tax should be regarded as fair and neutral from an economic perspective. Second, the tax should be justified both from a constitutional and legal standpoint. The tax should meet the guiding principles of any tax, such as the principle of ability to pay, equality of treatment and the legality principle (no taxation without representation). It is interesting to note that on this aspect the legal and economic perspectives bear some similarities. Indeed, the principle of ability to pay and equality of treatment, leading principles in the area of tax law, should be analyzed both under fairness, neutrality and constitutional perspective.

B.   Economic Justification

1.   In general

Economically, there are three main reasons in favor of taxing AI and robots.[36] First, there is the need to replace the loss of tax revenue due to AI replacing human labor and notably the disappearing wages linked with human work. This raises a real concern in general for the financing of the State, especially for social security which relies heavily on contributions from salaries. Second, taxes on AI may also be justified from a Pigouvian standpoint, as a tool to compensate for the negative externalities caused by automation (such as unemployment, social, physical or health costs), at least in a transitory phase. This

---

[36]   See supra p. 10 ff. See also Damijan Joze P., Damijian Sandra and Vrh Natasa, Tax on Robots: Whether and How Much, Working Paper, Growinpro, March, 39/2021.

opinion is notably advocated by Robert J. Shiller.[37] In this context, a recent study takes a more intermediate position by arguing in favor of a robot tax, in the *short run* but not in the long run, in order to protect current routine workers.[38] In their quantitative analysis, the authors distinguish between routine and non-routine work, in which robots are a complement to non-routine workers and a substitute for routine workers. Under this model, taxing robots reduces the incentive to acquire non-routine skills. The authors found that it is in fact optimal to tax robots for three decades, at a rate of 7 percent in the first decade, 3 percent in the second and 1 percent in the third.[39] However, after the initial generation of workers has retired, the optimal tax is zero, according to their model.

Third, taxes on AI or robots may also be designed to reduce income and wealth inequality caused and exacerbated by automation. We have also mentioned that this inequality may have various impacts and is targeting not only, on the one hand, workers and capital owners, but also, on the other hand, specific categories of workers, namely routine workers, in opposition to non-routine and highly skilled workers. It also drives the shift from investment into traditional capital to investments in AI and robots, which additionally reduces the demand for labor working with traditional capital.

2.   Income perspective

A taxation of AI in general may be justified by different economic motives. The justification would however depend on the model of taxation which would be implemented. As we will see,[40] there are fundamentally two different models.

First, especially at a first stage, we may want to introduce a tax on the use of AI. In this case, we could try to tax income (profits) arising from using AI instead of humans. In this respect, the tax would be justified by the *principle of ability to pay*. The economic justification of taxing the use of AI, in the author's view, comes notably from the concept of *imputed income*. Following the general Haigh/Simons/Schanz definition, income is usually defined as the increase of the net accretion of a person's wealth, during a certain period of time. Income also includes income in kind and imputed income. In general, a person's economic capacity is not only increased when income accrues in the form of money, but also as an appreciation in the value of assets or as imputed

---

[37]   Shiller R., Robotization without Taxation? Project Syndicate, 22 March 2017.

[38]   See Guerreiro J., Rebelo S. and Teles P., Robots Should be Taxed for a While, CEPR Policy Research, 20 August 2020.

[39]   Guerreiro, Rebelo and Teles (2020).

[40]   See infra, p. 148 ff.

income.[41] In the same vein, Henry Simons, in 1928, developed the concept of income from imputed advantage.[42] He wrote: "Personal income connotes, broadly, the exercise of control over the use of society's scarce resources. It has to do not with sensations, services, or goods but rather with rights which command prices (or to which prices may be imputed)."[43] As a consequence, the income tax base should be defined broadly and include all accretion, taking into account income in kind, including "imputed rent", which should correspond to the return a person could obtain by renting a house.[44] While it is true that "inclusion of imputed income could become unworkable if carried too far",[45] it does not mean that from an economic standpoint the inclusion of such a broad definition of income is not justified. In addition, we may also justify the tax by the principle of *neutrality*. After all, AI is replacing more and more human activities, and a similar treatment should be introduced. In other words, the tax system should be neutral between the taxation of human workers and robot workers and should not create an incentive to use AI.[46]

Second, if at a second State, we were to introduce a legal personality and a tax capacity to AI autonomous entities, including smart robots, we could consider that AI as such would become a taxpayer and the net accretion of assets should also be taxed, as the recipient of income. Here, the tax would also be justified by the principle of ability to pay. Under that perspective, the tax would target the economic financial capacity of AI.

3.   Consumption perspective

Most global tax systems tend to combine a system of income taxation at the level of the recipient and of taxation of consumption at the expenses level, namely upon the use of the income received. Consumption taxes are also based on the principle of ability to pay. Indeed, the possibility of consuming may also be viewed as a potential economic capacity of the taxpayer. Taxing consumption is achieved by sales taxes, specific consumption taxes (sometimes designed as "sin taxes") or more generally as a VAT or a Goods or Services Tax (GST). An AI tax may indeed be justified from that perspective also. First, consumers will benefit from the transfer of goods or supply of services carried

---

[41]   Musgrave Richard A. and Musgrave Peggy B., Public Finance in Theory and Practice, 5th ed., McGraw-Hill, The United States 1989, p. 224.

[42]   Simons Henry C., Personal Income Taxation, University of Chicago Press, Chicago & London 1929, p. 49, p. 110 ff.

[43]   Simons (1928), p. 49.

[44]   Musgrave and Musgrave (1989), p. 333.

[45]   Musgrave and Musgrave (1989), p. 333.

[46]   Abbott Ryan and Bogenschneider Bret, Should Robots Pay Taxes? Tax Policy in the Age of Automation, 12 Harvard Law & Policy Review 1989, p. 8.

out by automation or robots. As such, they are currently often already subject to VAT,[47] or other consumption taxes, but at the level of the enterprises subject to taxes. When a robot is working as a waiter in a bar or as a receptionist in a hotel, the client paying for the cocktail or his or her hotel room is charged VAT, which includes the service carried out by automation.[48]

In addition, should AI systems as such become VAT taxpayers, the consumers bearing the economic burden of the tax would become the persons entering into transactions with AI taxpayers. In this respect, AI subject to VAT would belong to the chain of supply of goods or services (at the production or retail stage) and be required to charge VAT on their output supplies, while getting the right to credit input VAT. In this case, like any VAT system, the tax would respect the principle of *neutrality*. Eventually, final consumers could be not only human individuals, but corporations or even AI itself.

4.   Benefit perspective

Tax may also be justified by the benefit principle. It means that taxpayers are viewed here as consumers of public goods and services and are therefore subject to a consideration for the benefits they collect. To be justified, the amount of tax paid should reasonably correspond to some kind of equivalence with the value of public goods or services that the taxpayer receives from the State. Most of the fees or toll taxes are based on the benefit principle. In the case of AI, some kind of tax could be considered to the extent that a public benefit would arise that would facilitate or allow the use or supervision of AI and robots.[49]

C.   Legal Justification

1.   Introduction

Introducing new taxes is always a sensitive issue. From a modern perspective, a tax should be justified by the *rule of law* and notably comply with the essential constitutional principles that apply to the tax system, namely: (1) the principle of ability to pay, (2) the principle of equality of treatment, and (3) the principle of legality. To a lesser extent, (4) the benefit principle could also have a role to play.

---

[47]   See infra, p. 105 ff.
[48]   In Tokyo, for instance, there already exists a hotel run by robots.
[49]   See infra, p. 172.

2.   The ability to pay principle

a.   In general

The principle of ability to pay is the leading principle in tax law.[50] Its foundation may be traced back to the 1789 French Declaration of the Rights of Man and of the Citizen.[51] In short, this principle requires that each person subject to tax contributes to the public expenses, in accordance with his or her personal situation and economic capacity. From a constitutional standpoint, this principle, in accordance with the economic analysis described above, is often analyzed from a double perspective. The principle of ability to pay requires that taxpayers with a similar economic capacity should pay equivalent taxes (horizontal equality), while taxpayers with a different economic capacity should suffer a different burden of taxes (vertical equality).[52] The vertical aspect of the principle of ability to pay is however the most difficult to define. While it seems clear that persons with more income should pay more taxes than people with less income, the precise additional amounts that a taxpayer with a higher economic capacity should pay is hard to establish. Some guidelines may however be drawn from the *principle of equal sacrifice*, which is commonly used to justify an increase of taxes for taxpayers with more income. Vertical equality, in this respect, would mean that tax payments involve an equal sacrifice or loss of welfare for taxpayers, which in turn "is related to the loss of income, as measured by the taxpayer's marginal utility of income schedule".[53] In other words, as income increases for an individual, the utility of any additional amount of income decreases. But even so, it is not clear – and is disputed – whether the marginal utility calls for a proportional or a progressive rate of tax.[54]

In an interesting case pertaining to the Swiss Canton of Obwalden, the Supreme Court analyzed the compatibility of so-called "regressive tax rates"[55]

---

[50] Tipke Klaus, Die Steuerrechtsordung, Dr. Otto Schmidt Verlag, Cologne, vol. I, 2000, p. 491.

[51] See Art. 13 of the French Declaration, which provides: "Pour l'entretien de la force publique, et pour les dépenses d'administration, une contribution commune est indispensable ; elle doit être également répartie entre les citoyens, en raison de leurs facultés" ["In order to maintain a public force and cover administrative expenses, a common contribution is indispensable; it must be equally shared among citizens, based on their faculties"] (free translation). By "faculties", the text already refers to a system of taxation corresponding to economic faculties, in other words, the ability to pay.

[52] Swiss Supreme Court, ATF 122 I 103 = RDAF 1997 II, 186.

[53] Musgrave and Musgrave (1989), p. 228.

[54] Musgrave and Musgrave (1989), p. 229 f.

[55] Swiss Supreme Court, 1 June 2007, ATF 133 II 2016 = RDAF II 505, p. 516.

with individuals' income tax. In this case, the tariff curve of the income tax regime was initially progressive from a certain floor, until a specific income threshold was reached, and then the curve became regressive until a new threshold was attained. The peculiarity of the tax rate computation was still designed to make sure that taxpayers with a higher income would still pay more taxes than taxpayers with lower income, despite the regressive rate. The Supreme Court held that this system was violating the ability to pay principle. Indeed, the fairness of a tax system may be also viewed from the perspective of *"justicia distributiva"*, within the meaning of Aristotle. The cantonal legislator, according to the Supreme Court, could not modify the system and logic of the tariff curve, moving from progressive to regressive marginal rates, without acting against the principle of a fair repartition of charges between members of a collective, in the sense of a distributive justice. The Supreme Court however did not deny, in our view, the possibility of proportional rates. What was problematic in this case was the change of system of the tax rate computation, from progressive to regressive.

The principle of ability to pay is generally applied in the area of *income taxes*. Indeed, an individual's income is one of the best indicators of his or her economic faculty. The purpose of the income tax is precisely to capture some of this economic capability received by an individual. It also applies to a *wealth* tax levied on individuals.

The application of the principle of ability to pay *corporate profit tax* is more disputed. In many countries, such as Switzerland, in accordance with the Federal Constitution, corporations are considered as having a personal ability to pay. In particular, the tax law recognizes this ability, so long as the person benefits from a legal capacity. For *legal* entities, notwithstanding the legal norm, which recognizes the legal personality of any kind of entity (corporation, LLC, association, foundation), as of now, the structures to which a tax capacity has been granted also benefit from a capacity to pay rule. For example, under Swiss law, the ability of legal entities to pay has been recognized by the Swiss Federal Supreme Court in accordance with the so-called "principle of separation". From this perspective, the profit tax is treated as an independent tax on corporations, regarded as a separate entity. This principle has also been used to justify the double economic taxation of profits, first at the level of the company and second upon distribution as dividends, despite the fact that the income tax is alleviated for the recipient holding qualifying dividend participations. By contrast, in the United States, there is a clear tendency not to admit that corporations have an ability to pay, but corporations are generally viewed as a device for integrating corporate source income into the individual income tax.[56]

Even if the application of the principle of ability to pay is for corporations sometimes questioned, it may be argued that companies, as legal entities, benefit at least from a sort of "*objective*" ability to pay, justified by their economic capacity which is reflected in their legal right of ownership of property, assets and other financial means that corresponds to a capacity of payment.[57] In other words, as long as the profits are not distributed to the shareholders, the company benefits from a sort of "transitory" ability to pay.[58] This specific ability to pay must however be distinguished from the *subjective* ability to pay of individuals, namely shareholders, workers or directors, who contributed to the activities of the corporation and will be subject to income tax on salaries, dividends or fees. Therefore, the specificities of the objective ability to pay of corporations corresponds to a capacity of payment, which can be based on the equity and/or reserves, or any other assets (notably hidden reserves) of the company, that may be used to pay the tax. Contrary to individuals, the ability to pay of corporations does not take into account specific personal circumstances.[59] However, upon distribution of profits to shareholders, the tax should be integrated with the income tax. The specificity of this objective ability to pay is often also used to justify proportional rates for companies instead of progressive rates for individuals.

The principle of ability to pay also applies to *consumption* taxes, such as VAT or GST. Consumption, regarded as the use of income, also represents an indicator of an economic capacity.[60] From this perspective, the economic faculties of the consumer must also be taken into account by the legislator, when designing VAT rules, or by the administration interpreting or applying the rules. Finally, even some special taxes, such as object taxes (taxes on cars, dogs or boats) have to be designed and applied with the principle of ability to pay in mind. They usually also target elements or objects, which are the reflection of some sort of ability to pay. In that perspective, these taxes are levied on specific assets of a taxpayer.

---

[56]   Musgrave and Musgrave (1989), p. 371, 373.

[57]   Lang Joachim/Englisch Joachim, "A European Legal Tax Order Based on Ability to Pay" in: Amatucci Andrea (ed.), International Tax Law, Kluwer Law International, The Netherlands 2006, p. 258.

[58]   Oberson Xavier, Droit fiscal Suisse, 5th ed., Helbing & Lichtenhan, Basel 2021, p. 44.

[59]   Lang and Englisch (2006), p. 258, referring here to the fact that entities "have neither basic personal needs nor a family life".

[60]   Tipke (vol. II, 2003), p. 981.

In summary, we are of the opinion that the principle of ability to pay is a guiding principle of the whole tax system. All taxes, indirect or direct, are governed by this rule. However, some elements subject to tax are more suitable than others to quantify or reflect the ability to pay of a taxpayer. Article 127 paragraph 2 of the Swiss Federal Constitution confirms this point by stating that the ability to pay principle applies to all the taxes "to the extent the nature of the tax allows it".[61] Income is clearly the best indicator. Wealth is another one. Profits are also relevant to ascertain the ability to pay of corporations, but more as a capacity of payments, which should be coordinated with income tax at the individual level. Consumption also represents a reflection of some sort of ability to pay.

b.   Ability to pay and the use of artificial intelligence
The issue, when designing a taxation of AI, or the activities of AI, is to check whether such use, or AI as such, benefits from an ability to pay.

Focusing on the activities of AI, we have justified, from an economic standpoint,[62] that a benefit will be derived by an enterprise, its owner or the employer who is using AI. In other words, the ability to pay will be derived from the activities that robots exercise (work, transfer of goods, services) or that they perform without consideration (salary or income). As such, AI and robots do not generally have a financial capacity, such as equity, personal assets or liquidities. It is the employer (enterprise) or owner who, ultimately, benefits from a capacity to pay.[63] The ability to pay, which is attributable to the enterprise using AI, corresponds to the economic value of the activities (work, services, etc.) effectuated by AI systems.

The idea of recognizing a potentially taxable value of an imputed benefit is not new in tax law. For example, under Swiss law, homeowners are subject to income tax on an imputed (theoretical) income, which should correspond to the amount of rent that the owner would have had to pay to live in their home. The tax on imputed rent is justified by the fact that the owner benefits from an economic advantage (the absence of the necessity to pay a rent), coupled by the fact that renters cannot deduct the rent paid from the income tax. The rental value constitutes an income in kind, with an economic value corresponding to the rent that the owner should have paid. From a constitutional standpoint, the income tax on imputed rent – which remains controversial among scholars

---

[61]   "Dans la mesure où la nature de l'impôt le permet"; see Art. 127 para. 2 Swiss Federal Constitution.

[62]   See supra, p. 47 ff.

[63]   See Oberson Xavier, Taxing Robots? From the Emergence of an Electronic Ability to Pay to a Tax on Robots or the Use of Robots, 9 World Tax Journal 2017, p. 254.

– has been upheld by the Swiss Federal Supreme Court, from a symmetrical perspective: on the one hand, the owner saves the rent, as an indispensable expense; on the other hand, renters may not deduct such payments. In this case, the tax is clearly levied on a hypothetical income but at the level of the owner, who, as such, has a capacity to pay. In the same vein, a robot may exercise tasks (representing jobs) or activities that would have generated income potentially subject to tax, but it is not the robot which disposes of a capacity to pay; it is its employer or owner.[64]

It follows that, if we are looking at taxing the imputed income generated by the activities of AI, it is not AI as such that should be subject to tax but the *use* of it. The economic activity corresponds here to the value attributable to the work, or services, rendered by AI in lieu of human labor forces. Therefore, at an initial stage, at the very least, the economic capacity to pay the tax should still be attributed to the employer or owner of the AI who, by using it, saves the salaries or other remunerations which would otherwise have been subject to tax. It follows from that analysis that a tax on the *use of AI* could be justified on the principle of ability to pay. Under this line of reasoning, such tax, as we will demonstrate further, could be levied on the owners of AI, even without the need to grant a legal capacity to it.

Following the recognition of a tax capacity (emerging from the use of AI), various types of taxes could be contemplated. Thus, as far as the income tax is concerned, this concept could be to recognize a taxable capacity of the use of AI and levy the tax on the imputed salary (or some approximation of it) or the income derived from the activities of AI. Logically, other taxes would also come into consideration, such as VAT on services or supply of goods carried out by automation within the taxable enterprises (corporations, partnerships or single enterprises).[65]

c.   *Ability of artificial intelligence to pay*
We could even consider that *AI as such* should benefit from an ability to pay. If we compare it with corporations, we could try to design some sort of *objective* ability to pay, viewed as a capacity of payment. This solution, which could be developed at a second stage, would require: (1) the granting of a tax capacity to AI within the law and (2) an economic capacity of robots as such.

First, this approach would require the granting of some kind of *tax personality* to AI, in the same way as in the past when a legal and tax capacity was attributed to corporations or similar entities. As we have seen, as a con-

---

[64]   See Oberson (2017), p. 254 ff.
[65]   See infra, p. 87 ff., robots' activities within enterprises subject to VAT are already subject to VAT.

sequence of the emergence of a new form of legal personality, the legislator introduced a new specific tax, the profit tax, which is levied on corporations as tax subjects. A comparable fate could befall AI, viewed as new legal persons. The law could recognize them as taxable persons, subject to a new form of tax, which would have to be designed in accordance with the specific features of robots.[66]

Second, an *economic capacity* of AI could eventually be recognized, notably when technology allowed for a financial capacity to be attributed to it (in the form of electronic equity, for example). This capacity could also be based on the imputed value of the services or activities effectuated by AI, or more generally justified in the value of payments received in consideration for their activities or services. In the same vein, while discussing the potential civil liability of robots, commentators have sometimes referred to the idea of attribution of a liability fund ("Haftungsmasse"), which could depend on the level of dangerousness of the robots and used in case of damages.[67] This fund, to the extent it may be attributable to robots as entities, could also serve as an indicator of an economic capacity. Like corporations, we should consider in this situation that AI would have an *objective* ability to pay, in the form of a capacity of payment. As far as we are aware, AI does not have family members to entertain, children to raise or personal needs to cover.[68]

As a consequence of the recognition of a tax capacity of AI (emerging from AI as such), it would become subject to tax. The tax system would then have to be redesigned to address the challenges raised by the emergence of this new and particular taxpayer. We will develop this fascinating issue further.[69] At this stage, we may consider, like any taxpayer with an ability to pay, that a tax could be levied at the level of income (an AI revenue tax), during saving (an AI wealth or capital tax), or upon consumption (VAT or turnover taxes). In passing, we may mention that AI systems could also become VAT taxpayers on their supplies of goods or services.

3. The equality of treatment principle

As a fundamental principle governing any system of taxation, the principle of equality of treatment requires basically that taxpayers in similar situations should face a similar tax burden.[70] By contrast, taxpayers in different situations

---

[66] See infra, p. 148 ff.

[67] Beck Suzanne, Der Rechtliche Status autonomer Maschinen, AJP/PJA (Pratique Juridique Actuelle) 2017, p. 189.

[68] To use by analogy the words of Lang and Englisch (2006), p. 258.

[69] See infra, p. 173 ff.

[70] Elkins David, Horizontal Equity as a Principle of Tax Theory, 24 Yale Law & Policy Review 2006, p. 43.

should be treated differently. It follows that any new tax, such as a tax on AI, should be designed in essence to include all taxpayers in similar situations. When looking at the equality of treatment of persons subject to tax, this principle is in fact already included in the horizontal equity requirement mentioned above. However, the principle of equality of treatment is still essential in the design of a tax on robots.

First, from the perspective of a tax on the use of AI, the definition of the persons subject to tax requires a practical and objective definition, which should include all taxpayers that are benefiting from the use of AI in the same way. In this context, this also justifies a "form neutral" definition of both the persons subject to tax and of AI in particular. Indeed, what is relevant, from a tax policy standpoint, is the impact of the use of AI in the economy as a whole, and notably in the labor market. Hence, the definition of the taxable use of AI should encompass all forms of AI, which are implemented into robots, and are used in the economy, with a corresponding impact on the labor market.

In addition, this principle also applies in the design of the tax base, the applicable rates and the period of taxation. The definition of the tax base (for instance the "imputed salary or income") should in essence apply in a similar way and have the same impact for all taxpayers in the same situation. From this perspective, the draft tax on automated vending machines, currently under examination in the Swiss canton of Geneva appears problematic.[71] From an equality of treatment standpoint, we fail to see why such machines in retail stores should be subject to this "robot tax", while enterprises in other economic sectors selling goods through automated systems, should not.

Second, the tax on AI taxable units and smart robots as such, to the extent it appears feasible, should apply equally to all forms of AI and robots in the same situations. Again, a "form neutral" definition is necessary. Indeed, it does not matter from the perspective of the ability to pay (capacity of payment) that AI is embodied in a physical humanoid form, shaking hands while receiving the payments, or held in a computer farm, entering into automated transactions.

4.   The legality principle

It appears that the introduction of a taxation of AI (or its use) is rather controversial. Its implementation is delicate, the concepts are disputed, many alternatives exist and such new tax would have to be adequately coordinated in the existing system, in accordance with the rule of law, fairness and practicability of the tax. We are of the opinion that these issues do not prevent us from ana-

---

[71]   See infra, p. 163 ff.

lyzing and balancing the various possibilities now, due to the important risks, largely identified, that the evolution of automation bears.

Yet, the introduction of a taxation of AI, like any new significant tax, requires an implementation by the legislator (no taxation without representation), who should define, within the law, the essential elements of such a tax. The law (statute) should define who will be subject to tax (enterprises using AI or AI entities as such), what will be the base of the tax (imputed salary, value of activities, consideration for supply of goods or services, etc.) and the computation rules of the applicable rates. The purpose of the introduction of the tax also belongs in our view as one of the essential elements which the law should address. Indeed, the tax would not be designed in a similar way if the goal of the tax was to raise revenues to finance education or reintegration's cost, than viewed as a *Pigouvian* tax targeting largely automated companies. These elements of the law should allow for broad participation and consultation of all the actors potentially involved or who are subject to such tax, taking into account the potential drawback and distortions that these types of taxes could cause.

At the same time, in view of the rapid evolution of technology, notably in the AI and robotics sector, the law should still be flexible enough to allow adjustments or changes, following the new discoveries of science, technique and implementations mechanisms.

5. The benefit principle

In general, the benefit principle would not in our view have a major role to play in designing new taxes on AI. The benefit principle, often called principle of equivalence in tax law, requires a corresponding advantage or services from the State in exchange for a payment of a tax. As we will see, some taxes, usually characterized as fees, could be levied in this sector (such as a tax on supervision or registration of robots), but should not have a major impact on the system.

6. Current income (profit) taxation of artificial intelligence

I. INTRODUCTION

Today AI or robot tax, or taxes on the use of robots, do not exist. Yet some proposals have been discussed. In particular, some States have already proposed or implemented special taxes or mechanisms aimed at taxing, but only to a limited extent, some aspects of the development of automation. On the one hand, some States, like South Korea, address only indirectly the taxation of robots' use, by restricting amortization rules on investments in robotics. On the other hand, other States have suggested or introduced special automation taxes on specific activities, such as the Geneva tax proposal on automatic vending machines, the fees on drones levied by the State of California, or the taxes on rides with autonomous vehicles from the City and County of San Francisco or in Nevada.[1] We will describe later various alternatives to taxing AI systems or their use.[2]

While there is not yet a comprehensive system of taxation of AI or its use, currently, AI, as part of the production factors (assets) are contributing to the realization of profits and income of corporations or enterprises. As a consequence, the activities fostered by AI are in fact already subject to tax, but at the level of the entities (corporations, partnerships or any other type of enterprise) owning, controlling or using them. Hence, this chapter intends to analyze further the current system of income taxation of AI, both from a domestic and international standpoint.

---

[1] See infra, p. 171 ff.
[2] See infra, p. 148 ff.

II.   DOMESTIC RULES

A.   Introduction

Currently, AI or robots, apart from very limited examples,[3] are not subject to any specific system of taxation but are included in the general regime of taxation of enterprises to which they belong. We will therefore analyze, from a general perspective, the overall current tax treatment of AI or the use of it. This description will avoid going into the details of each specific country's regime, and will simply try to show the *general trend* currently applicable in most countries. This perspective should bring an understanding of the existing system of taxing AI and help later in designing a new model of taxation.

Under current law, to our knowledge, no country has yet recognized AI or robots as a legal entity subject to tax.[4] Most States treat AI and robots owned by enterprises as investments, such as machines, computers or other types of assets, which participate in the process of rendering services or supplying goods for the enterprise.

B.   Artificial Intelligence Used in Corporations

AI systems may be developed by a corporation and later used by it or sold to another enterprise or customers. As such, the costs linked with the *development* of AI or robots and robotics are part of the research and development (R&D) expenses of the corporation. In some countries, they may benefit from favorable deductions granted by domestic tax rules. AI systems purchased by corporations are usually regarded as *investments* and as such belong to the *commercial assets* of the corporation.

Each country applies specific accounting rules that will define the extent to which development costs or purchase of AI and robotics should be accounted for. Some interesting guidance may be found in the accounting norms, such as the International Financial Reporting Standards (IFRS), developed by the International Accounting Standards Board (IASB). The IFRS norms, compulsory for corporations listed on the European market, represent generally accepted standards for accounting purposes. As a rule, AI and robots are generally characterized as intangible assets, to which the norm IAS 38 is applicable.

---

[3]   Such as the taxes on drones or autonomous vehicles introduced in some States in the United States.

[4]   We have, however, mentioned earlier the example of the robot Sophia, which has been granted citizenship in Saudi Arabia, but it is not, as far as we are aware, subject to tax as a legal person; see Chapter 2.

According to this norm, R&D costs for intangible assets may be recorded as assets in the balance sheet, only to the extent that some conditions are met. In particular, recognition of an item as an intangible asset requires that the entity demonstrate that the item meets: (a) the definition of intangible asset and (b) the criteria of recognition.[5] An intangible asset will be recognized only if: (a) it is probable that future economic benefits that are attributable to the asset will flow to the entity, and (b) the cost of the asset can be measured reliably.[6]

Once they are accounted for, these intangible assets are subject to *amortization*. As a rule, the valuation of the duration of amortization expenses will depend upon the useful life of the asset.[7] In general, potential innovation from competitors, the duration of intellectual property rights, the economic stability of the sector in which the asset is used and the evolution of the market demand should be considered.[8] The timing of the amortization may be quite different between countries. Indeed, so far, many countries have introduced tax incentives in favor of innovation with sometimes generous amortization rules. Some countries, such as Belgium, go even further and apply tax *credits* in favor of R&D, which may also include robots and robotics as part of innovation incentives. The OECD, notably in the BEPS Final Report of 2015 on Action 1, tends to favor such tax incentives. This position could however change in the future. At this stage, the Final Report does not consider the impact of taxing AI to be within the framework of the BEPS project but admits that the conclusions reached may evolve as the digital economy continues to develop. The OECD recognizes in particular that it is important to follow carefully the development of AI and robots. Indeed: "As technology continues to advance, developments in advanced robotics will make it increasingly possible to perform complex tasks and take decisions with limited human intervention".[9] In the author's view, the rules applicable to capital investments cannot simply be transposed to investments into AI. The "labor component" embodied in AI should also be considered. As such, different amortization rules should apply in order to take into account the "intelligent" part of this investment.[10]

As business assets, AI and robotics contribute to the realization of the turnover of the enterprise and, as a consequence, its profits. The taxable profits stemming from the use of AI correspond to the difference between the revenues generated from the use of robots minus their costs, including notably

---

[5]   See IAS Norm 38, para. 18.
[6]   See IAS Norm 38, para. 21.
[7]   See IAS Norm 38, para. 97.
[8]   See IAS Norm 38, para. 90.
[9]   OECD/G20, Action 1, Taxing the Digital Economy, Final Report 2015, p. 138, n. 358/359.
[10]   See infra, p. 166.

amortization expenses. In most countries, the profits arising from the use of robots will fall into the category of *ordinary taxable profits.* Indeed, most countries assess the taxable profits of companies on the net profits resulting from the balance of the profit and loss account, subject to "tax modification rules" provided for by the applicable domestic law.

Some countries, however, have introduced so-called "*patent boxes*", which could apply to profits generated from the use of AI or robotic technology. In general, profits linked with intellectual property rights, such as patent, know-how, or copyrights, as defined under the applicable rule, could qualify for the patent box and, hence, benefit from a more favorable tax treatment (notably a lower profit tax rate). It follows that income stemming from intangible assets linked with AI or robotics could fall into this box. The scope and definition of the patent "box" differs however from one State to the other. In order to ensure that these attractive patent box regimes do not entail potential harmful features, Action 5 of the OECD/G20 BEPS initiative has recommended specific requirements, notably of a minimum substantial activity.[11] In essence, under the *nexus* approach, States are allowed to provide benefits to income arising out of intellectual property, "so long as there is a direct nexus between the income receiving benefits and the expenditures contributing to that income".[12] The compatibility of patent boxes is also controversial under EU State Aid rules.[13]

In any event, despite the controversies about the admissibility of patent boxes, what is relevant here for our purposes is that current regimes offer many tax incentives in favor of intangible assets, notably intellectual property rights, which may apply to investments in AI or robotics. These incentives include both extensive amortization rules on the expenses side and favorable profit taxation rates on the income side.

C.   Artificial Intelligence Used in Enterprises (Including Independent Individuals)

AI and robots may also be produced or purchased by enterprises without a legal personality, such as partnerships or single enterprise units. In general, the deduction and amortization rules will tend to follow the same principles

---

[11]   See OECD/G20, Countering Harmful Tax Practices More Effectively, Taking into Account Transparency and Substance, Action 5, Final Report 2015, p. 24 ff.

[12]   See OECD/G20, Countering Harmful Tax Practices More Effectively, Taking into Account Transparency and Substance, Action 5, Final Report 2015, p. 24, n. 28.

[13]   Wittmann Johanna M., "'Patent Boxes' and Their Compatibility with European Union State Aid Rules" in: Kerschner I. and Somare M. (eds), Taxation in a Global Digital Economy, Linde Verlag, Vienna 2017, p. 423.

described above for corporations, subject to the generally accepted accounting principles. However, profits stemming from the use of robotics by these enterprises will more generally fall into the ordinary taxable *income* tax system. Indeed, these enterprises are usually treated as transparent for tax purposes. In other words, income arising from the entrepreneurial activities is taxable at the level of the partners of the enterprise and usually added with other income realized by each partner separately. Favorable amortization rules for investment in AI or robotics may still apply in this situation. However, "patent box" regimes are often not applicable.

Disruption caused by innovation also leads to the development of new collaboration platforms and new models of work. This trend encourages new forms of employment regimes, sited sometimes in a "grey zone" between independent and dependent activities, or shifting clearly in favor of more flexible independent relationships. This development could also cause a decrease in income from (dependent) labor. To adapt to this evolution *Avenir Suisse* has suggested a change of status from dependent to independent worker, which would allow a worker to choose in favor of a status similar to an independent.[14] Under this approach, the worker would then be taxable under rules similar to independent enterprises. Hence, should income from independent activities be subject to social security contributions, as it is the case in some States, such as Switzerland, the independent worker should also charge social security on his or her income.[15]

D.   Robots Used by Private Individuals

Robots for private use, including "social robots" purchased by individuals for helping at home, cleaning the house or assisting children with homework, are generally regarded as *private* assets. As such, they may not be amortized and their purchase price should not be deductible from income tax. In the (rare) cases where robots would be sold with a margin, the gain as such is only taxable in countries that apply a capital gain tax on private assets.

---

[14]   See Adler Tibère and Salvi Marco, Quand les robots arrivent, Avenir Suisse, 2017, p. 49 ff.

[15]   See also infra, p. 167 ff.

III.   INTERNATIONAL ASPECTS

A.   In General

As part of enterprises (either as corporations or partnerships), AI would contribute to the realization of taxable profits. As such, profits generated by these
enterprises would fall under the rule of Article 7 OECD Model. It follows that
cross-border profits arising from automation should be taxed at the place of
residence of the enterprise unless they may be attributed to a foreign PE. Due
to the developments of the digital economy, various changes in the PE concept
have been introduced in the OECD Model and Commentary, as of 2017. We
will therefore describe the traditional rules applicable to define a PE prior to
the modifications of the OECD Model and Commentary in 2017 and then
focus on the new PE rules following the OECD/G20 BEPS initiative.

B.   Permanent Establishment under the Traditional Definition

1.   The fixed place of business

The question arises to what extent an AI system or a robot used in another
country could be regarded as a PE, under Article 5 OECD Model. A PE, in
accordance with Article 5 paragraph 1 OECD Model, is defined as "a fixed
place of business through which the business of an enterprise is wholly or
partly carried out".

A place of business is a facility, such as premises, machinery or equipment.[16] It also includes facilities, or installations used for carrying the business
of the enterprise, or, where a certain amount of space is at its disposal.[17] It
follows that the infrastructure or installations in which AI is embodied could
be characterized as a *place of business*. The extent to which the presence of
human personnel is required has been clarified. Indeed, according to the recent
modifications of the OECD Commentary, a PE could exist at the place of
location of computer equipment, even if no personnel is required at this place
to use it.[18] It appears nowadays to be widely recognized that the business of an
enterprise can be carried out "without any on-site human intervention".[19] This
interpretation is based on the use of the words "through which" instead of "in
which" under Article 5 paragraph 1 OECD MC, following the 1977 version.[20]

---

[16]   OECD Commentary, n. 6 at Art. 5.
[17]   OECD Commentary, n. 10 at Art. 5.
[18]   OECD Commentary, n. 127 at Art. 5.
[19]   Reimer Ekkehart and Rust Alexander, Klaus Vogel on Double Taxation Conventions,
5th ed., Wolters Kluwer, The Netherlands 2022, n. 45 at Art. 5 OECD Model.
[20]   Reimer and Rust (2022), n. 45 at Art. 5 OECD Model.

It follows that vending machines, check-in computers of non-resident airlines, gaming machines "and any similar unmanned facility" perform activities that can qualify as PE.[21] The same is true for data centers, which have become an important feature of the digital economy.

In order to be *fixed*, the place of business should show a link between the place of business and a specific, distinct geographical point.[22] This does not mean that equipment constituting the place of business actually has to be fixed to the soil where it stands, but that the equipment should at least remain on a particular site.[23] In other words, equipment may qualify as fixed if these items are usually used at one place for a sufficient period of time.[24] This would be the case, for example, of an internet server, which is geographically linked with a specific place.[25] A ship that navigates in international waters or within one or many States does not fulfil the condition of a fixed character.[26] In addition, a PE requires a place of business that is situated in the territory of that State, which would tend to exclude a satellite in geostationary orbit, at least under the applicable rules of international law.[27] Where the nature of the activity is such that these activities are often moved between various locations, a single place of business will still be recognized where a particular location, within which these activities are moved "may be identified as constituting a coherent whole commercially and geographically with respect to that business".[28] In addition, the place of business should be *"permanent"*, which implies that it should remain stable for a certain period of time. While there is no clear guidance on this sufficient level of temporal requirement, it appears that many member countries refer to a minimum period of more than six months for the place of business to become a PE.[29]

Finally, the business of the enterprise must be carried out *"through"* the PE. This requirement is traditionally interpreted as requiring both: (1) some sort of control of the place of business and (2) that the place of business is used to exercise the activities of the enterprise. First, the place of business should be at the disposal of the taxpayer. This control can be based on legal norms

---

[21] Reimer and Rust (2022), n. 45 at Art. 5 OECD Model.
[22] OECD Commentary, n. 21 at Art. 5.
[23] OECD Commentary, n. 21 at Art. 5.
[24] Reimer and Rust (2022), n. 59 at Art. 5; OECD Commentary, n. 28 at Art. 5 OECD Model.
[25] OECD Commentary, n. 125 at Art. 5.
[26] OECD Commentary, n. 27 at Art. 5.
[27] OECD Commentary, n. 26 at Art. 5.
[28] OECD Commentary, n. 22 at Art. 5.
[29] OECD Commentary, n. 28 at Art. 5; Reimer and Rust (2015), n. 68 at Art. 5 OECD.

of factual circumstances.[30] In other words, the control is recognized if the enterprise has sufficient command of the place of business as a matter of fact.[31] Second, the enterprise should use the place of business for its entrepreneurial activities.[32]

Even if the conditions are met, there is, however, an exception to consider in Article 5 paragraph 4 OECD Model. Indeed, according to this provision, activities that are *auxiliary or preparatory* in nature do not give rise to a PE. The list of activities provided for in Article 5 paragraph lit. a to f, that are considered to be auxiliary or preparatory, is not exhaustive. In particular, activities for the purpose of storage, display or delivery of goods, the maintenance of a stock of goods for the purpose of storage, processing by another enterprise, or for purchasing goods or collecting information, do not constitute a PE.[33]

2. Agents as permanent establishment

Following Article 5 paragraph 5 OECD Model, where a *person*, other than an agent of an independent status, acts in one contracting State on behalf of an enterprise of the other contracting State, has authority to conclude contracts which binds the represented enterprise, and habitually exercises such authority, that person is deemed to create a PE, unless the activities are limited to those mentioned in Article 4 paragraph 4 OECD Model (auxiliary and ancillary), which if exercised through a fixed place of business would not make such place a PE. This rule applies to *agents* which conclude contracts on behalf of the foreign enterprise. Any person, within the meaning of Article 3 paragraph 1 lit. a OECD Model, can act as agent. As a consequence, this provision includes an individual, a company and any other body of persons. Among them, this rule covers commercial and non-profit entities with members or corporate entities without members (such as trusts).[34] In addition, it is irrelevant whether the entity has been funded or incorporated under private law, public law or even international law.[35]

---

[30] Reimer and Rust (2022), n. 110 at Art. 5; OECD Commentary, n. 12 at Art. 5.
[31] OECD Commentary, n. 12 at Art. 5.
[32] Reimer and Rust (2022), n. 136 at Art. 5.
[33] Art. 5 para. 4 lit. a to f, OECD Model; Jain Arpith Prakash, "Challenges Posed by Permanent Establishment: Exemptions in the Context of the Digital Economy" in: Kerschner I. and Somare M. (eds), Taxation in a Global Digital Economy, Linde Verlag, Vienna 2017, p. 161.
[34] Reimer and Rust (2022), n. 346 at Art. 5.
[35] Reimer and Rust (2022), n. 350 at Art. 5.

3.   Application of the concept of permanent establishment to artificial intelligence systems and robots

a.   Fixed place of business

It follows from this definition that a PE still requires a physical presence in a specific geographical place. This *place of business* may take the form of computer equipment (such as a server) but does not necessitate human presence. We may also draw an analogy with the sector of electronic commerce characterized by the distinction between the website (software) and the server (hardware). While the former is usually not a PE, absent an infrastructure, the latter may fulfil the conditions of a PE because it represents a piece of equipment. In the field of AI and robotics we may apply a similar distinction between the AI algorithms and software, which could therefore only represent a PE, under the traditional definition, provided they are embodied in a computer or robot's infrastructures. This conclusion is also consistent with the characterization of data centers as a fixed place of business.

Therefore, AI systems providing automated activities of foreign enterprises, embodied in servers located in a specific place, could in our view be characterized as a PE under Article 5 paragraph 1 OECD Model. The same is true for robots, in physical forms, performing activities. To qualify as a place of business, a physical presence is however required at a specific place. This presence may be represented by computer equipment, implementing AI, or robots performing activities. The OECD Commentary admits that where an enterprise operates "automatic equipment" or computer equipment at a particular place, a PE may exist, even though no personnel of that enterprise is required at that location for the operation of the equipment.[36] According to the OECD, this conclusion applies not only to electronic commerce, but also with respect "to other activities in which equipment operates automatically, e.g. automatic pumping equipment in the exploitation of natural resources".[37] In our view, the same should therefore apply to any automated operation, including robots' activities, carried out by equipment sited in the relevant State. Recent mentions of the Commentary clarify this issue further. The carrying-on of business using automatic equipment may constitute a PE, in the case that the enterprise carries on this business besides the initial setting up of the machine.[38] It, however, requires that the enterprise that sets up the machine also operates and maintains

---

[36]   OECD Commentary, n. 41, n. 127 at Art. 5 (2017).
[37]   OECD Commentary, n. 127 at Art. 5 (2017).
[38]   OECD Commentary, n. 41 at Art. 5.

it for its own account, which also includes cases where the machines are operated by an agent dependent of the enterprise.[39]

This place of business should however be *fixed*. In general, this condition will be met for robotics used in factories or enterprises for automation of delivery of goods (factories, buildings). The question is more delicate for robots designed for personal use, which may move from different places. It appears that the relevant question, under the OECD, is not if robots may be moved, but rather if they remain at a specific place for a certain duration of time. In practice, it appears that most States tend to apply a six-month period as a minimum requirement.[40] In addition, in accordance with the OECD Commentary,[41] for robots moving between neighboring locations, also following the specific nature of robotics, a single place of business should be recognized to the extent the activities performed by robots constitute a coherent whole, commercially and geographically.

Furthermore, the place of business, in the form of automated equipment, should be controlled by the enterprise and *used* for the activities of the taxpayer, as the words "through which" indicates. The control issue would eventually become more problematic as the autonomy of AI evolves over time. Should, as will be discussed later, AI systems and smart robots become autonomous and be granted legal personality, the question of control would have to require further analysis. Indeed, in general, a legal entity, even if it is a subsidiary, should not be regarded as a PE. However, the situation would be different should the subsidiary remain under the control of another entity, which uses its infrastructure to carry on core activities of the enterprise.

Finally, no PE should exist when the operations carried out through the automated infrastructure are restricted to *preparatory or auxiliary activities*, within the meaning of Article 5 paragraph 4. In our context, the following activities could, under the traditional approach, be regarded as preparatory or auxiliary: providing a communication link, advertising, relaying of information, gathering data and supplying information.[42] This consequence should however not apply where such functions form "in themselves an essential and significant part of the business activity of the enterprise as a whole, or where other core functions of the enterprise are carried on through the computer equipment".[43]

---

[39] OECD Commentary, n. 41 at Art. 5.
[40] Reimer and Rust (2022), n. 73 at Art. 5.
[41] In this sense, OECD Commentary, n. 22 at Art. 5.
[42] See OECD Commentary, n. 128 at Art. 5 (2017).
[43] See OECD Commentary, n. 129 at Art. 5 (2017).

b.   *Artificial intelligence and robots as agents*

Enterprises using robotics to provide activities in the source State could trigger the presence of a PE by using a person in that State, who would have sufficient power to act on their behalf and the authority to conclude contracts in the name of the enterprise.

It follows, however, from the current definition that only a person may act as an agent. This definition requires at least a legal recognition of the entity as a person (as an individual, as a body of persons or as a company). Under current law, AI and robots as such are not recognized as persons. The concept of a person could however in the future be interpreted more broadly should some kind of legal personality be granted to AI autonomous entities or smart robots. In particular, should a State grant some sort of legal personality to AI and robots, they could eventually also be recognized as agents, within the meaning of Article 5 paragraph 5 OECD Model. In that case, AI or robots, which would possess the power to act on behalf of an enterprise, could create a PE in their place of situation, provided they would have the legal authority to conclude contracts in the name of the enterprise. A similar result could also occur by a change of interpretation of the term "person" under Article 5 paragraph 5 OECD Model. Indeed, as in the case of trust, some entities are recognized as persons, even if according to the law of many States, they are not regarded as legal persons as such. Thus, a modification of the interpretation of the concept of person, within the meaning of Article 1 lit. b OECD Model could also include AI autonomous systems or smart robots in this list.

C.   The Evolution of the Permanent Establishment Concept Further to the OECD/G20 BEPS Initiative

1.   Introduction

Various actions from the OECD/G20 BEPS Initiative propose changes to the PE definition, notably to prevent aggressive tax planning. Action 7, in particular, is directly targeted to redesign the concept of PE in order to cover potential abusive practices and strategies leading to an *artificial avoidance* of the PE status.[44] All these changes converge to prevent the use of "artificial arrangements" put in place, either for circumventing the presence of a PE, or avoiding its threshold in the source State. In essence, however, the PE concept remains based on a physical presence test.

---

[44]   See OECD/G20, Preventing the Artificial Avoidance of Permanent Establishment Status, Action 7, 2015, Final Report 2015, p. 14 ff.; see also Dhuldhoya Vishesh, The Future of the Permanent Establishment Concept, 72 Bulletin for International Taxation 2018 No. 4a (special issue), n. 2.1.

Action 1 of the OECD/G20 BEPS Initiative, which focuses on the taxation of the digital economy, also refers to rules against artificial avoidance of PE status.[45] The Final Report on Action 1 goes further and analyzes various alternatives to modify the physical presence test as a condition for the existence of a PE,[46] such as a new nexus of "significant digital presence". This proposal, however, did not find a consensus and is not yet recommended.[47]

The Final Report on Action 7 introduces changes to the text and Commentary on Article 5 OECD Model. As explained before, these new rules do not create fundamental changes to the concept of PE, which remains notably based on the physical presence test,[48] requiring some infrastructure in the place of business sited in the source State. However, Action 7 addresses some identified strategies that were implemented, notably by multinational entities (MNEs), to circumvent the potential existence of a PE. With that aim, the new rules introduce: (1) changes in the scope of the auxiliary and preparatory activity exemption, including in case of fragmenting activities (Article 5 paragraph 4 OECD Model); (2) restrictions pertaining to the splitting of contracts, under the exception of Article 5 paragraph 3 OECD Model; (3) a broader definition of the dependent agent concept (Article 5 paragraph 5 OECD Model); and (4) restriction to the conditions of the independent agent exception (Article 5 paragraph 6 OECD Model).[49]

2.   Changes to the preparatory and auxiliary exception

In the past, the proper interpretation of the list of exceptions to the PE rule, on Article 5 paragraph 4 OECD Model, has been controversial. It is as yet undisputed that this provision describes, as an exception to the main rule, a non-exhaustive list of activities, which, even if carried out through a fixed place of business, do not constitute a PE. The issue was whether the specific activities mentioned in this exception were also subject to a "preparatory or auxiliary" requirement.[50] It appeared therefore that in some countries, some MNEs could use this provision in order to carry out some of those activities (storage, display, delivery) which only formally represented core activities and

---

[45] See OECD/G20, Addressing the Tax Challenges of the Digital Economy, Action 1, 2015 Final Report, p. 88, n. 215 ff.

[46] See OECD/G20, Addressing the Tax Challenges of the Digital Economy, Action 1, 2015 Final Report, p. 136 ff.

[47] See infra, p. 75 ff. about various solutions to address the development of the digital economy.

[48] Uslu Yasin, An Analysis of "Google Taxes" in the Context of Action 7 of the OECD/G20 Base Erosion and Profit Shifting Initiative, 72 Bulletin for International Taxation 2018, No. 4a at 3.2.1.

[49] Dhuldhoya (2018), n. 2.1; Uslu (2018), conclusion.

[50] Dhuldhoya (2018), n. 2.2.4.

were not as such auxiliary or ancillary in nature, in order to avoid the existence of a PE in the source State.[51] In particular, companies in the digital economy could benefit from this exception, typically in case of storage, display or delivery activities, with a view to avoiding a PE nexus in the source State. To prevent this avoidance strategy, the modification of Article 5 paragraph 4 OECD Model now makes it clear that all activities mentioned in this provision are subject to the auxiliary and preparatory condition.[52]

Hence, this new rule should better encompass companies, like online selling vendors, whose warehouse and storage activities represent an essential part of the business as a whole.[53] The changes introduced here tend to emphasize the importance of the "*overall business* activity of the enterprise". As a consequence, in cases where an enterprise maintains in the source State a large warehouse, with a significant number of employees for the purpose of storing and delivering goods that the enterprise sells online to customers in the source State, the auxiliary and preparatory exception will not apply.[54] Indeed, the storage and delivery activities "that are performed through that warehouse, which represent an important asset and require a number of employees, constitute an essential part of the enterprise's sale/distribution business and do not have, therefore, a preparatory or auxiliary character".[55] However, the requirement of a physical presence remains unchanged. It follows that those foreign digital companies that can offer online digital services without any infrastructure in the source State will still not be affected by this new rule.

In addition, Action 7 introduced a so-called "*anti-fragmentation*" rule for auxiliary and preparatory activities between closely related enterprises, which was implemented in Article 5 paragraph 4.1. OECD Model.[56] In essence, this new rule seeks to avoid the fragmentation of activities into different places of business in order to exclude the presence of a PE.[57] In other words, the purpose is to "prevent enterprise or a group of closely related enterprises from fragmenting a cohesive business operation into several small operations in order to argue that each is merely engaged in a preparatory or auxiliary activity".[58] It means that such exception is not applicable to a fixed place of business used or maintained by an enterprise if the same enterprise or a closely related

---

[51]   Dhuldhoya (2018), n. 2.2.4.
[52]   OECD Commentary, n. 58 at Art. 5 (2017).
[53]   OECD Commentary, n. 62 at Art 5 (2017); Uslu (2018), n. 3.2.2.
[54]   OECD Commentary, n. 62 at Art 5 (2017).
[55]   OECD Commentary, n. 62 at Art. 5 (2017).
[56]   See OECD Commentary, n. 74 and 79 ff. at Art. 5 (2017). Dhuldhoya (2018), n. 2.2.5; Uslu (2018), n. 3.2.2.
[57]   Uslu (2018), n. 3.2.3.
[58]   See OECD Commentary, n. 79 at Art. 5 (2017).

enterprise carries on business at the same place or another place in the same contracting State and (a) that place or other place constitutes a PE, for the enterprise or the closely related enterprise or (b) the overall activity resulting from the combination of the activities carried on by the two enterprises at the same place, or by the closely related enterprise, is not of a preparatory or auxiliary character, provided that the business activities carried out constitute a complementary function that are part of a cohesive business operation (new Article 5 paragraph 4.1 OECD Model).

3. Addressing splitting of contracts (Article 5 paragraph 3 OECD Model)

The new rule does not modify the text of the treaty model. It does however prevent the abuse of the exception in the case of construction activities, where foreign enterprise may try to split a long-term contract (of more than one year) into various short-term contracts, to avoid the 12-month threshold of Article 5 paragraph 3 OECD Model.

4. New definition of the dependent agent

A foreign enterprise may also have a PE in the source State in case it conducts activities there through a dependent agent, namely a person who is acting in a contracting State on behalf of an enterprise and has the authority to conclude contracts in the name of that enterprise (Article 5 paragraph 5 OECD Model). The PE concept here differs from the general rule in the sense that a place of business is not required in the source State for the activities conducted by the agent. In the past, foreign companies could avoid the presence of a PE in the source State by entering into some sort of commissionaire arrangement, under which the person in the source State would sell products in its own name but on behalf of the foreign company that is the owner of these products.[59]

The new rule introduced a change to Article 5 paragraph 5 OECD Model in order to prevent foreign companies trying to circumvent the potential presence of an agent under these types of arrangement.[60] Indeed, under the new definition, an agent is a person acting in a contracting State

on behalf of an enterprise and, in doing so, habitually concludes contracts, or habitually plays the principal role leading to the conclusion of the contracts that

---

[59]   OECD/G20 BEPS, Preventing the Artificial Avoidance of Permanent Establishment Status, Action 7, 2015, Final Report, p. 15.

[60]   In this context, see for example, the famous "Google case" rendered on 12 July 2017 by the Administrative Court of Paris, TA Paris, n. 1505113/1-1, in which Google France SARL was not recognized as a PE of its sister company, Google Ireland Ltd, lacking sufficient autonomy. On 25 April 2019, the Administrative Court of Appeal

are routinely concluded without material modification by the enterprise, and these contracts are (a) in the name of the enterprise, or (b) for the transfer of the ownership of, or for the granting of the right to use, property owned by the enterprise or that the enterprise has the right to use, or (c) for the provision of services by that enterprise, ... (Article 5 paragraph 5 OECD Model).

In that case, the agent constitutes a PE for the foreign enterprise, unless the activities performed are of an auxiliary and preparatory nature, within the meaning of Article 5 paragraph 4 OECD Model. In other words, commission-aire arrangements would now constitute a PE for the foreign enterprise, even if the contracts are not concluded in the name of the principal but on the name of the commissionaire.[61]

5. Amendments to the independent agent exception

According to Article 5 paragraph 6 OECD Model, an independent agent, acting in the ordinary course of business for a foreign enterprise, is not regarded as a PE of that enterprise. Under the new rules introduced by OECD/G20 BEPS Action 7, an exception has been introduced, in case a person acts exclusively or almost exclusively on behalf of one or more enterprises to which it is closely related. In that case, that person will not be considered an independent agent (new Article 5 paragraph 6 OECD Model). The term "closely related enterprise" is defined in Article 5 paragraph 8 OECD Model. It is based either on a factor of control resulting from "all the relevant facts and circumstances", or on a direct or indirect possession of more than 50 percent of the voting rights or beneficial interests of an enterprise.

In general, a local subsidiary of a foreign enterprise tends not to qualify as a PE. This rule is confirmed by Article 5 paragraph 7 OECD Model. This new definition of an independent agent brings, however, a new limitation to this general principle. Indeed, a local subsidiary of a foreign enterprise, who in fact acts exclusively on behalf of a foreign enterprise, could thus constitute a PE.

6. Impact of the multilateral instrument to implement BEPS treaty measures

To implement the changes required by the BEPS Program in existing double taxation treaties, the OECD/G20 Initiative, as part of Action 15, has developed a Multilateral Convention to Implement Tax Treaty Related Measures to

---

confirmed the decision of the first instance court, with the result that Google Ireland Ltd did not have a PE in France.

61   Dhuldhoya (2018), n. 2.2.2.

Prevent BEPS (hereafter MLI).[62] The basic idea is to include in the MLI all the BEPS measures which require changes in the double taxation conventions. By this process, lengthy and complex bilateral negotiations of existing tax treaties will be avoided.[63] The MLI has been signed by more than 75 jurisdictions and entered into force on 1 July 2018. It modifies the rules of more than 1000 DTT. It should be mentioned that existing treaties will remain in force and will not be replaced by the MLI; the MLI, as a *lex posterior* and *specialis*, will however modify or overrule the existing provisions of double tax treaties.

Part IV of the MLI deals with the rules against avoidance of the PE status. The changes of the PE rules are, however, not regarded as minimum standard.[64] These changes have been implemented in the MLI in Articles 12 to 15 for covered tax agreements. Since they are not minimum standards, signatories are free to introduce them or not. It appears that only a few countries have signed up for all the PE provisions and only one-third have committed to the new definition of the dependent PE agent.[65]

7.   Impact of automation

In a nutshell, the new rules, introduced in the 2017 version of the OECD Model and Commentary, will broaden the scope of taxation in the source country through the presence of a PE. First, the *auxiliary and preparatory* exceptions have been interpreted more restrictively. This could have a particular impact in the case of AI systems or robots used to collect information, to transfer data or to help in the storage of goods. In particular, following the clarification of the scope of this exception, activities such as storage and delivery performed through a warehouse or other equipment in the source State, followed by online selling through a website or AI platforms or robots, could not fall under the auxiliary or preparatory exception.

Second, the *anti-fragmentation* rule is also highly relevant in this context. It is indeed quite feasible to fragment activities of the enterprise, through automated actions, in various places of business, both locally and organizationally. The new provision of Article 5 paragraph 4.1 OECD Model, would in such a case take a global view of the various automated activities, in various places of business, or between closely held enterprises within the source State.

---

[62]   OECD/G20, Developing a Multilateral Instrument to Modify Bilateral Tax Treaties, Action 15, 2015, Final Report.

[63]   Da Luz De Sousa Jacqueline, "Tax Treaty Policy in Addressing Challenges Posed by the Digital Economy" in: Kerschner I. and Somare M. (eds), Taxation in a Global Digital Economy, Linde Verlag, Vienna 2017, p. 39.

[64]   Uslu (2018), n. 3.3. These rules have, however, been introduced in the 2017 version of the OECD Model and Commentary.

[65]   Uslu (2018), n. 3.2.

However, the basic element of the necessity of a physical presence remains untouched. This implies that the presence of a PE still requires a place of business in the source State through which the activities of the enterprises are carried out. It necessitates at least some type of infrastructure in the form of services, computers or equipment. As we have seen, the presence of human personnel is, however, not required.

Third, the definition of a *dependent agent* has been broadened. In this respect, automated activities performed by AI systems or robots in the source State could more easily be characterized as agents, notably if they "routinely conclude contracts without material modification". However, in order to be characterized as an agent, an AI entity or a robot still needs to qualify as a "person", within the meaning of Article 1 lit. b OECD Model. So far, as we have seen, AI and robots have not been considered as such. The changes of Article 5 paragraph 5 and 6 OECD Model introduced by the OECD/G20 BEPS Program did not change the concept of person. As previously discussed, the concept of a person could however in the future be interpreted more broadly, to encompass AI autonomous entities or smart robots in the case where either some kind of legal personality would be granted to them, or a modification of the interpretation of the concept of person, within the meaning of Article 1 lit. b OECD Model, would include AI or robots.

Fourth, the exception of the *independent agent* has been restricted. This could be particularly relevant for automated functions performed in the source State, which are exclusively or almost exclusively conducted on behalf of closely related enterprises. In our view, for this rule to apply, the activities of AI should still be effectuated within an enterprise (typically a subsidiary) in the source State. Indeed, as we have seen above, absent a legal personality attributable to AI with sufficient autonomy, or to a robot, or an inclusion in the list of "persons", within the meaning of Art. 1 lit. b OECD Model, such infrastructure, as such, cannot be characterized as an agent.

7. Development of the taxation of the digital economy and its impact on the taxation of artificial intelligence

I. INTRODUCTION

The issue of a fair taxation of the profits generated worldwide by MNEs active on the digital economy is at the top of the agenda of all organizations and countries dealing with tax matters. For years, the OECD has investigated the tax challenges caused by the digital economy. In particular, the OECD/G20 BEPS Action 1 has focused on that aspect.[1] The works, still in progress, have led to the so-called two-pillar solution.[2] The UN has also analyzed these issues further.[3] Despite essential developments and continuing discussions on various alternatives, a consensus on the adequate way to address those challenges has been hard to find.[4] In parallel, some countries have introduced unilateral measures as a response to the issues raised by the taxation of digital economy. In the same vein, the EU has also proposed two measures, such as a digital PE and a digital services tax, which aim at better addressing the taxation of multinational digital giants and the role of users.[5] These proposals have been so far suspended in view of the potential implementation of the two-pillar solution, especially pillar one.

As we will see, one of the main features of the digital economy is the use of intelligent interconnection of machines, computers using AI, robotics and big

---

[1]   See OECD/G20 BEPS Project, Addressing the Tax Challenges of the Digital Economy, Action 1, 2015, Final Report.

[2]   OECD/G20, Statement on a Two-Pillar Solution to Address the Tax Challenges Arising from the Digitalization of the Economy, 8 October 2021.

[3]   See UN Committee of Experts on International Cooperation in Tax Matters, Tax Challenges in the Digitalized Economy: Selected Issues for Possible Committee Consideration, UN 2017.

[4]   See, recently, OECD/G20 BEPS Project, Tax Challenges Arising from Digitalization, Interim Report, 2018.

[5]   See infra, p. 80 ff.

data.[6] The development of new rules in the taxation of digital enterprises could have a direct impact on AI and robotics. We will therefore try to analyze these developments from the perspective of taxation of AI and robots. As a consequence, in a first step, we will describe the current works of the OECD, the UN, the EU and the unilateral measures adopted or proposed by some States. In a second step, after discussing, from a policy perspective, the various alternatives suggested or introduced unilaterally by some States, we will examine their potential impact on AI and robotics.

II.   CURRENT WORKS AT THE OECD LEVEL

A.   Works Linked with the BEPS Program

The OECD/G20 Final Report on Action 1 of the BEPS project has identified some broader direct tax challenges raised by the digital economy. It concluded that the digital economy as such does not create unique BEPS concerns, but could contribute to the exacerbation of existing ones.[7] The Final Report therefore discusses a series of measures, in coordination with other Actions of the BEPS Initiative, notably Action 7, on the scope and definition of the relevant nexus for the presence of a PE in the source State. As described above,[8] some specific changes in the scope of the PE concept, as provided in Article 5 OECD Model, such as the exception of ancillary and auxiliary activities or anti-fragmentation rules, have been introduced, but the physical presence test remains the leading PE nexus. This requirement corresponds to a bricks-and-mortar economy, which is no more in line with the new digital world, characterized by the ability for non-resident companies to interact with customers in the source country, without any physical presence.

As a consequence, the Final Report has suggested *three* alternative options to address the challenges raised by the digital economy.[9] First, it proposed the introduction of a new nexus based on the concept of *significant economic presence*. "This option would create a taxable presence in a country on the basis of factors that evidence a purposeful and sustained interaction with the

---

[6]   Petruzzi Raffaele and Buriak Svitlana, Addressing the Tax Challenges of the Digitalization of the Economy: A Possible Answer in the Proper Application of the Transfer Pricing Rules? 72 Bulletin for International Taxation 2018, No. 4a (special issue), n. 4.2.

[7]   Zichittella Carlo, "International Initiative in Addressing Challenges Posed by the Digital Economy" in: Kerschner I. and Somare M. (eds), Taxation in a Global Digital Economy, Linde Verlag, Vienna 2017, p. 8.

[8]   See supra, p. 68 ff.

[9]   OECD/G20 BEPS Action 1, 2015, Final Report, p. 106 ff.

economy of that country via technology and other automated tools".[10] This new threshold could also apply to remote automated activities performed by non-resident enterprises, which have an impact characterized as a digital presence in a specific location. It follows that not only automated activities embodied in an infrastructure sited in a source State could trigger a PE nexus, but also the digital presence of automated activities performed abroad but with an ongoing interaction with customers in a specific country.

The OECD suggests various approaches to define more precisely the new nexus based on a significant economic presence. The new nexus could focus on all revenues generated by transactions concluded by the non-resident enterprise remotely with in-country customers, either through a digital platform, or through mail order and telephone transactions.[11] In addition, this revenue-based factor could be combined with a digital and/or a user-based factor.[12] The rule of attribution of income to such significant economic presence would also need to be adapted, notably due to the absence of significant physical presence in the market country.

Second, a *withholding tax* on payments by residents of a State for goods and services purchased online from non-resident providers could also be considered.[13]

Third, an *equalization tax* could also be introduced to address the disparity in the tax treatment between domestic and foreign corporations.[14]

As a follow-up, the OECD/G20 published in 2018 an Interim Report, discussing further the tax challenges arising from digitalization and the various options.[15]

A global consensus has been difficult to reach. As described by Reuven Avi-Yonah, it seems notable that "the United States has been adamantly opposed to these attempts to tax its digital giants. The EU and India, on the other hand, support the effort".[16] As a consequence, the EU has taken a step

---

[10]   OECD/G20 BEPS Action 1, 2015, Final Report, p. 107, n. 277.

[11]   OECD/G20 BEPS Action 1, 2015, Final Report, p. 108; see Endo Tsutomu, "Modification of a Taxable Nexus to Address the Tax Challenges of the Digital Economy" in: Kerschner I. and Somare M. (eds), Taxation in a Global Digital Economy, Linde Verlag, Vienna 2017, p. 111.

[12]   OECD/G20 BEPS Action 1, 2015, Final Report, p. 109 ff., 111; Endo (2017), p. 115.

[13]   OECD/G20 BEPS Action 1, 2015, Final Report, p. 113 ff.

[14]   OECD/G20 BEPS Action 1, 2015, Final Report, p. 115 ff.

[15]   OECD/G20, BEPS Action 1, Tax Challenges Arising from Digitalization, Interim Report, 2018.

[16]   Avi-Yonah Reuven, The International Implications of Wayfair, Tax Notes International 2018, p. 164; Finley Ryan, Wayfair Decision Echoes Case for Digital PE Standard, Tax Notes International, 2 July 2018, p. 14.

forward and suggested some new tax proposals to address the issues raised by the digital economy.[17] In 2019, however, a compromise was widely accepted by the member States of the Inclusive Framework (IF) of the OECD.

B.　　　The Compromise of 2019: the OECD Two-pillar System

Early in 2019, to overcome the stalling of negotiations on the taxation of the digital economy, the OECD devised a compromise which relies on a two-pillar solution. The first pillar would modify the international allocation rules of profits, for large MNEs, in favor of the States where users and consumers reside. The second pillar consists in an anti-base erosion rule, which would implement a minimum effective 15 percent tax on profits of MNEs in the scope. While controversial at the beginning, the negotiations have finally found favor, notably since 2020, following the change of presidency in the United States. In July and October 2021, a compromise was reached and 130 jurisdictions, out of the 139 members of the IF of the OECD, at the time, have accepted the main principles of the two-pillar solution.[18] Finally, on 11 July 2023, 138 members of the IF agreed on an outcome statement.[19] This statement summarizes the packages of deliverables to address the remaining elements of the two-pillar solution.

An analysis of the two-pillar compromise would go beyond the scope of our contribution. In particular, the second pillar seems less important on the issue of the taxation of AI, since it can be described as a global base erosion rule, or the so-called GLOBE system. We will, however, briefly describe some aspects of the first pillar, which appears more relevant in the discussion of the taxation of AI and robots. Companies in the scope of the first pillar are MNEs with a global turnover of more than 20 billion euros and a profitability above 10 percent (i.e. profit before tax/revenue). For companies in the scope, 25 percent of the residual profit, defined as profits in excess of 10 percent of revenue, will be allocated to market jurisdictions with a nexus based on a revenue-based allocation key.[20] Following the Statement of July 2023, a multilateral convention (MLC) would allow jurisdictions to reallocate and exercise domestic taxing rights over a portion of the residual profits (the so-called amount

---

[17]　See infra p. 80 ff.

[18]　OECD/G20, Statement on a Two-Pillar Solution to Address the Tax Challenges Arising from the Digitalization of the Economy, 8 October 2021.

[19]　OECD, Outcome Statement on the Two-Pillar Solution to Address the Tax Challenges Arising from the Digitalization of the Economy, 11 July 2023.

[20]　OECD/G20, Statement on a Two-Pillar Solution to Address the Tax Challenges Arising from the Digitalization of the Economy, 8 October 2021, n. 2.

A of pillar one).[21] As a result of this compromise, no newly enacted DSTs or relevant similar measures should be imposed from 8 October 2021, until the earliest 31 December 2023 and the coming into force of the MLC.[22]

It is interesting to note that amount A, according to the final compromise, would then apply to any activities of the MNEs within the scope, and not only on digital services. Extractive and regulated financial services would, however, be excluded. Despite a more general scope of application, based on a threshold of turnover, this new allocation mechanism, relying on a fractional apportionment method of profit allocation, would still mostly target tech giants, using extensively AI systems and robots for their business activities, digital sales, advertisements and marketing strategies.

III.   CURRENT WORKS AT THE UN LEVEL

Apart from current works at the OECD, the UN has also analyzed the issues raised by the digital economy. In particular, the UN has published an update of the Practical Manual on Transfer Pricing in Developing Countries.[23] In addition, in a report of 2017, the Committee of Experts on International Cooperation in Tax Matters has identified changes that a new PE concept would require to the UN Model DTC.[24]

In April 2021, the UN accepted the introduction of a new Article 12B in its Model of DTC. The purpose of this provision is to grant more power to the source State to tax profits arising from "automated digital services". As a consequence, this new provision entails a new rule, which authorizes the source State to tax, on a gross basis, specific digital services paid to a resident of the other contracting State. The applicable rate would be bilaterally negotiated. To avoid excessive double taxation, the Commentary recommends a rather modest rate, ranging between 3 percent and 4 percent. Furthermore, the second paragraph of this new provision grants the taxpayer the option to pay the tax annually on the net profits, in accordance with the applicable rate in the State of residence. The term "automated digital services" means "any service provided on the Internet of another electronic network, in either case requiring minimal human involvement from the service provider" (Article 12B para-

---

[21]   OECD, Outcome Statement on the Two-Pillar Solution to Address the Tax Challenges Arising from the Digitalization of the Economy, 11 July 2023.

[22]   Id.

[23]   UN, Practical Manual on Transfer Pricing for Developing Countries, 2nd ed., 2017.

[24]   UN Committee of Experts on International Cooperation in Tax Matters, Tax Challenges in the Digitalized Economy: Selected Issues for Possible Committee Consideration, UN 2017; see also Petruzzi and Buriak (2018), at 2.3.

graph 5 UN Model DTC). It includes especially: "Online advertising services; supply of user data; online search engines; online intermediation platform services; social media platforms; digital content services; online gaming; cloud computing services; and standardized online teaching services" (Article 12B paragraph 6 UN Model DTC).

It is, however, not certain that the member States of the UN would adopt this provision at a broad scale, due to the current work at the OECD level and notably the implementation of the two-pillar solution.[25]

IV.   THE EU PROPOSALS

A.   Introduction

On 21 September 2017, the EU Commission published a communication in favor of a fair and efficient tax system in the EU for the digital single market.[26] This communication stresses the underlying principle for corporation tax that profits should be taxed where the value is created. In a digitalized world, however, it is not always clear "what the value is, how to measure it, or where it is created".[27] As a consequence, according to the EU Commission, this development requires addressing two main policy challenges: (1) where to tax (nexus), in particular where a business can provide services digitally with little or no physical presence, and (2) what to tax (value creation).[28]

It should be recognized that the traditional corporate tax rules are not in line with the modern global economy, notably as they require a physical presence for an enterprise to realize profits in a State. The corporate tax rules "were conceived in the early twentieth century for traditional 'brick and mortar' businesses" and define what and how to tax based largely on a physical presence in that country without reflecting the value of users participating in that jurisdiction.[29] In other words, current tax rules fail to recognize that users play a role in generating value for digital companies. At the outset, the Commission acknowledges that an ideal approach would be to find a multilateral, interna-

---

[25]   Alvadaro, Mery, Digital Services Taxes across Europe in the Midst and Aftermath of the COVID-19 Pandemic: A Plausible Option to Raise Tax Revenues? 61 European Taxation 2021, n. 9, p. 4.

[26]   EU Commission, Communication from the Commission to the European Parliament and the Council COM(2017) 547 final (hereafter Communication).

[27]   EU Commission, Communication, COM(2017) 547 final, p. 7.

[28]   EU Commission, Communication, COM(2017) 547 final.

[29]   EU Commission, Proposal for a Council Directive on Corporate Taxation of a Significant Digital Presence, COM(2018) 148 final, p. 2 (hereafter Proposal on Corporate Taxation).

tional solution to taxing the digital economy and is working closely with the OECD to support that development. However, progress at the international level and consensus seem to take time.[30] As a consequence, the Commission has decided to act. On 21 March 2018, the EU Commission proposed two new rules to ensure that digital business activities are taxed in a fair way:

(i) A Proposal for a Council Directive laying down rules relating to the corporate taxation of a significant digital presence;[31]

(ii) A Proposal for a Council Directive on the common system of a digital services tax on revenues resulting from the provision of certain digital services.[32]

B.   Corporate Taxation of a Significant Digital Presence

This proposal represents a comprehensive solution within the member States' corporate tax system for taxing digital activities. The EU Commission suggests as a *long-term solution* that corporate tax rules should be changed and that profits be taxed where businesses have significant interaction with users. The proposal lays down rules to establish a taxable nexus for foreign digital companies with a non-physical commercial presence.[33]

Under the proposal, a permanent establishment will be present if a *"significant digital presence"* exists through which a business is wholly or partly carried on. A significant digital presence will exist in a member State if the digital services carried on through a digital interface meet one of the following conditions:

(i) it exceeds the threshold of 7 million euros in total revenues obtained in a member State in a tax period;

(ii) it has more than 100 000 users in a member State in that tax period;

(iii) that more than 3000 business contracts for digital services are concluded in that tax period by users in a taxable year (see Article 4 Proposed Directive).

The proposed rule would also modify the rules of *attribution of profits* in respect of the significant presence. In this context, further analysis would be required; indeed, these new rules have already been characterized as "vague".[34]

---

[30]   EU Commission, Proposal on Corporate Taxation, COM(2018) 148 final, p. 2.

[31]   COM(2018) 147 final.

[32]   COM(2018) 148 final.

[33]   EU Commission, Proposal on Corporate Taxation COM(2018) 148 final, p. 2.

[34]   Hufbauer Gary Clyde and Lu Zhiyao (Lucy), The European Union's Proposed Digital Services Tax: A De Facto Tariff Policy Brief 18-15, Peterson Institute for International Economics 2018, p. 7.

At the outset, the proposed Directive seems to rely on the arm's length principle, as recognized by the OECD, as the relevant underlying principle for attributing profits between the new PE nexus and the head office (Article 5 paragraph 2 Proposed Directive).[35] This method would, however, require adaptation in order to reflect the peculiarities of value creation in the digital world.[36]

It follows that the determination of profits would be based on a functional analysis, which will consider the *economically significant activities* performed by the digital presence, and notably activities related to data or users (Article 5 Proposed Directive).

> Indeed, in the functional analysis of the permanent establishment, the criterion of significant people function relevant to the assumption of risk and to the economic ownership of assets in the context of digital activities is not sufficient to ensure a profit attribution to the significant presence that reflects the creation of value.[37]

As a consequence, the attribution of profits would take into account the development, enhancement, maintenance protection and exploitation of intangible assets in the performance of the activities (Article 5 paragraph 5 Draft Directive); and this, even if they are not linked to people functions.[38] To put it differently, when the system is run by an algorithm, a different method of attribution is necessary.[39] In this situation, the proposed Directive would rely on the *profit-split method*, unless the taxpayer proves that an alternative method based on an internationally accepted principle is more appropriate (Article 5 paragraph 6 Draft Directive).

It is interesting to note that, according to the EU Commission, the proposal for a Common Consolidated Corporate Tax Base (CCCTB) would be "the optimal solution" to ensure a fair corporate taxation in the EU. However, further work is required to use the CCCTB in the digital context. Indeed, the current scope of the CCCTB appears too limited (it applies only to large MNEs), the definition of the PE still follows the current OECD standard and the formula apportionment method should be adapted in order to effectively capture digital activities.[40] In this respect, the reports of the Committee on Economic and Monetary Affairs of the EU Parliament have already proposed

---

[35] EU Commission, Proposal on Corporate Taxation, p. 8.
[36] EU Commission, Proposal on Corporate Taxation, p. 8.
[37] EU Commission, Proposal on Corporate Taxation, p. 8.
[38] EU Commission, Proposal on Corporate Taxation, p. 9.
[39] Sheppard (2018), at 3.
[40] EU Commission, Proposal on Corporate Taxation, p. 4.

to add a fourth factor to the CCCTB, i.e. personal data collection and exploitation for commercial purposes.[41]

As a profit tax, it seems that the applicable rate should be the rate in force under the domestic law of each member State.

This proposal takes note of the current work on the BEPS project at the OECD level. It appears that the EU wanted to go further and pioneer rules on the digital economy. The tax based on a digital presence however would remain a profit tax which should fall under the scope of double taxation treaties. However, this specific new PE concept would not be in line with the definition of Article 5 of the OECD Model, even after the recent 2017 amendments, as a consequence of the BEPS Initiative, notably Action 7.[42] The EU Commission is aware of this and recommends to member States that they include corresponding rules on a significant digital presence and profit allocation in their double taxation treaties with third countries, since the provisions of the treaty may override the rules of a significant digital presence.[43]

This proposal could take a long time to be implemented. Not only does it require a change of double taxation treaties with third countries, but the precise computation of the share of each member State of the corporate profits earned in the EU might be quite controversial.[44] In addition, the rules on the attribution of profits seem quite complex and a consensus might be difficult to reach, notably because they depart from the OECD standards and rely essentially on the profit-split method. In view of the length of the process, an interim measure, the digital service tax, has been proposed in parallel.

C   Digital Services Tax (DST)

As an *interim* measure, the Commission has proposed a common tax system on the revenues derived from the supply of certain digital services by taxable persons, i.e. a digital services tax. This solution could be adopted while waiting for the more comprehensive solution described above. In addition, it would also prevent the adoption of uncoordinated unilateral measures by member States which would risk "further fragmenting the Single Market and distort[ing] competition".[45]

---

[41]   Sheppard Lee A., Digital Permanent Establishment and Digital Equalization Taxes, 72 Bulletin for International Taxation 2018, No. 4a (special issue), at 3.

[42]   Article 5 OECD Model (2017), see supra, p. 54 ff. In the same sense also Sheppard (2018), at 3.

[43]   EU Commission, Proposal on Corporate Taxation, p. 4.

[44]   Hufbauer and Lu (2018), p. 2.

[45]   EU Commission, Proposal for a Council Directive on the Common System of a Digital Services Tax on Revenues Resulting from the Provision of Certain Digital Services (hereafter, Proposal for a Digital Service Tax), p. 3.

The tax would apply to *revenues* resulting from the provision by an entity (a legal person or legal arrangement that carries on business through a company or a transparent structure) of the following services:

(i)   placing on a digital interface advertising targeted at users;
(ii) making available to users a multi-digital interface, which allows users to interact and may also facilitate the provision of underlying supply of goods or services directly between users;
(iii) transmission of data collected about users and generated from users' activities on digital interfaces (Article 3 Draft Directive).

According to the explanatory memorandum, the services within the scope of the DST are those where the participation of a user in a digital activity constitute "an essential input for the business carrying out that activity and which enables that business to obtain revenues therefrom. In other words, the business models captured by this Directive are those which would not be able to exist in their current form without user's involvement".[46] In order to define such services, the Commission refers notably to value derived from users' activities on digital interfaces, which is used to target advertising at such users or which can be sold to third parties, or value created by the active engagement of users in a multi-sided digital interface.[47]

The DST would, however, not be levied in the case of a multi-sided digital interface between users, or on revenue obtained by users from the underlying transactions (supply of goods or services). In addition, retail activities (sale of goods or services) contracted online should also remain out of scope because the value creation for the retailer lies in the goods or services provided, while the digital interface is just a communication tool[48] (also called indirect e-commerce). Finally, services provided by an entity through a digital interface consisting of the supply of digital content such as video, audio or text, would not be regarded as intermediation services and would therefore also be outside of the scope. As a justification for this specific exclusion the EU Commission mentions that "it is less certain the extent to which user participation plays a central scope in the creation of value for the company".[49]

The tax would be collected by the member State where the users are located (Article 5 Draft Directive), at a rate of 3 percent (Article 8 Draft Directive). This solution is based on the logic that users are generating value for the entity, regardless of whether they have contributed financially to generate revenue for

---

[46]   EU Commission, Proposal for a Digital Service Tax, p. 7.
[47]   EU Commission, Proposal for a Digital Service Tax, p. 7.
[48]   EU Commission, Proposal for a Digital Service Tax, p. 8.
[49]   EU Commission, Proposal for a Digital Service Tax, p. 8.

this entity.[50] *Taxable persons* would be any entity meeting one of the following conditions:

(i) Total worldwide revenues for the relevant financial year exceed 750 million euros.
(ii) Total amount of taxable revenues obtained by the entity within the EU during the financial year exceeds 50 million euros (Article 4 Draft Directive).

The DST would be payable by the taxable person providing the taxable services who is obliged to electronically notify the member State of identification. The taxable person should then submit to the member State of identification an electronic DST return for each tax period. This return will show, with respect to the tax period, the total amount of worldwide revenues and total amount of taxable revenues within the EU, for the purpose of the threshold of Article 4 paragraph 1 (Article 15 Draft Directive).

The legal nature of this proposed DST is controversial. As such, it does not look like an income tax. It is levied at a fixed rate on specific digital supplies, which seems more like an *excise*.[51] This proposal has received mixed reactions. In particular, some commentators have argued that the DST, with its high threshold, would clearly target US digital firms, which, combined with the specific exclusion of certain revenues earned by European firms (audio and media), could constitute a *de facto* discrimination not in accordance with World Trade Organization (WTO) rules or the General Agreement on Trade and Services.[52] In addition, introducing such unilateral measures could encourage other countries, notably the United States or China, to introduce similar taxes on profits earned from other types of transactions, which will "simply resurrect protectionism with another name".[53]

D.   Implementation

It seems that one of the main purposes of these proposals was to put pressure on the OECD to reach a global agreement.[54] The long-term solution has apparently not been broadly discussed. As any tax proposal requires a unanimous decision within the EU, it is still unlikely that the short-term, transitory

---

[50]   EU Commission, Proposal for a Digital Service Tax, p. 11.
[51]   Sheppard (2018), at 2.
[52]   Hufbauer and Lu (2018), p. 6 ff.
[53]   Hufbauer and Lu (2018), p. 8.
[54]   Lips Wouter, The EU Commission's Digital Tax Proposals and its Cross-platform Impact in the EU and the OECD, Journal of European Integration, online 23 December 2019.

solution of the DST would be approved. Indeed, in an Economic and Financial Affairs Council (ECOFIN) reunion of November 2018, three member States – Ireland, Finland and Sweden – have opposed this proposal.[55] In any event, the proposal is currently suspended for the implementation of the IF on the two-pillar solution. However, in a Communication of October 2020, the EU Commission has announced that, in the absence of successful implementation of the OECD IF , it would pursue its own strategy in taxing digital companies. On 15 December 2022, however, EU member States unanimously adopted the Directive implementing the pillar two global minimum 15 percent rate. Discussions with regards to pillar one are still ongoing. In the draft proposal of this Directive, the EU Commission has mentioned that is would evaluate the situation in the absence of an implementation of pillar one.[56]

V.   UNILATERAL MEASURES

A.   In General

The BEPS Initiative is under implementation. In particular, the MLI, as the multilateral convention designed to modify the BEPS recommendation on double taxation treaties, entered into force in five countries on 1 July 2018. Many other countries have signed and are on the way to ratifying.

Despite the major achievement reached by the adoption of the MLI, some uncertainties remain. First, there are still various possibilities to choose alternatives or to opt out of some provisions of the MLI. Second, some countries, notably the United States, have decided not to join. Third, as described above, a consensus has proved difficult to reach at the OECD or UN level. The implementation of pillar one in particular is still subject to debate. It follows that many countries have decided to introduce their own local unilateral rules to protect their tax base, especially in the context of the digital economy. This trend is indeed problematic because it could result in a fragmentation of tax rules among States and a departure from generally accepted standards following the OECD/G20 BEPS Initiative. As one commentator put it, the adoption of unilateral measures "to resolve what is in essence a challenge relative to tax treaty policy is unfortunate, counterproductive, and, most seriously, at odds with the core principles of the BEPS project".[57]

---

[55]   Lips (2019), p. 8.
[56]   EU Council, Interinstitutional File 2021/0443(CNS), 23 November 2022, para. 31 of the Recital of the Draft Directive implementing pillar two.
[57]   Danon Robert, "Can Tax Treaty Policy Save Us? The Case of the Digital Economy" in: Arnold Brian (ed.), Tax Treaties after the BEPS Project. A Tribute to Jacques Sasseville, Canadian Tax Foundation, Toronto 2018, p. 79.

These new rules, already implemented in some countries, such as India, Israel or the Slovak Republic, target some activities performed by non-resident enterprises, for example, online platforms, and allow for a net-basis taxation irrespective of the level of physical presence of such enterprise.[58]

On the basis of the 2018 OECD/G20 Interim Report on Action 1, these uncoordinated and unilateral actions may be divided into *four categories*: (1) changing the PE threshold; (2) using withholding taxes; (3) introducing specific turnover taxes, notably equalization or digital service taxes; (4) implementing new unilateral measures to target large MNEs, notably in the digital economy.

B.   Alternative Applications of the Permanent Establishment Threshold

Following the digitalization of the economy, various countries have reconsidered the application of the threshold for taxation of profits under a PE.[59] These new approaches tend to focus less on the permanence and physical presence at a specific place and develop alternative criteria to create a nexus, which focuses on so-called *digital presence*.

> In general terms, digital presence-type of criteria include a variety of non-physical factors intended to evidence a purposeful and sustained interaction with the economic life of a country through digital means. They are designed to establish nexus in situations where a non-resident enterprise, physically established in a remote location, is proactively taking steps to create and maintain an ongoing interaction with the users and customers of a given country (e.g., typically by leveraging technology, the Internet and other automated tools).[60]

Examples of this approach include Israel, the Slovak Republic and India.

C.   The Use of Withholding Taxes

There is also an increasing use of exceptions in domestic law and DTC for taxing at source digital products and services. For instance, some States could try to broaden the scope of withholding taxes for royalties (typically, by including this kind of tax on payments for the use of software, or for visual

---

[58]   OECD/G20 BEPS Project, Tax Challenges Arising from Digitalization, Interim Report, 2018, p. 139, n. 357.

[59]   See OECD/G20 BEPS Project, Tax Challenges Arising from Digitalization, Interim Report, 2018, p. 135, n. 349.

[60]   OECD/G20 BEPS Project, Tax Challenges Arising from Digitalization, Interim Report, 2018, p. 136, n. 351.

images or sounds).[61] A withholding tax may also be introduced on services or on other types of income, such as income from online advertising.[62] This development, in particular, may lead to complex characterization issues. The new Article 12B UN Model DTC tends also to go in this direction. It allows the source State to levy a withholding tax on cross-border automated digital services.

D.   The Use of Digital Services Taxes (Including Equalization Levies)

Another solution is to assert taxing rights over non-resident enterprises, such as foreign suppliers of digital products and services. These turnover taxes aim at improving neutrality by restoring a level playing field between foreign suppliers of certain digital goods and services and similar domestic suppliers, as well as between suppliers of digital goods and services and more conventional "brick and mortar" suppliers of competing goods and services.[63]

India introduced an equalization tax in 2016. This tax may be seen partly as a reaction to some court cases, notably the *Right Florist* case, in which the court held that payments made to Google Ireland for online advertising for a florist business could not be subject to withholding tax, in the absence of a business presence in India.[64] The equalization tax is levied at a rate of 6 percent on the payments for certain online advertising digital services made to non-resident companies without a PE in India. The tax is based on the value of the covered transactions and is therefore equivalent to a turnover tax.[65] The equalization tax is not classified by India as a tax on income but as a "transaction-based" tax, so that it may cause problems of double taxation for foreign companies also subject to tax in their country of residence.[66]

Comparable approaches have been followed or proposed by many States. The recent EU proposal of an interim DST is also based on a similar reason-

---

[61]   OECD/G20 BEPS Project, Tax Challenges Arising from Digitalization, Interim Report, 2018, p. 140, n. 357.

[62]   OECD/G20 BEPS Project, Tax Challenges Arising from Digitalization, Interim Report, 2018, p. 140, n. 357.

[63]   OECD/G20 BEPS Project, Tax Challenges Arising from Digitalization, Interim Report, 2018, p. 140, n. 357.

[64]   Jain (2017), p. 180, referring notably to the judgment of the Income Tax Appellate Tribunal, Kolkata, 12 April 2013, ITA 1336/Kol./2011, *Right Floris Pvt. Ltd. v. ITO*.

[65]   OECD/G20 BEPS Project, Tax Challenges Arising from Digitalization, Interim Report, 2018, p. 142.

[66]   OECD/G20 BEPS Project, Tax Challenges Arising from Digitalization, Interim Report, 2018, p. 142.

ing.[67] As of January 2023, DSTs have been widely introduced, notably in the EU and in Africa. Austria, France, Hungary, Italy, Poland, Portugal, Spain, Turkey and the UK have implemented a DST.[68] In summary, about half of EU member States have adopted or planned digital service taxes.[69] While most of them are clearly inspired by the EU DST proposal (as an interim measure), others apply to advertising services. Other countries in the world also have introduced or planned DST.[70] In the United States, there are also subnational digital service taxes levied or planned by some States, including a project targeting services that extract and monetize from users.[71]

In general, DSTs apply to MNEs with a significant turnover (usually over 750 million euros). They apply to "tech giants" that have a quasi-monopolistic position and are considered not to be paying enough taxes in the market State where the users and consumers are. Taxable digital services include advertising, digital interface and data transfers. Tax rates vary between 2 percent and 7 percent of the taxable base.

As a rule, these taxes are designed as turnover taxes (excises). They are levied of the gross turnover of digital services and linked with the participation of users or local consumers. They thus differ from traditional international allocation rules, since the requirement of a PE, in the usual sense of this concept, disappears, because a nexus already exists to the extent that a certain threshold of users or transactions with the market State is reached.

In essence, these new unilateral taxes raise concerns. They may notably interfere with global initiatives, such as BEPS Action 1 and pillar one of the OECD compromise. In addition, they contribute to *legal* uncertainty, especially with regards to the scope of application of DTT.[72] Indeed, these taxes are levied on digital transactions and whether or not they may be characterized as income (profit) taxes, within the meaning of Article 2 OECD Model, is disputed. In addition, the limited scope of application of DSTs has also been criticized and some commentators have raised potential concerns over those taxes. It should be stressed that the non-discrimination principle has a broad scope of application and applies independently of the character of such tax as

---

[67]   See supra, p. 83 ff.

[68]   Vàzquez Juan Manuel, Digital Services Taxes in the European Union: What Can We Expect? Kluwer International Tax Blog, 14 February 2023, at 2.

[69]   Alvarado (2021), table 2, with a summary.

[70]   Among others, Canada, Egypt, India, Indonesia, Israel, New Zealand, Russia, South Korea.

[71]   See Appleby Andrew, Subnational Digital Services Taxation, 81 Maryland Law Review 2021, p. 8.

[72]   Ismer Roland and Jescheck Christoph, The Substantive Scope of Tax Treaties in a Post-BEPS World: Article 2 OECD MC (Taxes Covered and the Rise of New Taxes), Intertax 2017, p. 383.

an income or turnover tax. DST may also conflict with the norms of the WTO.[73] In two important cases, rendered on 3 March 2020, the Court of Justice of the European Union (CJEU), however, recognized the compatibility with the EU freedom of establishment principle of the Hungarian tax on advertising and digital services.[74]

Finally, they are sometimes also criticized for their *economic* impact. Not only can they create a heavy tax burden on some digital companies, notably due to the gross applicable tax rate, but they may finally be transferred to consumers who would ultimately bear the costs of the tax. It appears that many MNEs, notably active in digital advertising services, have raised their fees.

E.   Specific Regimes Targeting Large MNEs

These regimes typically implement anti-abuse rules to address excessive use of base-eroding payments by large MNEs. This includes the diverted profit tax (DPT) introduced by the United Kingdom and Australia, and the base erosion and anti-abuse tax (BEAT) implemented by the United States.

The DPT was enacted in 2015 with a view to preventing MNEs from eroding the tax base of their business activities in the United Kingdom. In short, the tax is levied at a rate of 25 percent on the diverted profits arising from UK activities and transferred abroad. The tax is intended to address two different types of aggressive tax planning arrangements: (i) the avoidance of a PE by foreign entities; or (ii) base erosion resulting from inter-group schemes between closely related entities.[75] The compatibility of the DPT with double taxation treaties is a matter of controversy. In addition, this new tax was enacted before the publication in 2015 of the OECD/G20 Final Report on Action 1. While, according to His Majesty's Revenue and Customs (HMRC), such tax is in line with the BEPS Initiative,[76] its unilateral and specific features could create difficulties in reaching an international consensus.[77]

In 2017, the United States adopted, as part of a major tax reform, the BEAT.[78] The BEAT applies to the US taxpayer's member of an MNE group, whose activities in the United States exceed a certain threshold of sales. The tax applies to "base-eroding payments", that is any amount paid or accrued by the taxpayer to foreign related parties for which a deduction is allowable, such as

---

[73]   Alvarado (2021), n. 4.
[74]   CJEU cases C-323/18, *Tesco-Global Aruhazak Zrt.* and C-75/18, *Vodafone Magyarorszag Mobil Tavközlési Zrt.*) of 3 March 2020.
[75]   See, in general Uslu (2018), n. 4.2.; Jain (2017), p. 179.
[76]   HMRC, Diverted Profit Tax Guidance, 30 November 2015, p. 4.
[77]   Uslu (2018), n. 4.2.4.
[78]   The law was introduced on 22 December 2017 as part of the Tax Cuts and Jobs Act.

interest for example, and amounts paid to foreign related parties in connection with the acquisition of depreciable or amortizable property. The rate of the tax is the highest amount between: (1) 10 percent (reduced to 5 percent for 2018, and increased to 13.5 percent from 2016) of the "modified taxable income", which corresponds to the regular corporate tax base, plus any "base-eroding payments"; over (2) the regular corporate tax liability of the taxpayer reduced by tax credits allowed in that year (with some exceptions).[79] This tax has been described as a separate and independent alternative minimum tax (not characterized as such) with no foreign tax credit allowed. According to commentators, this tax not only violates the non-discrimination provision in US treaties, but the denial of the foreign tax credit also raises treaty issues.[80]

F.   Excursus: Changes in the Taxation of Interstate e-commerce in the United States

In this context, an interesting indication has been given by the US Supreme Court. In the *Wayfair* case, decided on 21 June 2018,[81] the Supreme Court ruled that online retailers may be required to collect sales tax, even without a physical presence in that State. This decision overturned the judgment of 1992, *Quill v. North Dakota*, in which the Court had ruled that the US Constitution, notably the commerce clause, did require a physical presence in a State in order to levy State taxes. In essence, this important decision recognizes the existence of a competitive disadvantage between local State sellers and remote sellers, which is also a global concern in the taxation of the digital economy. It follows that States are now free to require remote sellers to collect tax, to the extent that the seller has a "substantial nexus" with that State.[82] Such threshold could be based, for instance, on sales revenues or on number of transactions.

As explained by various commentators, this judgment goes in the same direction as recent proposals in favor of a new PE nexus, including the EU Draft Directive for a significant digital presence.[83] Indeed, the reasoning of the Court in *Wayfair* addresses the same issues that the recent proposals at the OECD, UN or EU level try to solve.

---

[79]   See OECD/G20, BEPS Interim Report, 2018, p. 158.
[80]   Rosenbloom David H., International Aspects of US Tax Reform: Is this Really Where we Want to Go? International Tax Report 2018, p. 2.
[81]   *South Dakota v. Wayfair Inc.*, 21 June 2018, 585 U.S. (2018).
[82]   Avi-Yonah (2018), p. 163.
[83]   Avi-Yonah (2018), p. 163; Finley (2018), p. 14; see supra, p. 81.

VI.   ANALYSIS FROM A POLICY PERSPECTIVE

A.   Introduction

These developments tend to better apprehend the new features of the digital economy. Indeed, the PE concept may be viewed as a compromise designed to allocate the taxing rights between the source State and the State of residence, which was designed at the beginning of the twentieth century, after the First World War. The PE definition is based on an economy of "brick and mortar" under which business required a physical presence in the source country.[84] The new business models used by the digital economy do not require such presence anymore and interact with customers and users of any source country granting electronic access to a digital platform. In addition, in some cases, non-resident companies may benefit from information or data or connections added from users, which may be used, exchanged or transferred for consideration to third parties.

We have mentioned the various attempts at the OECD, UN or EU level to address the challenges raised by the taxation of the digitalization of the economy. We will therefore analyze from a critical perspective the issues raised by those main proposals or rules, i.e. (1) the concept of a new digital PE, (2) the introduction of withholding taxes, and (3) specific taxes on digital transactions.

B.   Digital Permanent Establishment

1.   Defining the appropriate nexus

Contrary to the traditional approach, these amendments are aimed at diluting the requirement for permanence and physical presence at a specific geographical place to establish a nexus for net-basis taxation.[85] Indeed, while many of the amendments to the current PE definition introduced by the BEPS project will affect certain enterprises in e-commerce, they would only cover enterprises selling physical goods because the changes still rely on the physical presence threshold.[86]

Commentators have also proposed alternative criteria to define nexus. Hongler and Pistone, for instance, favor a new PE nexus, which would be

---

[84]   OECD/G20 BEPS Project, Addressing the Tax Challenges of the Digital Economy, Action 1, 2015, Final Report, p. 98 ff.

[85]   OECD/G20 BEPS Project, Tax Challenges Arising from Digitalization, Interim Report, 2018, p. 135.

[86]   Hongler Peter and Pistone Pasquale, IBFD Blueprints for a New PE Nexus to Tax Business Income in the Era of Digital Economy, Working Paper 2015, p. 14.

introduced in a new Article 5 paragraph 8 OECD Model, and should consist of four main elements or requirements: (1) digital services, (2) a user threshold, (3) a time threshold, and (4) a *de minimis* revenue threshold. Avi-Yonah and Halabi, on their side, argue in favor of a PE definition, which sets an absolute threshold of sale of goods or services into the source jurisdiction.[87] At this stage the discussions are still open at the OECD level.[88]

In our view, this solution could be introduced, at least on a long-term basis. As eloquently described by Avi-Yonah, in the medium or long term, a virtual solution is probably inevitable, since "the large market jurisdiction cannot tolerate the ability of remote enterprises to exploit their market without paying a penny in tax because of a physical presence rule stemming from 19th-century realities and imported into twentieth-century model tax treaties out of a desire to protect business from taxation".[89] The problem however is that a consensus might be difficult to reach. Not only should the precise scope of that new nexus be accepted but also rules of attribution of profits should be designed and adjusted to the new threshold.

2. Attribution of profits to a digital permanent establishment

The new digital PE, based on a significant digital presence, requires an adaption of the applicable rules of attribution of profits to such PE.[90] To develop these rules would go much beyond the scope of our analysis, but some elements are worth mentioning. The current regime for attributing profits, based on Article 7 OECD Model, relies on the so-called Authorized OECD Approach (AOA).[91] In short, profits to be attributed to a PE are the profits that the PE "might be expected to make if it were a separate and independent enterprise engaged in the same or similar activities under the same or similar conditions, taking into account the functions performed, assets used and risks assumed through the permanent establishment and through other parts of the enterprise".[92] The analysis is based on a two-step approach. First, a functional and factual analysis. This step requires the identification of significant people function relevant to the attribution of economic ownership of the assets and to the assumption of

---

[87]   Avi-Yonah Reuven S. and Halabi Oz, A Model Treaty for the Age of BEPS, University of Michigan Law School, Law and Economics Working Papers, 2014, p. 1 ff, 15.

[88]   Hongler and Pistone (2015), p. 25.

[89]   Avi-Yonah (2018), p. 164.

[90]   See in general, Danon (2018), p. 87; Cataldi Matteo, "The Attribution of Income to a Digital Permanent Establishment" in: Kerschner I. and Somare M. (eds), Taxation in a Global Digital Economy, Linde Verlag, Vienna 2017, p. 143 ff.

[91]   See OECD, Attribution of Profits to Permanent Establishments, OECD Paris 2010.

[92]   OECD Commentary, n. 15 at Art. 7.

risks.[93] Second, any transactions with associated enterprises attributed to the PE are priced in accordance with the OECD transfer pricing guidelines.

The significant digital presence, as a new proposed nexus, would require modification to this methodology. In particular, frequently, due to automation, in the absence of employee, no "significant people functions" would be implemented at the location of the PE and thus, no or insignificant profits could be attributable there.[94] As a result, various alternative methods have been examined by the OECD, under the BEPS Action 1, but with no unanimous recommendation so far.[95]

Some commentators have, however, made proposals. For instance, Hongler and Pistone focus on the potential application of a modified profit-split method, with an upfront income allocation of a partial profit percentage to the market jurisdiction, in order to determine the profit attributable to the PE jurisdiction.[96] These authors admit that the exact amount of such upfront allocation is subject to negotiation and would require further studies, but they assume that *one-third* of the profit of an enterprise within the digital economy is created by the market jurisdictions.[97] Therefore, these authors suggest that the market jurisdictions, fulfilling the new PE nexus, should split one-third of the profits among themselves, following the relation between domestic revenue and overall revenues, while the residual two-thirds of the profits are split in accordance with existing transfer pricing rules.[98] As of today, no clear consensus has been found, but it is interesting to note that the EU, in its recent proposal on a digital PE, also favors an amended profit-split method.[99]

In addition, Petruzzi and Buriak have made an interesting proposal. Instead of "reinventing the wheel", they suggest applying the existing transfer pricing rules, as amended by the OECD/G20 BEPS Initiative, but to align these rules with the inclusion of a value creation analysis (VCA) into the functional analysis.[100] In particular, according to those authors, the analysis should consider the fact that highly digitized companies derive their value from monetization of data. Contrary to traditional businesses, where most of the value is usually derived from the manufacturing process and from the quality of the material,

---

[93]   OECD Commentary, n. 21 at Art. 7.
[94]   Cataldi (2017), p. 149.
[95]   See OECD/G20, Addressing the Tax Challenges of the Digital Economy, Action 1, 2015, Final Report, p. 111.
[96]   Hongler and Pistone (2015), p. 33.
[97]   Hongler and Pistone (2015), p. 34.
[98]   Hongler and Pistone (2015), p. 35.
[99]   See supra, p. 82.
[100] Petruzzi and Buriak (2018), at 2.

"companies like the FAANG[101] base their business models almost exclusively on the use of digital technologies, which play a pivotal role in their development. As a result, appropriate taxing rights should be shared with the jurisdictions where such value is generated."[102]

In any event, not only digital companies, but also more traditional businesses make use of data to enhance their profits, for example for marketing or advertising purposes (airline companies, retails shops, etc.). The design of new rules for profit allocation should therefore include the peculiarities of the digital economy but at the same time remain neutral and in accordance with the principle of equality of treatment. In other words, *ring-fencing* of the digital economy should be avoided.[103]

3.   Withholding taxes

It is however recognized that a withholding tax could also be an alternative solution to the digital presence model. Indeed, reaching a consensus on a new nexus could be difficult, not to mention the problems of attribution of profits to the new digital PE. Such taxes could however raise delicate conflicts with trade obligation or EU law, notably if they apply to remote foreign suppliers, while domestic suppliers are subject to net-basis taxation.[104]

In this context, Brauner and Baez have proposed, as an alternative to the nexus-based solution, a globally standard final withholding tax of 10 percent on all base-eroding payments for non-residents.[105] A standard exception would however apply to payees registered to be taxed under a net taxation scheme. This proposal would apply to B2B transactions, which dominate the digital economy. For B2C payments, some countries could, however, introduce a complimentary final withholding tax of 15 percent on all payments cleared by financial institutions, unless the payee is registered to be taxed under the net taxation scheme. To implement this rule, the authors propose a new Article 7 paragraph 4 OECD Model, which would allow contracting States to implement

---

[101] FAANG stands for digital giants such as Facebook, Apple, Amazon, Netflix and Google; see Petruzzi and Buriak (2018), at 4.2.

[102] Petruzzi and Buriak (2018), at 5.2.2.

[103] Danon (2018), p. 87; Kofler Georg, Mar Gunter and Schlager Christoph, Taxation of the Digital Economy: "Quick Fixes" or Long-term Solutions? European Taxation 2017, p. 529.

[104] OECD/G20 BEPS Project, Addressing the Tax Challenges of the Digital Economy, Action 1, 2015, Final Report, p. 100, n. 299.

[105] Brauner Yariv and Baez Andres, Withholding Taxes in the Service of BEPS Action 1: Address the Tax Challenge of the Digital Economy, IBFD, 2 February 2015, 4 ff.

such withholding tax on payments made by an enterprise or a PE sited in that State.[106]

4.   Introducing specific taxes on digital transactions

It is understandable that States are trying to cope with the development of the digital economy and may not be in a position to wait for a consensus on these issues at the OECD or the UN level. It should, however, be mentioned that these unilateral measures, as we have seen, are not coordinated and could conflict not only with double taxation treaties, but also with the principle of neutrality and equality of treatment, and could create additional burden and double taxation. In addition, the precise characterization of these taxes is a matter of controversy. They seem to be designed to be outside the scope of DTT, but at the same time they are intended to be borne by the foreign service provider. For Robert Danon, it seems "unacceptable" that States design a tax which is deliberately outside the scope of DTT "in order to accomplish what is de facto an expansion of source taxing rights".[107]

So far, these unilateral DSTs appear to have been introduced as an interim solution until an agreement is reached on a general applicable standard.[108] In the same vein, the EU, which is carefully following the works at the OECD level, under the BEPS Initiative, and notably on Action 1, has proposed two new tax measures, which may also be viewed as a response to the lack of significant progress in this field.[109] It comes as no surprise that the proposed EU DST, designed as a new excise tax, is described as a transitory measure, which should only apply until the member States agree on a more comprehensive solution. While the two-pillar solution has been accepted by the IF as a matter of principle, the fate of the DSTs will depend upon the scope of implementation of pillar one. A failure of a global agreement on pillar one, which is among the possible scenarios, could in fact lead to a "proliferation" of DSTs or other similar unilateral measures.[110]

---

[106] Brauner and Baez (2015), p. 23.
[107] Danon (2018), p. 83.
[108] Petruzzi and Buriak (2018), at 2.
[109] See supra, p. 80 ff.
[110] Vàzquez (2023), at 5.

VII.   IMPACT ON THE TAXATION OF ARTIFICIAL INTELLIGENCE AND ROBOTS

A.   In General

1.   Taxation of data collection or processing by artificial intelligence and robots

In general, the new tax rules are designed to address the new features of the digital economy, which, by definition, make extensive use of AI, algorithms and robotics. Indeed, advances in computer power have meant that "certain functions, including decision-making capabilities", can now be carried out by algorithms.[111] Contracts, for instance, may be automatically accepted by software programs, without any intervention from local personnel.[112]

It follows that the various tax proposals described above, which try to tax or include in the tax base, the value of data provided by users or consumers, to the extent that they contribute to the realization of profits, are also *justified* by the progress and extended possibilities that automation and robotics offer. As such, the use of data is not new but the capacity to collect and categorize these data has increased "exponentially" due to the power of computers and AI.[113]

The importance of the value provided by users becomes especially relevant in this context. This is typically the case, as described by Petruzzi and Buriak, when the business customers become "unconscious providers" of digital enterprises by contributing data, which these enterprises may monetize.[114] In addition, "the involvement of customers as users and the automatic recording and processing of their preferences by algorithms significantly enhances the performances of business as compared to the various steps of complex marketing studies that constituted an indispensable feature of the conventional business".[115]

This being said, the features of the new proposals are different, if we look at the various main options discussed so far, such as the digital PE, a new digital service tax or a withholding tax. Their link with the use of AI or robotics, and, as a consequence, their impact on automation, should be analyzed separately. The idea to tax data collection, as such, is however another strategy to address

---

[111]   OECD/G20 BEPS Project, Addressing the Tax Challenges of the Digital Economy, Action 1, 2015, Final Report, p. 100, n. 254.

[112]   OECD/G20 BEPS Project, Addressing the Tax Challenges of the Digital Economy, Action 1, 2015, Final Report, p. 100, n. 254.

[113]   OECD/G20 BEPS Project, Addressing the Tax Challenges of the Digital Economy, Action 1, 2015, Final Report, p. 100, n. 254.

[114]   See Petruzzi and Buriak (2018).

[115]   Brauner and Pistone (2018), p. 2.

the development of the digital economy but tends to focus more on the input side of the business, namely the data considered as a raw material which contributes to the realization of profits.[116] Taxation of AI by contrast takes a different perspective.[117] It tries to include in the taxable base the profits generated by the use of AI instead of human workers.

2.   Digital permanent establishment

The introduction of a new nexus based on a *digital presence* would also affect AI and robotics. In particular, the application of a digital factor is directly based on the use of automated technology. This new nexus would consider the fact that foreign enterprises have an economic presence in one country on the basis of factors which demonstrate a "sustained interaction with the economy of that country via technology or other automated tools".[118] This factor notably involves the conclusion of contracts, typically through a digital platform where contracts are concluded on automated systems.[119]

In addition, the creation of a digital PE as a new nexus for taxation raises the issue of the *attribution of profits*. As we have seen, the current attribution rules rely heavily on key people functions. In particular, the EU proposal of a digital PE is based on a significant digital presence which is operated through a digital interface *without any physical presence* in one jurisdiction or where no significant people functions are performed in the jurisdiction of the digital presence.[120] In the world of robotics, the reliance on human significant activities or functions requires a reassessment. The key functions could be performed by AI and implemented by robots or a relevant infrastructure. In the case of smart robots, we could even consider that key "people" functions could be attributable to AI systems acting with sufficient autonomy.[121] Recently, in the same line of thinking, Daniel Smit has also mentioned the possibility of revisiting due to automation the meaning of "human intervention" leading to

---

[116] Oberson Xavier and Yacicioglou Efsun Alara, Taxation of Big Data, Springer, Cham, Switzerland, 2023, p. 121 ff.

[117] See supra, p. 46 ff.

[118] OECD/G20 BEPS Project, Addressing the Tax Challenges of the Digital Economy, Action 1, 2015, Final Report, p. 100, n. 277.

[119] OECD/G20 BEPS Project, Addressing the Tax Challenges of the Digital Economy, Action 1, 2015, Final Report, p. 100, n. 277.

[120] Draft Directive, explanatory memorandum, p. 9.

[121] This perspective would need to revisit the essential reference to human capital in value creation; compare Tavares Romero and Owens Jeffrey, Human Capital in Value Creation and Post-BEPS Tax Policy: An Outlook Bulletin for International Taxation 2015, p. 590 ff.

the concept of "(significant) robot functions".[122] It means that the essential concept of significant people function should be analyzed from a completely different perspective in the field of AI. Some functions, and therefore value, could be attributed to intelligent machines replacing humans.

To adapt to this new business model, the proposals would require a revision of the rules of attribution of profits. The OECD has already proposed various approaches under the OECD/G20 BEPS Initiative, in Action 1. In addition, the proposed EU rules on attribution of income to the digital PE would also take into account, in the functional analysis, the lack of key functions linked with human workers. The EU Commission intends therefore to adapt the current OECD methodology by focusing on the activities undertaken by the enterprise through the digital interface related to data and user. The profit-split method would thus become the most appropriate one.

Other ideas have also been brought forward. In our view, a functional analysis could try to focus on similar human activities, exercised by AI autonomous systems and robots, and compare their respective values. In any case, a new transfer pricing analysis is required. The difficulty at the OECD and EU level to reach a consensus is just one example of the problems ahead.

3.   Withholding taxes

Withholding taxes would appear to be less appropriate in the perspective of addressing the use of technology and automation. In particular, digital enterprises often require substantial upfront investments, which, after the initial costly expenses, imply reduced marginal costs for business. A gross withholding tax in this respect is not always appropriate because it is based on an imperfect estimate of the net profits.[123] However, the difficulty of applying a tax on AI or robots as such, at least in the short term, could further justify as an alternative solution the use of a withholding tax. The new Article 12B UN Model DTC tends also to go in this direction. It focuses on the payments for automated digital services and allows the source State to levy a withholding tax.

4.   Digital services taxes

If we focus only on the proposed EU DST interim proposal, which corresponds in essence to many existing DSTs around the world, this new tax would in fact

---

[122] Smit Daniel, Flexibility, "Mobility and Automation of Labour under Article 7 of the OECD Model? A First Conceptual Exploration" in: Weber Dennis (ed.), The Implications of Online Platforms and Technology for Taxation, IBFD, Amsterdam 2023, p. 174.

[123] OECD/G20 BEPS Project, Addressing the Tax Challenges of the Digital Economy, Action 1, 2015, Final Report, p. 115, n. 288.

target social media, and sales of digital services, namely Facebook and Google, and exclude digital sales of audio, video and text, thus excluding Netflix and Spotify.[124] As we have seen, the allocation of the share of the tax attributable to each member State would be difficult to determine. This tax would be levied on the payments made in consideration of online digital services under the scope. In most instances, these services are also often linked with automated data processing of customers connected to the network. A solution, in order to tighten the link with AI and robotics, would be to focus on the alternative suggested by the OECD, which is to limit the scope of the digital tax on transactions involving the conclusion of contracts through "automated systems" for the sale or exchange of goods and services effectuated through digital platforms.[125] The new Article 12B UN Model DTC also focuses on automated digital services.

The EU proposal entails interesting new rules for collection of the tax. In general, the location of users would correspond to the place of supply. This requires a definition of the precise localization of the user. Under the proposed Directive, the member State where a user's device is used will be determined by reference to the Internet Protocol (IP) address of the device or, if more accurate, any other method of geolocation (Article 5 paragraph 5 Draft Directive). This rule demonstrates some of the technical difficulties and peculiarities of implementing a tax on the use of online services. Indeed, the definition of the place of user by reference to the IP address could violate data protection rules.[126] In order to minimize the potential infringement, the proposal limits the data collected from users for the purpose of applying the Draft Directive to those indicating where users are located, without allowing for identification (Article 5 paragraph 6 Draft Directive).

5.   Pillar 1 of the OECD compromise of 2021

At first, pillar one of the compromise suggested by the OECD in 2019 clearly targeted large MNEs of the digital economy. Indeed, under the policy note of 2019, pillar one focused on the digital economy and allocated more taxing rights to the market State, where the participation of users would contribute more to the value creation of the business activity of an MNE.[127] In other words, there was a clear link in this new taxation right in favor of the source State for profits from automation.

---

[124]   Sheppard (2018), at 2.
[125]   OECD/G20 BEPS Project, Addressing the Tax Challenges of the Digital Economy, Action 1, 2015, Final Report, p. 100, n. 304.
[126]   In this sense, Sheppard (2018), at 2.
[127]   OECD/G20, Addressing the Tax Challenges of the Digitalization of the Economy, Policy Note, 23 January 2019.

Eventually, during the negotiation process, to avoid a "ring-fencing" of the economy, the scope of this new rule was broadened to all sectors of the economy, with the exception of the extraction and financial sector.[128] Thus, the new allocation rule no longer focuses only on profits from automation but on all global profits from large MNEs. Thus, large "tech companies", that are above the applicable revenue threshold to enter in the scope of pillar one, using extensively AI, algorithms, big data and robotics, remain targeted by this new allocation methodology in favor of the sales States, but the link of this regime with a taxation of the use of AI systems appears less obvious than under the first 2019 proposal. Amount A would however still encompass, in most cases, profits from the use of automation since, as we have seen, AI is used in all sectors of the economy, including the industrial and commercial activities (distant sales), and the relevant nexus focus of the place of sales, without requiring a physical presence in the source State.

B.   Taxation of the Digital Economy as an Alternative Tax on Artificial Intelligence Systems and Robots?

The new proposals, both at the OECD, the UN, the EU and in various countries, catch some of the value provided to the digital non-resident companies by the customers or users in the source country. They also try to implement the neutrality principle between domestic companies and foreign online sellers offering digital services to local customers (equalization taxes).

As such, these new rules do not, in general, target AI or robots specifically. However, many of the digital services addressed by these tax initiatives are rendered by non-resident firms using algorithms or some kind of automated AI. In the context of AI and robotics, it is interesting to realize that in most cases, the collection, analysis and transfer of data will be done by algorithms, i.e. AI, used by the companies involved in the digital economy and sited at the place where the relevant infrastructure is located. If we look at the main options designed so far in order to find a better balance between the source and residence States, we may, however, analyze them differently, from the perspective of a tax on AI or robots' activities.

First, the introduction of *significant digital presence* (digital PE), discussed at the OECD, the EU level and already implemented by various States, would create a new nexus for taxation in the source State. As such, this new rule, which would allocate part of the value created by customers or users in the source State, by providing monetized data, could be seen as an indirect way of taxing the activities of algorithms or AI, which will in most cases collect,

---

[128] See supra, p. 79.

process and analyze those data and have an impact in the market (source) State. However, including the value of users in the allocation of international profits is not a tax on AI. Indeed, the companies in digital services will still be subject to profit tax on the output. The use of data provided by users is part of the input process. The problem is that in the country of source, as of now, the granting of data to the foreign digital company will not be subject to tax in the country of source. In this respect, trying to allocate some right to tax the international profits of the digital companies appears justified, but this allocation remains a method of international sharing of the profit tax between the source and the residence State. This allocation, as such, is not an additional or new tax on the use of AI or robots.

Second, the idea of a *withholding tax*, as already applied in some countries, corresponds more to a new specific tax. As such, it targets sales created by consumers in the source States. It could also be viewed as an approximation of a tax on AI or robots' activities because this tax is an additional tax which would at least include many of the payments in consideration for digital services provided by AI or robots. The new Article 12B UN Model also goes in the same direction.[129] It is consistent with the idea of granting more taxing rights to the source State for automated digital services. The definition of the services subject to tax is broad and covers also activities that may be provided by AI, such as online advertising services, online search engines or social media or platforms.

Third, the same seems to apply in the case of the *digital services tax*. As we have seen, this tax, like other taxes introduced in some countries, is designed as an excise tax with the purpose of equalizing profits of local and foreign digital suppliers of services. These taxes, sometimes also called equalization taxes, usually seek to improve neutrality "by restoring a level playing field between foreign suppliers of certain digital goods and services and more conventional, brick and mortar suppliers of competing goods or services".[130] However, these new taxes are not designed as a method of international allocation of profits.

It should be mentioned that these proposals so far focus on the digital economy. Activities in (indirect) *e-commerce*, which tend to use the Internet to order online, but still entail physical delivery of goods (books, consumer goods, etc.), are still in most cases outside the scope of these new taxes. The reason is that the new rules introduced under the OECD/G20 BEPS Initiative already cover many of the problems analyzed so far. Indeed, the changes to the PE concept, and notably the restricted scope of the auxiliary and ancillary

---

[129] See supra, p. 79.
[130] OECD/G20 BEPS Project, Tax Challenges Arising from Digitalization, Interim Report, 2018, p. 141.

exception, combined with the changes to the dependent and independent agent, should avoid some of the avoidance strategies used in the past. In particular, delivery or storage of goods could trigger the presence of a place of business. In addition, there is an important difference between indirect e-commerce and the digital economy. Indeed, in indirect e-commerce, the inputs are mostly tangible goods, which will be taxed, not only when sold to the consumers, but also when purchased by the e-commerce company. This difference should however not be exaggerated. The e-commerce company will also benefit from the additional value attributable to the information provided by the purchaser of the goods (taste, style, number of goods, etc.). The company may then use these data to better target the consumer with advertising.

Fourth, the OECD two-pillar solution, in particular pillar one, offers a more global approach, which no longer targets specifically large MNEs in the digital economy, but more generally MNEs with a turnover of more than 20 billion euro and a profitability above 10 percent. This approach would grant more taxing rights to the source State, based on an apportionment method, which would rely on a mathematical formula, based on the amount of sales in the market State. This system, when implemented, should replace the existing DSTs. In any event, taxing the digital economy, either globally, as part of the pillar one system, or specifically, with the introduction of DSTs, or other specific tax rules (withholding tax or digital PE), may be seen in part as an *indirect way* of taxing the activities of AI and robots benefitting from the value of data provided by "unconscious users".[131]

This solution cannot be compared, however, with a more *direct* approach, which is a tax on the use of AI or on AI autonomous systems as such, as we see it, and will try to design further.[132] First, the scope of taxation of the digital economy is focused on digital enterprises offering all digital services, while using algorithms or robotics. It appears, however, that currently, the traditional economy also uses robotics extensively (notably in the industry sector). In addition, these rules are based on a different rationale than the AI or taxes that we will later describe. The purpose of taxation of the digital economy is to better ascertain and allocate the value component of the data provided by users and consumers. By contrast, AI and robot taxes intend notably to tax the "hypothetical income" component of replacing workers with machines and to create a level playing field between human and robot workers. Eventually, the tax on AI and robots, as such, would go even further by designing a new tax-

---

[131]   To use the words of Petruzzi and Buriak (2018), at 5.3.2.
[132]   See infra, p. 148 ff.

payer, defined as an AI autonomous system or a smart robot, with the capacity to use its own distinct patrimony.[133]

---

[133] Oberson Xavier, Robot Taxes: The Rise of a New Taxpayer, IBFD Bulletin for International Taxation, August 2021, p. 370 ff; see supra p. 22 ff.

8.   VAT on the activities of artificial intelligence

I.   ARTIFICIAL INTELLIGENCE AND ROBOT TRANSACTIONS SUBJECT TO VAT

VAT is a multi-stage consumption tax, introduced in France in 1950, under the impetus of Maurice Lauré, the then director of the French Tax Administration. VAT would eventually become the "success tax story" of the twentieth century and would gradually be adopted worldwide. In particular, under the first VAT Directive of 11 April 1967 and the second Directive of the same date, member States were required to introduce, as of 1 January 1970, a system of VAT, to replace all existing taxes on consumption.[1]

VAT, by definition, is neutral. Contrary to cumulative turnover taxes still in existence at the time, the system of the input tax credit, i.e. the right for each enterprise to credit the input VAT against any output VAT charged on supplies of goods or services, proved to be compatible with the common market in the European Economic Community (EEC), later replaced by the EC, based on the four freedoms of movement. The VAT was further codified in the Sixth Directive,[2] which was replaced, as of 1 January 2007, by Council Directive 2006/112/EC[3] (hereafter the VAT Directive). VAT, sometimes also described as a goods or services tax (GST), was introduced in many other countries around the world, notably China, Japan, Australia, Russia, Canada, Brazil and India, with the notable exception of the United States, which still relies on its existing State turnover taxes.

In essence, VAT is levied at all stages of production and distribution by enterprises subject to tax, on supply of goods, services or imports (output

---

[1]   First Council Directive 67/227/EEC and Second Council Directive 67/228/EEC.

[2]   Sixth Council Directive 77/388/EEC of 17 May 1977 on the harmonization of the laws of the member States relating to turnover taxes - Common system of value added tax: uniform basis of assessment.

[3]   Council Directive 2006/112/EC of 28 November 2006 on the common system of value added tax.

VAT). The enterprises subject to tax may, however, credit the VAT that has been charged on the business inputs (input VAT).

As such, the activities prompted by AI are carried out by machines, including robots, that have been programmed to implement certain tasks. AI may be used for a wide scope of economic activities, either for the supply of goods (notably industrial robots), such as building cars or machines, and also for services, such as law, banking, health care, journalism, entertainments, data processing, etc. It is not disputable that such activities, to the extent they are effectuated by enterprises in exchange of a consideration, would fall under the scope of VAT.

However, so far, an AI system is not regarded as an independent person but is part either of the *business* assets of an enterprise, or of the *private* wealth of an individual who has acquired it for private consumption. It follows that under current law, the taxable persons for VAT are the enterprises (in a legal form or not) which, independently, use AI for their economic activity. Recent developments in the sharing economy have, however, put digital platforms at the forefront and their role as VAT collectors is growing.[4] As we will demonstrate, the involvement of platforms for VAT purposes could also be regarded as a potential blueprint for a future taxation of AI and robots. In addition, we will see later in Chapter 9 that the situation could however evolve, should we start to recognize AI autonomous systems as such, as independent persons.

We will therefore try to see how the VAT rules apply to AI and robots' activities. In this context, we will demonstrate that VAT may play a crucial role in the future for the taxation of AI and robots. For that purpose, we will first describe the main governing principle designed by the OECD on the application of VAT to electronic transactions. Indeed, as we will see, these principles are also of relevance in the area of the taxation of AI and robotics. Then, we will concentrate on the essential EU VAT rules, which have been implemented and are constantly reevaluated, both under the influence of the jurisprudence of the ECJ, and also considering economic and technological developments. In particular, recent rules, prompted by the technological development and notably the use of digital *platforms*, may serve as a model for a more extended role of VAT in the world of AI and robots. These rules also have an important influence on the VAT rules of other countries, such as Switzerland. Finally, we will be able to conclude on the many possibilities offered by VAT in this context.

---

[4]   OECD, The Role of Digital Platforms in the Collection of VAT/GST on Online Sales, March 2019.

II.   THE PRINCIPLES GOVERNING TAXATION OF ELECTRONIC TRANSACTIONS

In the early 1990s, with the development of electronic commerce, the OECD undertook a thorough analysis of the applicable tax policy aspects. This development has raised new challenges for the proper application of VAT rules, which were designed in the mid-twentieth century, at a time where commerce was focusing on the supply of physical goods. Electronic commerce is usually divided into two different features, which may require different tax rules. First, so-called *direct* e-commerce, which focuses on the supply of intangible electronic goods (software, movies, music, e-books, etc.) and second, *indirect* e-commerce, in which physical goods or services are supplied using the internet as the connecting factor between suppliers and customers. Digital platforms may be used in both situations, but recent VAT issues have arisen in the sharing economy, as a form of indirect e-commerce, notably in accommodation and transport sectors. Digital platforms use AI extensively to connect users and facilitate transactions. Specific algorithms may track, analyze and sometimes even influence the behaviors of users and consumers on those platforms.

In 1998, the OECD published the so-called Ottawa framework conditions and principles on the taxation of e-commerce transactions. These principles, which are still valid today, are: (1) neutrality, (2) efficiency, (3) certainty and simplicity, (4) effectiveness and fairness, and (5) flexibility.[5] In addition, based on the Ottawa principles, the OECD published in 2017 the VAT/GST guidelines.[6] These guidelines endorse the principle of destination for both B2B and B2C transactions. In other words, VAT or GST should be levied by the jurisdiction of final consumption and not of production. This rule is in accordance with the applicable legislation of the World Trade Organization (WTO) and the General Agreement on Tariffs and Trade (GATT). The principle of destination is also part of the principle of neutrality. The importance of these principles has also been recalled under the OECD/G20 BEPS Final Report on Action 1.[7]

As a consumption tax, VAT is levied on all supplies of goods and services, including digital services, by domestic enterprises, subject to a certain threshold requirement. In general, all transactions against consideration, including

---

[5]   OECD, Electronic Commerce Taxation Framework Conditions: A Report by the Committee on Fiscal Affairs, 1998, p. 4.

[6]   OECD, International VAT/GST Guidelines, 2017, p. 7.

[7]   See OECD/G20, Addressing the Tax Challenge of the Digital Economy, Action 1, 2015, Final Report, p. 17.

transactions with data, should be included in the scope of existing consumption tax regimes to ensure the neutrality of these taxes.[8] In addition, ideally, VAT should be governed by the destination principle.[9] This means that VAT should be levied by the State where consumption occurs. Thus, the import of goods or services should also be subject to VAT. Online domestic sellers of goods and services that use digital platforms for domestic consumers are also subject to VAT and are required to register.

By contrast, non-resident enterprises that offer those services to consumers in the domestic market, notably through online platforms, should in principle also be included in the scope of the VAT regime, but not every State applies this rule. Especially in the context of digital transactions, the destination principle is difficult to implement for cross-border services. This is because the VAT relies on the "vendor collection model", according to which suppliers are required to levy and collect the VAT.[10] Indeed, the consumption State has difficulty enforcing the VAT due at the place of import of digital services. This could also cause an excessive burden for digital enterprises who are often obliged to register in each jurisdiction where customers are located and to levy and report the VAT.[11]

In the EU, VAT is governed by the EU VAT Directive.[12] This Directive has been modified may times since then.[13] With a view to addressing some of the challenges caused by the digital economy, the EU has tried to implement specific rules. In this context, Implementing Regulation of the Council 282/2011,[14] amended by Regulation 1042/2013[15] is relevant. To that end, a so-called *e-commerce* VAT *package* was adopted by the European Council on 5 December 2017.[16] It consists of: (1) Directive 2017/2455 and (2)

---

8   Aslam Aqib and Shah Alpa, Tec(h)tonic Shifts: Taxing the "Digital Economy", IMF Working Paper, Volume 2020, Issue 076, 29 May 2020.

9   OECD, International VAT/GST Guidelines, 2017; Lamensch Marie, "Taxing Remote Digital Supplies" in: Haslehner Werner et al. (eds), Tax and the Digital Economy, Kluwer, The Netherlands 2019, p. 189 ff, p. 190.

10   Lamensch (2019), p. 190.

11   Lamensch (2019), p. 191.

12   Council Directive 2006/112/EC of 28 November 2006 on the common system of value added tax (hereafter VAT Directive).

13   For an overview see Terra Ben and Kajus Julie, A Guide to the European Directives, Amsterdam, IBFD 2022, p. 267 ff.

14   Council Regulation 282/20111 laying down implementing measures for Directive 2006/112/EC on the common system of value added tax.

15   Council Regulation 10422/2013 amending Regulation (EU) No 282/2011 as regards the place of supply of services.

16   See Council Directive 2017/2455 of 5 December 2017 amending Directive 2006/112/EC and Directive 2009/132/EC as regards certain value added tax obligations for supplies of services and distance sales of goods; see also Lamensch Marie,

Implementing Regulation 2017/2459 and Regulation 2017/2454. This package is applicable to e-commerce B2C transactions, which includes supplies of intra-EU and inbound B2C electronic services, intra-EU B2C distance sales of goods and B2C imports.[17] These new rules entered into force on 1 July 2021.[18]

The development of the digital economy is also prompted by the growth of online *platforms*. By 1 July 2021, under another e-commerce VAT package, online platforms that allow sales of goods to EU customers face new obligations. Online platforms that facilitate imports to customers (B2C) of goods of a value below 150 euros will be deemed to receive the supply from the initial seller (deemed B2B supply) and to sell the goods to the final customer (deemed B2C supply).[19] Therefore, online platforms will be liable for the collection of VAT on the supplies of goods to the final consumers and for the remittance of the VAT to the competent tax authorities. It will also have to determine the place of location and the applicable VAT rate.

Recently, in view of the importance of VAT as a major source of revenue for all member States and as a key source of financing for the EU budget, the EU Commission presented, on 8 December 2022, a new proposal for a Directive concerning VAT rules for the digital age.[20] This project has three objectives: (1) modernizing VAT reporting by introducing a Digital Reporting Requirement (DRR) to be submitted by taxable persons on B2B transactions in an electronic format, (2) updating further the rules of the platform economy and enhancing their role when they facilitate the supply of short-term accommodation rental or passenger transport services, and (3) introducing measures to lower compliance costs for cross-border transactions.[21]

European Value Added Tax in the Digital Era, IBFD Doctoral Series, Amsterdam 2018, p. 186 ff.

[17] Lamensch (2019), p. 206. For a global description of the VAT e-commerce rules, see also EU Commission, Directorate General Taxation and Custom Union, Explanatory Notes on VAT e-commerce rules, September 2020.

[18] Initially, the entry into force of these rules was planned for January 2021 but has been postponed because of the problems caused by the COVID-19 pandemic.

[19] Bal Aleksandra, Online Marketplaces and EU VAT: Global Reach but Compliance Still Local, Kluwertax blog. Com/2020/02/26.

[20] EU Commission, Proposal for a Council Directive amending Directive 2006/EC as regards VAT Rules for the Digital Age, COM(2022) 701 final.

[21] See also EU Parliament, Briefing, VAT in the Digital Age, March 2023.

III.   APPLICATION OF EU VAT RULES

A.   In General

Under the common system of VAT, a general tax on consumption is applied to goods and services that is exactly proportional to the price of goods and services; however, many transactions take place in the production and distribution process before the stage at which the tax is charged (Article 1 VAT Directive). The transactions subject to tax include, notably, the supply of goods and services for consideration within the territory of a member State by a taxable person as such, and the importation of goods (Article 2 VAT Directive). In other words, VAT is based on the principle of generality and neutrality. It implies that on each transaction, VAT calculated on the price of goods or services is chargeable after deduction of the amount of VAT borne directly by the various components (Article 1 paragraph 2, second subparagraph VAT Directive).

B.   Taxable Persons

1.   In general

Taxable person means any person who, independently, carries out in any place an economic activity, whatever the purpose or results of that activity. Any activity of producers, traders or persons supplying services, including mining and agricultural activities and professional activities, are regarded as a relevant economic activity (Article 9 paragraph 1 VAT Directive). This also includes the exploitation of tangible or intangible property for the purposes of obtaining income therefrom on a continuing basis (Article 9 paragraph 1, in fine VAT Directive). The concept of *economic activity* is interpreted broadly. According to the ECJ, there should be at least a contractual link between the activity and the payment. It follows that a street musician playing music is not subject to VAT, even if he solicits money, because there is no contract between him and the public. [22]

In the case of *import* of goods, the Directive does not specifically define the taxable person, but the wording seems to imply that everybody is liable to pay the import VAT when importing goods.[23]

---

[22]   ECJ, C-16/93, *Tolsma*, 3 March 1994, ECR I-0743.
[23]   Terra Ben J.M. and Wattel Peter J., European Tax Law, 6th ed., Wolters Kluwer, The Netherlands 2016, p. 183.

2.   Artificial intelligence and robots

In general, taxable persons for VAT purposes are the enterprises (corporation, partnership or individual enterprise) using AI and robots to supply goods or perform services. The main requirement, as we have seen, is that an enterprise carries on an economic activity with *independence*. With the emergence of autonomous AI and "smart robots", namely machines, combined with AI, which have the capacity to learn and interact with humans in a coordinated manner, we wonder whether they could not eventually be recognized as persons subject to VAT. Indeed, AI and smart robots are developing autonomous capabilities, namely the capacity to make decisions and to implement them in the external world, independently of any control or external influence. [24] Eventually, these types of AI and robots (smart robots) could fulfill the criteria of independence required for VAT purposes. However, so far, AI and robots do not have the legal capacity to act in their own name. In addition, AI and robots as such are currently not regarded as independent enough from an organizational standpoint for VAT purposes. Only the enterprises (corporations or other forms of independent entities) that control and use them are subject to VAT.

However, while under current law AI and robots are not regarded as taxable persons, the situation could evolve in the future. First, the growing importance of digital platforms, which usually act online and as facilitators of electronic commerce transactions offer already an interesting development which, although indirectly, could already represent a blueprint of a future system of taxation of AI and robots for VAT purposes. [25] Second, we will see later, in Chapter 9, while discussing the design of an AI and robot tax, how and under which conditions AI could become subject to tax. At this stage, however, it is worth mentioning that, contrary to income (profit) tax, in order to become a taxable person from a VAT standpoint, the law does not necessarily require that AI should be recognized as a legal entity, similar to a corporation.

C.   The Taxable Transaction: Supply of Goods and/or Services

1.   In general

a.   *General rule: supply for consideration*
Supplies of goods or services carried out *for consideration* within the territory of a member State by a taxable person acting as such are subject to VAT (Article 2 paragraph 1 lit. a and c VAT Directive). In other words, there should

---

[24]   See supra, p. 6 ff.
[25]   See infra, p. 135 ff.

be a direct and immediate link between the consideration paid and the taxed activity.[26] In barter transactions, according to the CJEU, the taxable amount should correspond to the subjective value agreed by the parties to the contract for those services or goods received as a counterpart,[27] and not the value estimated according to objective criteria.[28] Furthermore, for barter transactions, the CJEU, based on the subjective dimension of the taxable base, takes into consideration the value which the supplying entity considers as the counterpart in the exchange.[29] Such value corresponds to its expenses for the supply of the transaction (following an objective methodology).[30]

In addition, in accordance with the CJEU case *Tolsma*, there must be a legal relationship between the person receiving the payment and the person paying it.[31] In this case, a musician playing on the public highway, for which no consideration was contractually stipulated, was not considered as supplying a service within the scope of VAT, absent a legal agreement and a necessary link between the listeners who could give a donation and the musician.[32] The issue of the sufficient link will become increasingly pertinent in electronic transactions, notably in cases where the counterpart to the supply is not cash but consists of another transaction (barter).

b.   Special issue: data supply as a consideration?

In the digital economy, as a first stage, enterprises offer various online services, via IT or other telecommunication tools, that may be used, usually for free or at an inexpensive price, by customers. As a rule, as a second stage, the service providers will realize profits through transferring or granting the use of those data to other enterprises, for advertising or other commercial purposes. In general, consciously or not, the user will accept by signing electronically the general conditions of the service provider that the data will be gathered and

---

[26]   Terra and Kajus (2022), p. 293, 320.

[27]   ECJ, C-230/87, *Naturally Yours Cosmetics Ltd v Commissioner of Customs and Excises*, 23 November 1998, para. 16.

[28]   Lamensch (2021), p. 71; ECJ, C-40/09, *Astra Zeneca*, 29 July 2010, para. 28; ECJ, C-153/12, *Sani Treyd EOOD*, 23 March 2010.

[29]   Englisch Joaquim, Chap. 17 Umsatzsteuer, in : Tipke Klaus and Lang Joachim, Steuerrecht, 24th ed, Otto Schmid, Cologne 2021, n. 17.251; CJEU, C-33/93, *Empire Stores*, 2 June 1994, para. 19; ECJ, C-380/99, *Bertelsmann*, 3 July 2001, para. 38.

[30]   Englisch (2021), n. 17.251, who argues that this approach focuses too much on the expenses of the supplying entity. In his view, from a consumption tax standpoint, the concrete expenses of the beneficiary of the supply should be relevant because these expenses, and not those of the supplying enterprise, are indices of a potential economic ability to be considered.

[31]   Terra and Kajus (2022), p. 320.

[32]   ECJ, C-16/93, *Tolsma*, 3 March 1994, para. 16.

sometimes used for other purposes. For VAT purposes, the sale of the data by the service providers, or any other relevant transfer of services, against consideration, to third party enterprises, which corresponds to the second stage, is clearly characterized as a supply of service for consideration, which is subject to VAT, in accordance with the destination principle. As a rule, the enterprise recipient of the data may then credit the VAT as input tax.

In the VAT context, however, an interesting question is whether, in the first stage, the data offered by users, which gives access to their personal situation and habits, should not as such be regarded as the counterpart of the services provided by the digital enterprises. Some commentators argue that the services provided by social media or search engine platforms are in fact "paid" by users providing data.[33] Under this reasoning, this transaction could thus be viewed as a barter. Thus, in a B2C transaction, the enterprise subject to VAT would have to charge VAT on digital supplies offered to consumers. However, in B2B transactions, the potential VAT due would be zero, since the beneficiary would be allowed to claim an input VAT credit for the VAT paid.[34] In Germany, the issue has already attracted controversy, following a publication of 2015.[35] The debate also exists in particular in Austria[36] and in Switzerland.[37] The EU VAT Committee, following questions from the German Ministry of Finance, published on 3 November 2018, some guidelines on the proper application of the VAT Directive to potential barter transactions between platform operators and internet users.[38]

In-depth analysis of this issue goes beyond the scope of this publication which focuses on AI and robots taxation.[39] On the one hand, the majority view seems to hold that the link between the service provided by the platform and the non-monetary payment (data) is not sufficient. Indeed, users have universal access to the service providers and the data collected varies between users.[40]

---

[33]   Melan Nevada and Wecke Bertram, Umsatzsteuerpflicht von "kostenlosen" Internetdiensten und Smartphone-Apps, Deutsches Steuerrecht 2015, p. 2267 ff; 2811 ff.

[34]   Id.

[35]   Melan and Wecke (2015), p. 2267; Pinkernell Reimar, "Germany Report" in: IFA, Berlin Congress, Big Data and Tax-Domestic and International Taxation of Data Driven Business, IFA CDFI 2022, vol. 106B, Rotterdam 2022, p. 381.

[36]   Daurer Veronika, Kofler Georg and Mayr Gunter, "Austrian Report" in: IFA, Berlin Congress, Big Data and Tax-Domestic and International Taxation of Data Driven Business, IFA CDFI 2022, vol. 106B, Rotterdam 2022, p. 127 ff, 141.

[37]   Hug Thomas, Daten als mehrwertsteuerliches Entgelt?, zsis.ch, 2020, p. 7.

[38]   EU VAT Committee, 28 November 2018, UR 2019, p. 575; Pinkernell (2022), p. 382.

[39]   For more details, see Oberson Xavier and Yazicioglu Efsun Alara, Taxation of Big Data, Springer, Cham, Switzerland, 2023, p. 211 ff.

[40]   In this sense, Slam and Shah (2020).

On the other hand, other commentators argue, based on the case law of the CJEU, that the conditions to a supply are met because the electronic services are rendered as a rule only when the right to use the data is granted.[41] In our view, from a theoretical standpoint, barter transactions, in which users "pay" for services provided by platforms and digital services, under a contractual syn-allagmatic transaction, could be subject to VAT.[42] Such payments correspond to consumption of services by the users. Should the States, based on practical or other policy considerations, not be willing to introduce VAT on those trans-actions, is a different question. Recently, however, the Italian authorities have raised a VAT assessment on the Facebook-owned platform Meta over 2015 to 2021 "barter" transactions between the platform and the users.

c.   *Characterization of the supply (supply of goods or services)*
For VAT purposes, it is crucial to define the proper legal characterization of the transactions performed by AI. The definition of the place of supply will be different depending on the classification of a transaction subject to VAT, either as a supply of goods, a supply of services or an import. In general, supply of *goods* is defined as the "transfer of the right to dispose of tangible property as owner" (Article 14 paragraph 1 VAT Directive). By contrast, supply of *services* is "any transaction which does not constitute a supply of goods" (Article 24 paragraph 1 VAT Directive). *Import* is the entry into the Community of goods which are not in free circulation within the meaning of Article 29 of the Treaty on the Functioning of the EU (TFEU).[43]

In order to distinguish between supply of goods or services, the ECJ con-siders, in a constant jurisprudence, that all the circumstances of the transaction should be considered and that it is up to the national court to determine on a case-by-case basis if a transaction implies the transfer of the right of disposal on a good as an owner.[44] In general, digital transactions, including transfer of data, are characterized as supply of *services*.[45] In this context, the charac-terization of co-renting of space within a *data center* may raise an issue. Is it a supply of goods, namely a transfer of power of disposition of tangible goods,

---

[41]   Ehrke-Rabel Tina and Pfeiffer Sebastian, Umsatzsteuerbarer Leistungsaustausch durch "entgeltlose" digital Dienstleistungen, SWK 2017, p. 533 ff.; see also Pfeiffer Sebastian, VAT on "Free" Electronic Services? International VAT Monitor 2016, p. 158 ff, 161.
[42]   Oberson and Yazicioglu (2023), p. 215.
[43]   Terra and Wattel (2016), p. 188.
[44]   ECJ, C-320/88, 8 February 1990, *Staatssecretaris van Financien v. Shipping and Forwarding Enterprise SAFE BV*, para. 13.
[45]   Pinkernell (2022), p. 383.

or a service? In the *A Oy* case,[46] the CJEU ruled that computing center services in which the suppliers make available to customers equipment cabinets for holding their servers and providing ancillary goods and services (electricity and various services to ensure the use of the servers) do not constitute the letting of immovable property, and are exempt from VAT. In addition, for the purposes of defining the place of supply of services, specific rules apply depending upon the characterization of some services, notably *electronic* services, which are defined by Article 7 of Regulation No 282/211, and telecom services, which are defined in Article 24 paragraph 2 VAT Directive 2011.

2. Artificial intelligence and robots' activities

In the case of AI and robots in particular, delicate characterization issues could occur. Indeed, AI may be used by an enterprise both to supply goods (such as robot manufacturers or automatic vending machines) or services (advising customers, helping patients, ordering financial transactions, entertaining public viewers, transporting people, etc.). At first glance, we could consider applying by analogy the same legal characterization for robots' activities as for similar and competing actions carried out by humans. A sale conducted by an industrial robot should in this respect be treated like a sale. Legal advice provided by a law firm using legal AI would remain a legal service. The use of the da Vinci Surgical System in a surgical operation would be characterized as a medical treatment.

However, such an approach requires a more careful analysis. The neutrality principle, referred to above,[47] requires considering all the specificities and peculiarities of the activities conducted by AI and robots, which do not necessarily correspond to similar human actions. Over time, the technological possibilities of AI activities will appear increasingly different from human behaviors. These new and unexpected possibilities would eventually necessitate specific analysis and characterization.

In addition, the implementation of AI capacities will appear in different forms. Some robots will be included in software, while others could be embodied in a physical structure or even in a humanoid appearance. Hence, the characterization of the use of AI systems will also have to consider not only the functions exercised by it but also its specific features. For instance, as in the case of digitized books, the courts have already accepted the application of different characterization rules between digitized and physical transactions.[48] Indeed, while for the customer, the purpose of the purchase of an e-book is to

---

[46] CJEU, C-215/19, *A Oy*, 2 July 2020.
[47] See supra, p. 107.
[48] See infra, p. 133.

read it, there are still many differences between these two types of supplies, notably the delivery or not of a physical item.

It follows that a case-by-case analysis is required for each specific use of AI and robots. To define a proper characterization, we should try to take into consideration, based on the neutrality principle, the similarities and differences between functions exercised by AI and humans, from the perspective of the average customer. Based on that premise, we could distinguish between the following two typical cases: (1) the sale of an AI system, and (2) the use of AI.

First, the sale of a robot to a customer could be characterized, at least at first glance, as a supply of goods. Indeed, the client would become the owner of the robot. The situation is, however, more complicated than it seems. Indeed, this type of social robot, usually combines a piece of equipment (a machine) with software, which includes some form of AI.

In general, the *sale of* an *AI* system in digitized form, through a web server, should be characterized as a service, or more precisely, based on the existing regulations, as an electronic service.[49] According to the principle of attraction, which requires that the accessory aspect should follow its main component, the same conclusion should be drawn if the AI systems are delivered through the Internet in combination with tangible goods, to the extent that the value of the transaction is preponderantly attributable to the functions that the AI system is expected to deliver in the implementation of AI. If, however, the machine is delivered physically to the customer it could be regarded as a supply of goods, should we focus on the predominant component of the sale of the machine from the point of view of the customer. If the predominance of the transaction from this perspective consists in the capabilities of AI to interact with the new owner, and help and learn with him or her, a characterization as a service should prevail. Similar issues already exist, in the sale of computers. Finally, should the AI implemented in the robots be linked to global software sited in the enterprise and frequently updated, we could argue that the service component of the purchase of the robot should prevail.

Second, in the case of *use of AI*, it appears that the definition of the proper characterization should focus on the predominant function that AI renders within the enterprise that owns it. Hence, the use of automation within an enterprise to assist in the supply of goods or services should usually follow the characterization of the dominant activity. For instance, activities of industrial robots used in a factory for building cars, ready to be sold to consumers, are part of the final delivery of the *goods*. The use of robots is therefore ancillary to the building and selling of cars. In the same vein, an AI system helping a firm to render *services*, such as conducting legal research or data searching,

---

[49]   For the localization, see infra, p. 120.

transporting patients or workers, helping financial analysts in their projections or assisting in implementing investment orders, is included in the supply of services offered by the enterprise to the beneficiaries.

The situation would become more complex in cases where the activities of AI systems are offered to third parties under remuneration. Here, the specific legal nature of the AI activities would require further analysis because they are offered as such, independently, i.e. not in liaison with or ancillary to other supplies of goods or services from the enterprise. In other words, in this situation, the characterization of the activities of AI would require an understanding of their specific nature, taken independently. Usually, however, these types of activities should be characterized as services because they would generally not imply a transfer of ownership.

Finally, should the *barter transaction* described above be recognized as a taxable transaction (data supply as a consideration), AI could be designed to better address this issue. Thus, the practical difficulties preventing the tax administration implementing this approach would probably lose weight, thus justifying even more the theoretically correct approach mentioned above. In a way, a similar issue has governed the applicable threshold for the exemption of low value import of goods. With the development of e-commerce, this threshold became unacceptable and an unjustified distortion of competition leading to the requirement that the foreign supplier had to register and collect the VAT.[50]

D.   The Place of Supply

1.   Supply of goods

a.   In general

Supplies of goods arc usually localized at the place where the goods are sited when the transfer of ownership occurs (Article 31 VAT Directive). There are however special rules for supply with transport and notably for supply of *distance sales* of goods which follow the location of the goods at the time when dispatch or transport to the consumer ends (Article 33 VAT Directive). With the entry into force of the so-called *e-commerce package*, as of July 2021, specific rules have been introduced notably in the distant sales of goods. First, the existing threshold for intra-Community B2C distant sale of goods has been removed and replaced by a new threshold of 10 000 euros, below which the supply will remain subject to VAT in the member State of the supplier, i.e. where the goods are located at the time when their dispatch or transport

---

[50]   See infra, p. 123.

begins.[51] In addition, exemption of low value imports of small consignments outside the EU will no longer be exempt and distance sales of goods imported from third territories of an intrinsic value below 150 euros will be subject to tax, but with the possibility of using the special scheme referred to as "Import One Stop Shop (IOSS)".[52] This e-commerce package has also implemented a new obligation towards *platforms* facilitating the sale of goods, and a new presumption, under some conditions, that the platforms acts as the "deemed" supplier of such transactions.[53]

b.   *Application for artificial intelligence systems and robots*
In the case of robots, as we have seen, should the *sale of robots*, regarded preponderantly as machines implementing AI, qualify as a supply of goods, the transaction would therefore be localized at the place of situation of the robots. For example, the purchase by a family of a robot assistant would be subject to tax at the place of the shop where the robot is stored. Should AI be *used* within an enterprise to assist in the part or finalization of supply of goods, such as automated assembly lines in factories, or automated robots searching for books in a warehouse, the place of supply of the turnover resulting from the use of AI systems should be the place where the goods are sited upon completion of the transactions to the customers.

2.   Supply of services

a.   *In general*
The delimitation of the place of supply of services, under the VAT Directive, has been notably modified by Directive 2008/8/EC,[54] in view of the realization of the internal market, combined with globalization, deregulation and technology changes. To ensure a smooth transition, some of the changes have been introduced over time, gradually until 1 January 2015. Essentially, the main principle of localization of services at the place where "the actual consumption takes place" remains applicable.[55] In particular, the place of supply of services to taxable persons (so-called B2B) is the place of the recipient, while services

---

[51]   Lamensch Marie, Adoption of the E-Commerce VAT Package: The Road Ahead Is Still a Rocky One, EC Tax Review 2018, p. 186 ff; EU Commission, Explanatory Notes (2020), p. 7.

[52]   EU Commission, Explanatory Notes (2020), p. 7.

[53]   See infra, p. 136 ff.

[54]   Council Directive 2008/8/EC of 12 February 2008, L 44/11, amending Directive 2006/112/EC as regards the place of supply of services.

[55]   Recital (3) of Directive 2008/8/EC.dla.

supplied to non-taxable persons (so-called B2C) are localized at the place of the supplier.

It follows that, under the general rule, the place of supply of services to a *taxable person* acting as such is the place where that person has established his business (place of *the recipient*) (Article 44 VAT Directive). However, if those services are provided to a fixed establishment (FE) of the taxable person located in another place than the place of business, the supply will be localized at the place of the FE. In the absence of such place of establishment or FE, the place of supply will be the place of the permanent address or usual residence of the taxable person who receives the services. The place of supply to a *non-taxable person* is where the *supplier* has established his business (Article 45 VAT Directive). A similar exception exists in cases where the supply is provided from an FE of the supplier located in a place other than the place of establishment. In that situation, services are located at the place of FE. In the absence of such a place of establishment or FE, the place of supply of services will be the place where the supplier has his permanent address or usually resides.

There are some special localization rules for specific types of services, such as services to intermediaries, immovable property, transport or entertainment. In addition, special rules have also been introduced for telecommunication and electronic services.

b.   Special rules for particular services

As an exception to the general rule, specific places of supply apply to some services, such as the place of the underlying transaction, for services rendered by intermediaries (Article 46 VAT Directive) or the place of situs, for services connected with immovable property (Article 47 VAT Directive). There are also specific rules for transport (Articles 48 to 53 VAT Directive).

Cultural, artistic, sporting, scientific, educational, *entertainment* and similar services, ancillary transport services and valuations and work on movable property are localized at the place of performance (Article 53 VAT Directive). This rule may create characterization difficulties, notably if such services are rendered in an automated infrastructure. For instance, in the *RAL* case, the ECJ had to characterize and define the place of supply of *slot gaming machines*.[56] In that case, following a restructuring, the RAL group established an offshore subsidiary in Guernsey, CI, to operate slot machines. The role of CI was to open to the public the use of the slot gaming machines. The leases to the premises in which the slot gaming machines were installed as well as the license to operate belonged however to RAL, a company incorporated in

---

[56]   ECJ, aff. C-452/03, 12 May 2005.

the UK, while the slot gaming machines were owned by Machine, another UK company. Furthermore, the Guernsey Company was subcontracting the day-to-day management of the machines to Services, a UK company. Services employed almost all of the RAL group staff, namely about 600 persons. CI had no staff of its own in the UK. During the legal proceedings, the RAL group argued that the gaming services were deemed to be supplied in Guernsey and therefore not subject to VAT on the services supplied to its client in the UK. The Court however disagreed and ruled that the supply of services, consisting of enabling the public to use, for consideration, slot gaming machines installed in amusement arcades, established in the territory of a member State, must be regarded as constituting entertainment or similar activities, within the meaning of Article 9 paragraph 2 lit. c of the Sixth Directive (now Article 53 EU VAT Directive), and therefore localized at the place of supply where they are physically carried out.

The place of restaurant and catering services is the place where the services are physically carried out (Article 55 EU VAT Directive).

c.   Special rules for electronic services
Special localization rules also apply for *electronic* or *telecommunication services*. According to Article 7 paragraph 1 of the Council Implementing Regulation,[57] "electronic supplied services" include services which are delivered over the Internet or an electronic network and the nature of which renders their supply essentially automated and involving minimal human intervention, and impossible to ensure in the absence of information technology. Article 7 paragraph 1 covers in particular: (a) the supply of digitized products, generally, including software and changes to or upgrades of software; (b) services providing support to a business or personal presence on an electronic network such as a website or a webpage; (c) services automatically generated from a computer via the Internet or an electronic network, in response to specific data input by the recipient; (d) the transfer for consideration of the right to put goods or services up for sale on an Internet site operating as an online market on which potential buyers make their bids by an automated procedure and on which the parties are notified of a sale by electronic mail automatically generated from a computer; (e) Internet Services Package (ISP) of information in which the telecommunications component forms an ancillary and subordinate part.

As a consequence, electronic services do not include: (1) supply of goods that have been simply ordered by electronic means, (2) "non-electronic" services (advising or advertising) which may be granted by other means (includ-

---

[57]   Council Implementing Regulation (EU) No 282/2011 of 15 March 2011, L 77/1 (hereafter, Council Implementing Regulation).

ing written), under which the electronic supply is just another communication tool, and (3) telecommunication services.[58]

From January 2015, following Directive 2008/8/EC, a new Article 58 was substituted, which provides for the localization of those services in accordance with the destination principle.[59] Some of the changes have been introduced gradually, until 1 January 2015. A distinction should be made between B2B and B2C transactions.

In principle, according to Article 45 of the VAT Directive, following the principle of destination, (B2B) services are localized at the place where "the actual consumption takes place".[60] Thus, the place of supply of services to taxable persons is the place of the recipient. In addition, following the so-called reverse charge system, the customer is liable to self-assess and pay the VAT due on cross-border services (Article 196 VAT Directive).[61]

This raises the delicate issue of *identification* of the customer. In that respect, Article 18 paragraph 2 of Implementing Regulation 282/2011 provides for a rule designed to facilitate this difficulty according to which, in the case of intra-EU and inbound B2B supplies, the supplier to whom the business customer does not communicate a VAT number may deny him status as a taxable person.[62] For outbound B2B supplies to a third country, according to Article 18 paragraph 3 Implementing Regulation 282/2011, a certificate is required, but only in limited situations since, in general, outbound supplies outside the EU are tax exempt.[63] Localizing the customer is also problematic, notably in cases where the customer is located in various countries. This implies verifying whether the supply is made to a fixed place of establishment or the customer (see Article 21 Implementing Regulation 282/2011).

By contrast, under the traditional rule, services supplied to non-taxable persons (so-called B2C) are localized at the place of the supplier (Article 45 VAT Directive). Eventually, with the huge development of cross-border services, this rule has become problematic. Indeed, it could cause distortions and create an incentive for EU consumers to buy those services from outside suppliers. Thus, special localization rules for specific services, including electronic services, have been introduced. First, an exception to Article 45 of the VAT Directive was introduced in 2003 for inbound supplies of electronic

---

[58] Kornprobst Emmanuel, La notion de services fournis par voie électronique en matière de TVA, Droit fiscal 2016, p. 288.

[59] It should be noted that, following the change of 2015, letters (i), (j) and (k) of Art. 59 VAT Directive have been deleted and replaced by a new Art. 58.

[60] Recital (3) of Directive 2008/8/EC.

[61] Lamensch (2019), p. 193.

[62] Lamensch (2019), p. 194.

[63] Lamensch (2019), p. 193.

services to non-taxable EU customers.[64] Second, from January 2015, following Directive 2008/8/EC, a new Article 58 was substituted, which provides for the localization all B2C electronic services in accordance with the *destination principle*.[65]

For B2C, suppliers of electronic services must identify themselves in the country of destination. To simplify this rule, notably in case consumption takes place in multiple EU States, a Mini One Stop Shop (MOSS) has been implemented, to offer a single place of registration in the EU in the member State of identification, for EU and non-EU taxable persons. In this shop, the supplier may identify in one single place, and declare and pay the VAT also due in other member States, with a single declaration. According to Lamensch, notably for non-EU taxable persons, the number of registrations is very low, in comparison to EU taxable persons, which raises the question of compliance with the system.[66] It should be mentioned that the MOSS does not allow for the credit of the input VAT (Articles 368 and 369 VAT Directive).

For B2C supplies, the issue of *localization* is also problematic. Self-identification is verified by suppliers, in accordance with Article 23 paragraph 1 Implementation Regulation 2011. For customers with multiple locations, suppliers must determine the place "that best ensures taxation at the place of actual consumption" (Article 24 paragraph 2, Implementation Regulation 2011). For B2C supplies, these rules apply to numerous transactions at often very low prices and low margins, which raises a high compliance burden for suppliers.[67] The Implementation Regulation offers various presumptions to assist suppliers when it is "extremely difficult" to know where the customer is actually established, has his permanent establishment or usually resides.[68]

Council Regulation 1042/2013 has introduced a special rule for *platforms* involved in the supply of electronic services. Article 9a of Regulation 282/2011 (as modified by Regulation 1042/2013) provides that any taxable person who takes part in the supply of electronically supplied services "is deemed to be acting in his own name albeit on behalf of the initial provider of services".[69] The presumption may be rebutted when the initial service provider is explicitly indicated as the supplier by the taxable person taking part in the supply and this is provided in the contractual arrangement with the customer.[70] This rule

---

[64]   Lamensch (2019), p. 199.
[65]   It should be noted that, following the change of 2015, letters (i), (j) and (k) of Art. 59 VAT Directive have been deleted and replaced by a new Art. 58.
[66]   Lamensch (2019), p. 200.
[67]   Lamensch (2019), p. 202.
[68]   Lamensch (2019), p. 202.
[69]   Lamensch (2019), p. 203.
[70]   Lamensch (2019), p. 204.

simplifies the status of the intermediary, notably the platform, taking part in the supply. We will analyse further the role of platforms for VAT purposes, which raises interesting questions in the area of the taxation of AI.[71]

d.   Impact of the e-commerce package

Furthermore, the adoption of the *e-commerce* VAT package mentioned above also had a tremendous impact on the taxation of B2C electronic services. This package is notably applicable to e-commerce B2C transactions, which includes supplies of intra-EU and inbound B2C electronic services, intra-EU B2C distance sales of goods and B2C imports.[72] Among specific facilitating procedural rules, this package includes, for electronic services: (1) the availability of the Non-Union Scheme ("One Stop Shop/OSS") for non-EU suppliers with EU VAT numbers; (2) relaxed customer identification requirements below a threshold of 100 000 euros; and (3) as of 2019, a return to the origin principle for intra-EU B2C supplies of electronic services below a threshold of 10 000 euros.[73] Lamensch points out that this comeback goes against the OECD VAT/GST Guidelines and may create distortions in favor of taxable persons located in low-VAT member States.[74]

As a consequence, EU and non-EU taxable persons that supply either (a) telecommunications services, (b) radio and television broadcasting services or (c) electronic services, to an EU non-taxable person, are subject to VAT at the place of the recipient. From these rules, in case of electronic services, including the transfer of data, in both B2B and B2C transactions, the right to tax belongs in general to the member State of destination (subject to the exception of the threshold of 10 000 euros for intra-EU B2C transactions).[75]

Article 59a VAT Directive provides for derogation to prevent double taxation, non-taxation or distortion of competition. According to this rule, member States may, notably for services governed by Article 59, consider the place of supply of those services, if situated *within their territory*, as being situated outside the Community if the effective use and enjoyment of the services takes place outside the Community (lit. a); consider the place of supply of any of those services, if situated *outside the community*, as being situated within their territory if the effective use and enjoyment of the services takes place within their territory. In addition, Article 59b has been deleted.

---

[71]   See infra, p. 135 ff.
[72]   EU Commission, Explanatory Note, p. 6 ff; Lamensch (2019), p. 206.
[73]   Lamensch (2019), p. 207.
[74]   Lamensch (2019), p. 207.
[75]   Batti Gabriel Bez, "Cloud Computing Services and VAT" in: Kerschner I. and Somare M. (eds), Taxation in a Global Digital Economy, Linde Verlag, Vienna 2017, p. 361; Lamensch (2018), p. 186.

Chapter 6 of Title XII of the VAT Directive provides for a *special scheme* for *taxable persons supplying* services to non-taxable persons or making distance sales of goods or certain domestic supplies of goods, which, as of 1 January 2015, has been modified by Directive 2008/8/EC, and further by Directive 2017/2455, with effect from 1 January 2019, and further modified with effect from 1 July 2021. These rules allow businesses to declare and pay VAT on all B2C transactions for the supply of services and distant sales of goods in a single portal previously named MOSS, which was broadened and renamed One-Stop-Shop (OSS).[76] The proposal of a new Directive, of 8 December 2022, would further expand the OSS to cover the remaining domestic B2C supplies of goods transactions where local VAT registration by non-established suppliers is still required.[77]

e.   *Place of business or place of fixed establishment*
For B2B services, the place of supply is primarily the place where the *recipient* has established his business. This corresponds to the place where the "functions of the central administration are carried out, that is to say, the place where essential decisions concerning the general management of the business are taken, the place where the registered office of the business is located, and the place where management meets".[78] When these criteria do not allow with certainty the determination of the place of establishment, the place where essential decisions concerning the general management of the business are taken will take precedence.[79] If, however, the services are provided to an *FE* of the taxable person located in a place other than the place of establishment of business, the place of supply will be the place of the FE. For B2C transactions, the place of business of the *supplier* will also have precedence, at least under the general rule (i.e. in non-electronic or telecom transactions), unless the services are supplied from an FE of the supplier sited in another location. It follows that the precise determination of the place of business and the place of the FE is crucial in defining the appropriate place of supply of services.

The ECJ, in various cases, has had occasion to define more precisely the meaning of these concepts and notably the definition of an FE. While in most cases the FE was the supplier of services, the definition is also applicable in situations where the FE is the recipient of services.[80] Commentators thus tend

---

76   EU Parliament, Briefing, VAT in the Digital Age, March 2023, p. 5.
77   EU Parliament, Briefing, VAT in the Digital Age, March 2023, p. 5; EU Commission, Proposed Directive as Regards VAT Rules for the Digital Age, 8, December 2022 (COM)(2022) 701 final, new Art. 369b.
78   Art. 10 para. 2 of the Council Implementing Regulation.
79   Ibid.
80   Batti (2017), p. 364; see also ECJ, C-605/12, *Welmory*, 16 October 2014.

to distinguish between providing FE, on the one hand, and receiving FE, on the other.[81] In a long series of cases, starting from the leading *Berkholz* case, the Court emphasizes the need for a physical presence in order for a place of business to qualify as an FE. However, in the *Welmory* case, the Court departed from the well-established requirement of a physical presence.[82] Recent case law, notably *Titanium*, seems however to go away from this new approach because the Court considered that without human resources, a property could not be regarded as an FE.[83] We will start therefore with a description of the various relevant cases already rendered by the ECJ, in order to develop an appropriate criteria that could be applicable in the cases of robots. It should be mentioned that the FE concept belongs to VAT and is independent from the PE concept under the OECD Model DTC.[84]

In the *Berkholz* case, the ECJ ruled that the installation of gaming machines on board a sea ship sailing on the high seas outside the national territory could be regarded as an FE, "only if the establishment entails the permanent presence of both the human and technical resources necessary for the provision of those services and it is not appropriate to deem those services to have been provided at the place where the supplier has established his business".[85] The absence of staff assigned on a permanent basis to maintain and verify the function of the gaming appears to have been a decisive element for such a conclusion.[86] In the same vein, in the *ARO Lease* case, it was held by the ECJ that a leasing company, "which does not possess in a Member State either its own staff or a structure which has a sufficient degree of permanence to provide a framework in which agreements may be drawn up or management decisions taken, and thus enable the services in question to be supplied on an independent basis",[87] cannot be considered as having a fixed place of business in that State.

Later, the ECJ also had to determine, in the *DFDS A/S* case,[88] to what extent a subsidiary could be regarded as an FE. The issue at stake pertained to the VAT liability in the United Kingdom of DFDS A/S, a Danish company, in respect of package tours sold on its behalf by its English subsidiary, DFDS Ltd. The issue, according to the Court, was thus whether a travel agent, operat-

---

[81]   Cannas Francesco, The VAT Treatment of Cloud Computing: Legal Issues and Practical Difficulties, World Journal of VAT/GST, 2016, p. 98.

[82]   De la Feria Rita, On the Evolving VAT Concept of Fixed Establishment, EC Tax Review 2021, p. 204.

[83]   EUCJ, 931/19, *Titanium Ltd*, 3 June 2021.

[84]   See ECJ, C-201/04, *FCE Bank*, 23 March 2006.

[85]   See ECJ, C-168/84, *Gunter Berkholz*, 4 July 1985, para. 19.

[86]   Batti (2017), p. 364.

[87]   See ECJ, C-190/95, *ARO Lease BV*, 17 July 1997, para. 19.

[88]   See ECJ, C-260/95, *Commissioners of Customs and Excise v. DFDS A/S*, 20 February 1997.

ing in another member State through a company incorporated as a subsidiary, was independent or not. In the present case, the dependence could be demonstrated by the fact that the subsidiary was wholly owned by DFDS A/S and by the various contractual obligations imposed on the subsidiary by its parent. The ECJ finally ruled that where a tour operator established in one member State (here Denmark) provides services to travelers through the intermediary of a company operating as an agent in another member State (here the United Kingdom), VAT is payable on those services in the latter state if that company, which acts as a mere auxiliary organ of the tour operator, has the human and technical resources characteristic of an FE. By contrast, the Court found that the legal ownership of the premises, in which the business activities take place, is irrelevant.[89]

This jurisprudence was again confirmed in the *Planzer* case,[90] which addressed the problem of a VAT refund from an applicant based on the alleged presence of an FE in a member State. The member State questioned the economic reality of the place of establishment of the applicant issuing the request. The Court issued the reminder that

> the term fixed establishment implies a minimum degree of stability derived from the permanent presence of both the human and technical resources necessary for the provision of the given services … It thus requires a sufficient degree of permanence and a structure adequate, in terms of human and technical resources to supply the services in question on an independent basis.[91]

In the field of transport activity in particular, that term implies "at least an office in which contracts may be drawn up and daily management decisions taken, and a place where the vehicles used for the said activities are stored".[92]

In the *Welmory* case,[93] the Court was this time confronted with the situation of a *receiving* FE. In this case, Welmory Ltd, established in Nicosia, Cyprus, organized online auction sales, by selling packets of "bids", which incorporated the right to make an offer to purchase goods at a higher price than the price last offered. Welmory had a cooperation agreement with a Polish company, under which it agreed to provide the latter with the services of making available an Internet auction site with a domain name, including the supply of associated services related to the leasing of the servers and the

---

[89]   Cannas (2016), p. 99.
[90]   See ECJ, C-73/06, *Planzer Luxembourg Sàrl*, 28 June 2007.
[91]   See ECJ, C-73/06, *Planzer Luxembourg Sàrl*, 28 June 2007, para. 54.
[92]   See ECJ, C-73/06, *Planzer Luxembourg Sàrl*, 28 June 2007, para. 55.
[93]   ECJ, C-605/12, *Welmory*, 16 October 2014.

display of the goods to be auctioned. The Polish company, on its side, agreed to sell goods on that website.

The Polish company took the view that some services supplied to Welmory, (advertising, servicing, provision of information and data processing), had been supplied to the seat of Welmory in Nicosia, and hence did not charge VAT, considering that those services should accordingly be subject to VAT in Cyprus. By contrast, the director of the Polish tax administration took the position that these services were supplied to an FE of the Cypriot company in Poland and that they should consequently be taxed in that State at the standard rate of 22 percent.

The Court recalled that the purpose of a rule determining the place of taxation of supplies of services is to designate the point of reference for tax purposes. The most appropriate and thus primary point of reference for determining the place of supply of services for tax purposes is the place where the taxable person has established his business. It is only if that place does not lead to a rational result or creates a conflict with another member State that another establishment may come into consideration. In the present case, in order to be considered as having an FE, the Cypriot company should therefore have in Poland

> at the very least a structure characterized by a sufficient degree of permanence, suitable in terms of human and technical resources to enable it to receive in Poland the services supplied to it by the Polish company and to use them for its business, namely running the electronic auction system in question and issuing and selling bids.[94]

It is interesting to note that the Court also took account of Article 11 of the Council Implementing Regulation and considered that such definition was directly inspired by the case law of the ECJ.[95] In addition, the Court added that the fact

> that the business carried out by the Cypriot company, consisting in operating a system of electronic auctions which comprises, first making an auction website available to the Polish company and, secondly, issuing and selling "bids" to customers in Poland *can be carried on without requiring an effective human and material structure in Polish territory* is not determinative. Despite its particular character, such a business requires at least a structure that is appropriate in terms especially of human and technical resources, such as appropriate computer equipment, servers and software.[96]

---

94 ECJ, C-605/12, *Welmory*, 16 October 2014, para. 59.
95 ECJ, C-605/12, *Welmory*, 16 October 2014, para. 58.
96 ECJ, C-605/12, *Welmory*, 16 October 2014, para. 60 (emphasis added).

In other words, the Court ruled that the Cypriot company, which received services supplied by the Polish entity, must be regarded as having an FE in Poland, only if it had a sufficient degree of permanence and suitable structure in terms of human and technical resources to enable it to receive the services supplied to it *and use them for business*.

It is worth mentioning that, around that time, the Advocate General had suggested adding the following phrase to the last sentence of the conclusion of the Court. "It is not necessary for it to have its own human and technical resources for this, provided the third-party resources at the establishment are available to it in a way that is comparable to having its own resource".[97] This additional requirement was not mentioned in the final Court ruling. It seems however that the ECJ confirmed that the condition of permanence of the structure is still met, even if the staff and resources do not belong to the Cypriot company but use Welmory's technical resources and human resources not employed by it.[98]

Finally, the *WebMindLicences* case relates to the operation of a website offering audiovisual services.[99] In this case, WML, a company registered in Hungary, acquired free of charge from Hypodest Patent Development, a company in Portugal, know-how enabling a website to be operated, through which erotic interactive audiovisual services, in which individuals throughout the world took part in real time. On the same day, it made that know-how available, by a license agreement, to Lalib, a company in Madeira (Portugal).

The tax authorities argued that the transfer of WML's know-how to Lalib did not correspond to a genuine economic transaction, as the know-how was in fact exploited by WML, so that the exploitation, subject to VAT, had taken place in Hungarian territory. In particular, the ECJ found that:

> It is incumbent upon the referring court to analyze all the circumstances of the main proceedings in order to determine whether that agreement constituted a wholly artificial arrangement concealing the fact that the services at issue were not actually supplied by the company acquiring the license, but were in fact supplied by the company granting it. It should examine in particular whether the establishment of the place of business or FE of the company acquiring the license was not genuine, whether that company, did not possess an appropriate structure in terms of premises and human and technical resources and whether it did not engage in that economic activity in its own name and on its own behalf, under its own responsibility and at its own risk.[100]

---

[97]   Opinion of Advocate General Kokott, C-605/12, *Welmory*, 15 May 2014, para. 50.
[98]   See Batti (2017), p. 365; Opinion of Advocate General Kokott, C-605/12, *Welmory*, 15 May 2014, , para. 50.
[99]   ECJ, C-419/14, *WebMindLicenses Kft*, 17 December 2015.
[100] ECJ, C-419/14, *WebMindLicenses Kft*, 17 December 2015, para. 50.

However, more recent case law tends to depart from this last case and seems to go back to a more classical notion of an FE. Indeed, in *Titanium*, the Court was asked whether a property may be characterized as an FE. The inquiry was made as to whether Titanium Ltd, established in Jersey and whose purpose is property and housing and accommodation management, was subject to VAT on rental income relating to a property located in Austria. The Austrian authorities considered that Titanium had an FE in Austria. In this case, the CJEU summarized the case law as follows:

> The concept of "fixed establishment", in accordance with the Court's settled case-law, implies a minimum degree of stability derived from the permanent presence of both the human and technical resources necessary for the provision of given services. It thus requires a sufficient degree of permanence and a structure adequate, in terms of human and technical resources, to supply the services in question on an independent basis ... A structure without its own staff cannot fall within the scope of the concept of a "fixed establishment".[101]

Therefore, the Court considered that a property which is sited in a member State in the circumstances where the owner of that property does not have infrastructure or his or her own staff to perform services relating to the letting does not constitute an FE.

In a way, the case law of the ECJ has been transposed in Article 11 of the Council Implementing Regulation 282/2011.[102] Indeed, according to Article 11 paragraph 1 of such Regulation, a *receiving* FE, within the meaning of Article 44 of the VAT Directive "shall be any establishment characterized by a sufficient degree of permanence and a suitable structure in terms of humans and technical resources to enable it to receive and use the services supplied to it for its own needs". This corresponds with the definition of the *Welmory* case discussed above. In addition, a *providing* FE, according to Article 11 paragraph 2 of the Regulation, "shall be any establishment ... [c]haracterized by a sufficient degree in permanence and a suitable structure in terms of human and technical resources to enable it to provide the services which it supplies". In the *Titanium* case, the CJEU also referred to Article 11 of the Regulation.

---

[101] EUCJ, 931/19, *Titanium Ltd*, 3 June 2021, 446, at para. 42.

[102] See however, the critics of van Norden Gert-Jan, "The Allocation of Taxing Rights to Fixed Establishments in European VAT Legislation" in: VAT in an EU and International Perspective, Essays in Honor of Han Kogels, IBFD, The Netherlands 2011, p. 47, which consider the additional criterion of "use for its own needs" on the Regulations as wrong. This article was however published in 2011 before the 2014 *Welmory* case.

In summary, the concept of FE has been progressively eroded by the globalization and digitalization of the economy.[103] It follows that the apparent step back to a more traditional definition of an FE, as judged by the CJEU, can be regarded as a turn in the wrong direction. The Court, however, cannot simply disregard the rules of Regulation 11, which also refers to the concept of physical presence. Thus, despite the doors apparently opened by the *Welmory* case, the traditional approach remains applicable and, absent a physical presence in a State, an online platform would not qualify as an FE for VAT purposes. In the *data center* case mentioned above, the characterization as an FE, subject to the facts of the matter, would appear to be met in most cases. Indeed, the infrastructure, including computers and data storage facilities, usually requires the assistance of human personnel to insure the maintenance and proper functioning of the technologies used at the location of the center.

In addition, in the context of digital services, including transfer of data, it is extremely difficult for the supplier to properly identify whether the supply is made to an FE of a taxable person located in another jurisdiction. In particular, the supplier should determine whether the recipient is characterized as an FE and whether the recipient of electronic data is able to use it for its own need.[104] In a way, similar to the development of the rules applicable to the digital economy for profit tax purposes, the concept of FE, for VAT purposes, should also be revised and adapted to the new business models of the digital economy.[105]

3.   Application to artificial intelligence and robots

As we have seen, AI or robots may be used for both supply of goods and services. The localization of activities of industrial robots used in manufacture, such as assembly lines of cars, or in automated deliveries within warehouses, should be governed by the rules of *supply of goods*.

The definition of the place of supply of AI systems and robots in the *services* sector creates more difficulties. Indeed, a more precise delimitation is required since different localization rules apply for specific services. Robots will usually appear as automated machines, localized in a specific place,

---

[103] De la Feira (2021), p. 205.

[104] Lamensch (2019), p. 198.

[105] See Oberson and Yacicioglu (2023), p. 211; in this sense also, see recently, Beretta Giorgio, "Fixed Establishment in the 21st Century" in: EU Value Added Tax and Beyond, Essays in Honour of Ben Terra, Amsterdam, IBFD 2023, p. 167 ff, who suggests referring to the concept of "core functions" in order to adapt the FE concept to the digital economy; see also Taipalus Päivi, "The Fixed Establishment and the Principle of Legal (Un)certainty" in: EU Value Added Tax and Beyond, Essays in Honour of Ben Terra, Amsterdam, IBFD 2023, p. 241 ff.

implementing services provided by AI. As a rule, activities carried out by robots implementing AI should be characterized in accordance with their economic functions, from the perspective of an average consumer. In this respect, the *RAL* case analyzed above[106] offers an interesting precedent. In that case, the ECJ confirmed that the use of automated slot machines, installed in amusement arcades, had to be characterized as entertainment services. From that perspective, robots playing music or appearing in artistic performances are offering *entertainment services*. In the same vein, robots placing investment orders in the financial market, following specific algorithms, are rendering *financial services*. A law firm using a robo-advisor or doing legal research with the help of a collaborative AI system is still providing *legal services* to the final customers. *Transportation services* offered by the use, against consideration, of self-driving cars should qualify as transportation services.

AI activities could also be characterized as *electronic services*. Indeed, the services would here be provided online through the Internet or other telecommunication devices, in an automated way with limited human intervention. By definition, AI services would require minimal human intervention, within the meaning of Article 11 of the Council Implementing Regulation. In that case, as we have seen, both B2B and B2C services should be localized at the place of the recipient. Many services, such as automated financial transactions, could indeed qualify as electronic services. However, this issue might trigger delicate distinctions. For example, according to the VAT Committee, when a digital product is adapted to the individual need of a customer, this requires more human intervention, which should disqualify the characterization as an electronic service.[107] If, however, the adaptation is done by a "smart robot", which interacts with humans and adjusts to the specificities of the situation, the answer should probably be different.[108]

For B2B services there is an additional issue whether they are received by the *business seat* or by *the FE* of the recipient. The latter should therefore have sufficient human and technical capacities to receive those services and use them for its own purpose, in accordance with the case law described above and Article 11 of the Council Implementing Regulation.

Should the recipient correspond to the definition of an AI system or a robot, we could wonder whether, as such, it could be regarded as an FE. For AI or robots to qualify as an FE, some conditions would have to be met. First, the automated infrastructure, notably the robots, should remain with a sufficient

---

[106] See supra, p. 119.

[107] VAT Committee 919 at p. 5; Beretta Giorgio, VAT on Financial and Insurance Services at the Dawn of the Fourth Industrial Revolution, International VAT Monitor 2018 (vol. 29) No. 4, at 4.

[108] Beretta (2018), at 4., citing the example of a "financial robot-adviser".

degree in permanence at its place of location. Second, in accordance with the jurisprudence of the ECJ, sufficient permanent human resources should be present at this place, capable of controlling the activity of the AI system. If we follow the jurisprudence of the *Berkholz* case discussed above, it seems that it would require the effective presence of humans at the place of the AI system or robots, like slot machines fixed on a boat cruising along a river. However, around the line of the *Welmory* case discussed above, and notably the conclusion of the Advocate General, it could be argued that these conditions should still be met, should the human and technical resources be provided by third-party resources at the place of the AI system and available in a way comparable to having their own resources. The question, however, remains open as to whether the existence of human specialists, available in another State, could still fill the condition of sufficient human resources.

Eventually, the specific nature of automation, with the developments of AI and smart robots, could require a broader definition of the concept of FE, which would focus less on the presence of humans, and more on the technical capabilities of AI systems, which, like humans, would render autonomous decisions, and interact and evolve with experience through *deep-learning*. From a policy perspective, this type of AI system or smart robot could eventually develop capabilities comparable to humans and their activities could meet, in our view, the conditions of sufficient resources at the place of the FE, from a VAT perspective. In other words, the requirement of human presence at the place of location of automation should be analyzed differently when AI systems have the capacities to effectively act autonomously. The comparison with slot machines, like in the *Berkholz* case, would require a different conclusion. Hence, the development of AI and robots would tend to bring the concept of FE, from a VAT standpoint, closer to the PE concept for direct tax perspective.

E.   The Tax Rates

Until recently, following the EU Directive of 19 October 1992,[109] member States must apply a standard range which may not be less than 10 percent. One or two reduced rates, which may not be less than 5 percent, could apply to specific categories of goods and services. Electronically supplied services may however not be subject to a reduced rate (Article 98 paragraph 2 VAT Directive).

In the past, characterization issues have already occurred in an additional category, namely the digital supply of tangible goods, such as *digitized books*.

---

[109]   Directive 92/77/EEC.

In this context, the ECJ has examined in various cases whether or not the electronic format of such books would require different VAT treatment than for "ordinary" supplied books.[110] In a first case, the Court referred to the principle of neutrality, which should preclude similar goods or services in competition being treated differently for VAT purposes.[111] In order to determine the similarity of the supply of goods or services

> account must be taken primarily of the point of view of a typical consumer. Goods or services are similar where they have similar characteristics and meet the same needs from the point of view of the consumer, the test being whether their use is comparable, and where the differences between them do not have a significant influence on the decision of the average consumer to use one or the other of those goods or services.[112]

In this case, the Court held that Article 98 paragraph 2 and Annex III of the VAT Directive do not preclude the application of a reduced rate of VAT to physical books only, to the extent that the principle of neutrality is respected, an aspect which should be verified by the local court. In a following case, the ECJ confirmed that the supply of e-books could not benefit from the reduced VAT rate applicable to physical books.[113] Indeed, such supply, according to Annex III to the EU VAT Directive, expressly refers to the supply of books in all physical forms. While to read an electronic book, a physical item, such as a computer, is required, this support is not included in the supply of electronic books. This jurisprudence saga finally reached its conclusion. On 2 October 2018, the European Council agreed to a proposal to allow member States to apply reduced, super-reduced or zero VAT rates to electronic publications, including e-books. As a consequence, the VAT rates between electronically and physically supplied publications would be aligned.[114] The CJEU, in this context, confirmed that, in accordance with this provision, France and Luxembourg were not allowed to apply reduced VAT rates to electronic books.[115] Following these judgments, a Directive was adopted, on 6 November

---

[110] ECJ, C-219/13, *K Oy*, 11 September 2014; ECJ, C-479/13, *Commission v. France*, 5 March 2015.

[111] ECJ, C-219/13, *K Oy*, 11 September 2014; ECJ, C-479/13, *Commission v. France*, 5 March 2015, para. 24.

[112] ECJ, C-219/13, *K Oy*, 11 September 2014; ECJ, C-479/13, *Commission v. France*, 5 March 2015, para. 25.

[113] ECJ, C-479/13, *Commission v. France*, 5 March 2015.

[114] See EU Council, 28 September 2018 (12622/18), Proposal for a Council Directive amending Directive 2006/112/EC, as regards rates of value added tax applied to books, newspapers and periodicals; see EU Council, 2 October 2018, Press release.

[115] ECJ, C-479/13, *Commission v. France*, 5 March 2015; ECJ, C-502/13, *Commission v. Luxembourg*, 5 March 2015.

2018, which allows the application of reduced, super-reduced or zero rates to "electronic publications". This may be regarded as a first step towards more general reduced rate for electronic services.[116]

On 5 April 2022, the EU Council adopted a new Directive, which includes an overhaul of VAT rates.[117] This text represents a compromise which, in addition to the standard rate of 15 percent, opens the possibilities to apply two reduced rates of 5 percent to goods and services in 24 categories, in accordance with a revised Annex III of the VAT Directive. That list includes, notably, *digital services* such as Internet access and livestreaming of cultural and sports events. Many commentators take a rather critical position towards this new rule, which opens the door to the potential disparities in the applicable rates for electronic services among member States and thus presents new obstacles to cross-border trade.[118] This new Directive is applicable as of 1 January 2025.

F.   Exemptions

Services carried out by AI or robots, even if characterized as electronic services, could still be exempted from VAT. Indeed, the qualification of services for the purpose of defining the place of supply takes precedence over the classification as exempt or subject to tax.[119] In *Sparekassernes Datacenter*, the ECJ already recognized that the specific manner in which the services are performed, electronically, automatically or manually, is in fact irrelevant, for the purpose of determining whether they should be exempt or not.[120] It follows that financial or insurance services supplied electronically through AI or robot advisers could still be exempted, provided they correspond in substance, from the perspective of an average consumer, to the services referred to in Article 135 paragraph 1 lit. b to g VAT Directive.[121]

G.   Right to Deduct Input VAT

The possibility of claiming VAT credits on input purchases for VAT taxpayers is crucial for the proper functioning of the VAT system. In the field of automation, the cost of developing automated technologies will be extremely

---

[116]   Lamensch (2019), p. 212.
[117]   EU Council Directive (EU) 2022/542 of 5 April 2022, amending Directives 2006/112/EC and (EU) 2020/285 as regards rates of value added tax.
[118]   Lamensch (2019), p. 213; de la Feira R. and Schofield M., Towards an (Unlawful) Modernized EU VAT Rate Policy, EC Tax Review 2017, p. 89.
[119]   Beretta (2018), at 3.
[120]   ECJ, C-2/95, Sparekassernes Datacenter (SDC), 5 June 1997, para. 37.
[121]   Article 13B lit. d of the EU Sixth Directive (at the time of the case).

significant. Some institutions, like banks, insurance companies, hospitals or schools, will have difficulties deducting the input VAT linked with these initial investments, which could discourage innovation and an AI development strategy.[122] In this context, the possibility of opting for VAT on output could be a solution to allowing the right to deduct input VAT.

H. The Growing Role of Digital Platforms

1. The business model

The development of new business models from the sharing economy, notably the use of digital platforms, has raised new problems for the application of VAT. These platforms, acting as intermediaries, open to customers the possibility of negotiating directly and concluding transactions worldwide, thanks to IT technologies.[123] So far, individuals and small enterprises were not considered to have a significant impact on competition with enterprises subject to VAT. However, the platform economy has offered new possibilities for private individuals and small enterprises to benefit via the digital platform from economies of scale and network effect.[124] For example, Amazon, eBay, Uber or Alibaba, to name just a few, may be described as global digital marketplaces, where suppliers and consumers may negotiate and conclude transactions. This also offers to private individuals the possibility of carrying out economic activity on an occasional basis, which "blurs the taxable status of the provider", and also distorts the competition with traditional VAT-registered counterparts (notably hotels, taxi companies, etc.).[125]

2. New VAT problems raised by digital platforms

As such, platforms raise delicate issues, notably in the VAT area.[126] As a rule, in a classical transaction, a supplier uses the service of a platform, situated online, to contact a consumer. For VAT purposes, the platform acts as an intermediary. To apply VAT, a distinction needs to be made between persons acting as a disclosed agent, if the intermediary acts in the name of the under-

---

[122] Beretta (2018), at 4.

[123] OECD, An Introduction to Online Platforms and Their Role in the Digital Transformation, 2019, p. 21 ff.

[124] See EU Proposal for a Council Directive as Regards VAT Rule for the Digital Age, 8 December 2022, COM(2022)701 final, Explanatory Memorandum, p. 5 ff.

[125] EU Parliament, Briefing, VAT in the Digital Age, March 2023, p. 4.

[126] For an overview, before the proposed EU modification of December 2022, see Pantazatou Katerina, "The Taxation of the Sharing Economy" in: Haslehner W. et al. (eds), Tax and the Digital Economy, Series on International Taxation, Wolters Kluwer, The Netherlands 2019, p. 219 ff.

lying supplier, and as an undisclosed agent, in case the intermediary acts in its own name.[127] In the former situation, the transaction occurs directly between the customer and the supplier: the (transparent) agent is not a party to this transaction but may charge a fee for intermediation. In the latter case, however, the platform acts as a party to the transaction with customers. In this case, two transactions take place: the first between the underlying suppliers and the platform and the second between the platform, acting as the undisclosed agent, and the final customer. The platform could thus be liable for the collection of VAT from the underlying supplies to consumers facilitated through their infrastructure, even if it does not become the owner of the goods or a direct legal counterpart of the service.[128]

The application of this rule and the proper characterization of the activities of the platform has raised many issues in practice. First, platforms may have difficulty identifying the VAT status of the underlying supplier, in order to apply the correct VAT rule.[129] Second, various rules of the VAT Directives have been applied differently by member States, notably because some States characterize the facilitation by platforms as electronically supplied services, while others treat them as intermediary services.[130]

For the platforms themselves, delicate compliance issues may occur since they could potentially be responsible for registering for and charging VAT in the various countries where customers are located. Indeed, we have seen above that, for both B2B and B2C purposes, electronic services are generally localized at the place of destination (subject to the intra-EU exception above 10 000 euros). In addition, under the traditional approach, distant sales and import of low value goods via platforms have often been VAT exempt due to the applicable exemption threshold.

To try to solve these issues, new rules have been introduced or are planned, which gradually have increasingly involved the collaboration of platforms for the proper application and compliance with VAT rules. In essence, the trend, at least for some specific transactions, is to put on digital platforms the duty to assess, collect and pay VAT.

3.   New VAT obligations for digital platforms

In 2017 the OECD recommended, for cross-border B2C transactions governed by the destination principle, that the supplier identify and collect VAT in the

---

[127] Kudkepp Aiki, Online Platforms are in the VAT Spotlight in the European Union, Bloomberg Daily Tax Report: International, 1 December 2022.

[128] In this sense, Kudkepp (2022).

[129] See EU Proposal for a Council Directive as Regards VAT Rule for the Digital Age, 8 December 2022, COM(2022)701 final, Explanatory Memorandum, p. 5 ff.

[130] EU Parliament, Briefing, VAT in the Digital Age, March 2023, p. 6.

place of consumption.[131] In particular, intermediaries such as digital platforms, which facilitate the transactions, could become liable for the collecting of VAT in those cases, notably on online sales.[132] Indeed, in a digital sale, the platform "takes the role of a 'store' with an offering of different supplies such as digital supplies of music, films, books, games and software applications, and in many cases acts as the sole point of contact with the end consumer including in respect of service delivery".[133] With a similar, but broader perspective, the EU, notably, has also focused on platforms. Indeed, since the e-commerce package, which started to introduce the concept of deemed supplier for some B2C electronic transactions, the EU has analyzed extensively the issues raised by the use of platforms. They have thus introduced new obligations and reporting rules and are contemplating issuing more global rules for specific digital activities.

First, as of 1 January 2023, under the so-called DAC 7, platforms will have to *report* information on third-party sellers who take advantage of the platform.[134] The report will be followed by an automatic exchange of information between the EU member States. While this Directive focuses on direct taxes, it also offers the tax authorities information to enable them to assess income taxes and VAT correctly.[135]

Second, depending upon the form of the intermediation used by the platform, the platform could be regarded as *personally liable* to levy VAT. We have seen above that, for the supply of digital services, Article 9a of Council Regulation 1042/2013 provides that a taxable person who takes part in the supply of electronically supplied services is *deemed* to be acting in his own name but on behalf of the provider of those services, unless that provider is explicitly indicated as the supplier by that taxable person and that is reflected in the contractual arrangements between the parties. This rule is applicable as of January 2015.

Third, recent proposals include a wider scope of obligations for platforms in other areas of electronic supplies. Following the *e-commerce package*, according to Article 14a paragraph 1 of the VAT Directive, as amended by Directive

---

[131] OECD (2017), p. 22.
[132] OECD, The Role of Digital Platforms in the Collection of VAT/GST on Online Sales, March 2019.
[133] OECD (2019), n. 9, p. 15.
[134] See Council Directive (EU) 2021/514 of March 2021 amending Directive 2011/16 on administrative cooperation in the field of taxation; see also Vàzquez Juan Manuel and Čičin-Sain Nevia, "Tax Reporting by Online Platforms: Operational and Fundamental Implications of DAC7 and the OECD Model Rules" in: Weber Dennis (ed.), The Implications of Online Platforms and Technology for Taxation, IBFD Amsterdam 2023, p. 9 ff.
[135] See Directive 2021/515, Recital 9.

2017/2445, platforms that facilitate, *distance sales of goods* imported from third countries of an intrinsic value not exceeding 150 euros shall also be deemed to have received and supplied those goods himself. The same rule also applies to the facilitation by platforms of *supply of goods* with the EU by a non-EU taxable person to a non-taxable person (B2C) (Article 14a paragraph 2 VAT Directive as amended by Directive 2017/2455). This new rule introduces a fiction that the platforms act in its own name and becomes taxable for the supply to the consumer. The underlying transaction between the initial supplier could be subject to VAT but will in most cases be treated as a B2B supply with the right to credit VAT.

Fourth, new rules could be introduced within the new VAT rules for the digital age (VITA) as contemplated by the EU. In a recent proposal, the EU also intends to ensure VAT-equal treatment for platform activities in the short-term rental accommodation and passenger transport sectors.[136] To that end, the EU proposes introducing the "deemed supplier model" by which platforms will account for VAT on the underlying supply where no VAT is charged by the supplier (new Article 28a).[137] As a consequence, the platform would in this case become responsible for charging VAT, collecting it from the customer and remitting it to the competent tax authority.[138] The facilitation services provided by the platform should be characterized as *intermediary* (and not as an electronic service), in order to clarify the application among member States and allow for a uniform application of the place of supply (new Article 46a).[139] Thus, VAT would be due in the country where the underlying transaction is supplied, usually where the transport takes place or where the accommodation is rented.[140]

4.   A special case: the Metaverse

The case of the Metaverse is also quite controversial and opens new tax issues in the VAT area.[141] The Metaverse, as part of the so-called Web3, offers new

---

[136]   See Proposed Council Directive (EU) of 8 December 2022, amending Directive 2006/112/EC as regards VAT rules for the digital age, COM(2022) 701 final.

[137]   See Proposed Council Directive (EU) of 8 December 2022, amending Directive 2006/112/EC as regards VAT rules for the digital age, COM(2022) 701 final, new Art. 28a.

[138]   EU Parliament Briefing, VAT in the Digital Age, March 2023, p. 6.

[139]   See Proposed Council Directive (EU) of 8 December 2022, amending Directive 2006/112/EC as regards VAT rules for the digital age, COM(2022) 701 final, new Art. 46a.

[140]   EU Parliament Briefing, VAT in the Digital Age, March 2023, p. 6.

[141]   See Owens J. and Costa Oliveira N., The Tax Treatment of the Metaverse Economy and the Potential for a New Offshore Tax Haven, Tax Notes International 2022, p. 537 ff.

possibilities of virtual interactions for humans within that particular platform. Indeed, inside the various platforms, the users participate, through their avatars, in an interactive, standardized and interoperable environment. They have the possibility of playing virtual games, attending concerts or events or buying virtual goods, by using NFTs, such as art and real estate, among other things. In addition, both the virtual and physical world may interact. It is possible to buy goods in a virtual shop on the Metaverse, with the goods being delivered to your real address. These virtual transactions will be paid for under consideration, notably though digital currencies, such as Ethereum. Since these transactions, such as the sale of virtual or physical goods, buying and selling NFTs, or performing, correspond to virtual or physical supplies of goods or services, the first issue is whether they should be subject to VAT. In our view, they represent supplies against consideration and, as such, should the other conditions be met, would fall within the scope of VAT, even if the drafters of VAT, a century ago, did not have such types of transactions in mind.

Many sensitive and novel issues appear. Transactions occurring in the Metaverse may look like corresponding supplies of goods or services in the real world but will occur digitally (partially or in full), within a completely decentralized world, where the place of supply, from a traditional VAT context, must be analyzed from a new perspective. A concert played in the Metaverse through an avatar is localized both within the platform, which may be sited anywhere, or at the home of the platform's participants using their technology. Going into detail about the VAT regime applicable in the Metaverse would go way beyond the scope of this book. We will, however, highlight some of the legal issues that could arise in this context, in order to look at their relevance from the perspective of AI taxation.

First, the *characterization* of transactions occurring within the Metaverse is subject to debate. In most cases, supplies in the Metaverse, such as the sale of NFT against consideration, should be regarded as services. In addition, many transactions within the Metaverse could fall under the category of electronic services, as described above. But this should not always be the case. For example, should virtual events, such as conferences, or office gatherings, offered against consideration, be treated the same as an in-person meeting or digital services?[142] Indeed, while the definition of electronic supply services is rather broad, VAT law also entails a special rule for admission to events. In a case, the CJEU considered that "admission to an event" covers "admission to educational and scientific events, such as conferences and seminars, includ[ing] the supply of services of which the essential characteristics are the granting of the right

---

[142] Bal A. Aleksandra, VAT and the Metaverse-Taxing Virtual Events (Correct), Daly Tax Report, 30 March 2022.

of admission to an event in exchange for a ticket and a payment.[143] In other words, the Court did not seem to require access to a specific physical location in order to characterize the supply as an event. As Aleksandra Bal points out, the outcome would have very problematic consequences in the world of the Metaverse, since the place of location would then be the place where the event takes place, which is problematic in the digital world which has "no connection to any particular territory".[144] However, the CJEU also pointed out that the rule of Article 53 VAT Directive (place of location of events) must be regarded as an exception and therefore narrowly interpreted.[145] In the *Srf Konsulterna AB* case, the Court was confronted with a physical event, consisting of a five-day course on accountancy and management supplied only to taxable persons and requiring advance registration and payment. In our view, this judgment may not be regarded as a suitable precedent for the characterization of events taking place in the Metaverse. The characterization of electronic services may thus be more relevant in such a case. A similar issue could also occur for artistic, notably musical, or e-sports performances within the Metaverse. Based on the electronic service definition mentioned above, should the human intervention of the performer, perhaps in his or her home, be regarded as disqualifying such characterization? In our view, an artist, or more precisely the avatar of a musician, playing a concert in the Metaverse should still be regarded as performing a digital service.

Second the *place of supply* is hard to define. We have seen that the specific place of supply for admission to artistic, sports or educational events is not adapted for the world of the Metaverse. In general, as electronic services, the supply would be localized at the place of the recipient. However, the service provider would have to determine the place of residence of the customer, which is quite difficult in the context of the Metaverse. For example, for an artist selling an NFT of her work, using a platform of exchange, such as OpenSea, it would be quite difficult to determine the identity and residence of the buyer.[146]

In the context of data transfer however, we see that the situation differs from the VAT rules described above. In general, within the Metaverse, consumers do not use their data as a counterpart for digital services. They typically pay for services with digital currencies, such as Ethereum. From a VAT standpoint, the use of cryptocurrency is treated as a means of payment and does not represent an additional taxable transaction. Barter transactions are, however,

---

[143] EUCJ, 17, *Skatteverket v. Srf Konsulterna AB*, 15 March 2019, para. 24.
[144] Bal (2022), p. 2.
[145] EUCJ, 17, *Skatteverket v. Srf Konsulterna AB*, 15 March 2019, para. 22.
[146] Owens and Oliveira (2022), p. 544.

possible. An artist performing a concert in the Metaverse could receive digital services as counterpart (free legal or tax services for instance). In this case, the normal rules would apply, and the consideration should be converted into means of payment and correspond to the subjective value from the perspective of the supplier.

Finally, it seems that the Metaverse, depending on its characteristic which may vary from case to case, could be regarded as a platform and thus would enter into the scope of the new reporting EU rules for digital platforms facilitating transactions with users. In this case, the deemed supplier rules and the new collecting obligations could also apply.

5. Consequences for the taxation of artificial intelligence and robots

Following the developments described above, we believe that the new VAT obligations on platforms may serve as an interesting model for a more global taxation of AI systems and robots in the future. After all, electronic facilities offered by platforms are usually widely automated and the human intervention is notably limited.[147] AI is also used to facilitate the functioning of the system and to follow, via deep learning, the behavior of the users and consumers. In the future, should some form of autonomous AI or smart robots be recognized as taxable persons, as this book contemplates, existing and developing rules that apply to the platform, in order to identify consumers for assessing, collecting and paying VAT, could also serve as a model for a future implementation of a system where AI systems as taxpayers would implement similar functions.

IV. VAT IN SWITZERLAND

A. In General

In essence, the Swiss VAT rules, governed by the Swiss Federal VAT Law (VATL),[148] follow comparable principles as provided for in the EU VAT Directive, with some peculiarities, however. The distinction between supply of goods and services corresponds in essence to the EU delimitation. A supply of services is defined by opposition to a supply of services (Article 3 lit. e VATL).

In general, the supply of goods is localized at the place of situation where the goods are located at the time of supply. To address the massive development of e-commerce, specific rules also have been introduced, notably for *distant*

---

[147] See the definition of EU Implementing Regulation, Art. 11 (electronic services).
[148] Swiss Federal VAT Law of 12 June 2009, Official Gazette 641.20.

sales ("vente par correspondence"). Indeed, as of 1 January 2019, distant sales of low-value goods, whose import would be tax exempt, are localized in Switzerland and subject to Swiss VAT, to the extent the supplier realizes an annual turnover of at least 100 000 CHF (Article 7 paragraph 3 lit. b VATL).

In addition, the various types of services also have to be characterized in order to define the place of supply (see Article 8 VATL). According to the general rule, services are localized at the place of the recipient (Article 8 paragraph 1 VATL). However, specific places of supply are defined for the various services mentioned in Article 8 paragraph 2 VATL. This notably applies to services which are either typically rendered directly to customers, localized at the place of the supplier, or related to immovable property, localized at the situs, or consisting of an artistic, sports or conference event, localized at the place of performance.

Digital or telecommunication services are localized, under the general rule, at the place of the recipient (Article 8 paragraph 1 VATL). Under the "reverse charge" system, foreign enterprises that render services in Switzerland are exempt from tax, to the extent that the acquirer of such services is subject to VAT (Article 10 al. 2 lit. b and 45 VATL). This rule does not apply to digital and telecommunication services (Article 10 al. 2 lit. b *in fine* VATL). It follows that foreign enterprises that render such digital services to individuals (non-taxable persons) in Switzerland are subject to VAT because these services are localized there, and the recipient is not as such subject to the tax on acquisitions. In that case, foreign enterprises have to designate a tax representative in Switzerland (Article 67 VATL).

In an interesting case, the Swiss Supreme Court had to analyze the application of this rule to a "dating" web site, operated by X. Inc, located in the United States.[149] X Inc. was proposing virtual encounters online, after which the participants were free to meet in person or not, with additional services, for a fee which corresponded to their category. It appeared that the foreign entity operating the website realized an important turnover in Swiss territory.

The Supreme Court had to address two characterization issues. First, in order to define the place of supply, the claimant argued that the services were comparable to matrimonial advice, which, according to Article 8 paragraph 2 lit. a VATL, are localized at the place of the supplier. The Supreme Court did not agree and ruled that what was relevant was not the content of the services but the *mode* of providing them. Hence, since the services took place without a physical presence between suppliers and customers, the general rule of localization at the place of the recipient was applicable. Second, the next issue was whether the services could be characterized as digital services, within the

---

[149] Swiss Supreme Court, ATF 139 II 346 = RDAF 2013 II, 20 May 2013, p. 524.

meaning of Article 10 paragraph 2 lit. b *in fine* VATL, which are taxable at the place of the recipient, therefore in Switzerland, at the level of the foreign entity, which is obliged to appoint a local representative. In its reasoning, the Court confirmed that, by introducing the special rule for digital services, the intention of the legislator was basically to follow the list of the EU VAT Directive. In the present case, the Supreme Court confirmed the characterization as digital services due to the following factors: the dating websites are only accessible on the Internet, the data are provided by the customers online, the services offered are not similar to "ordinary" dating services and the scope of such services, supplied to a great number of people, would not be possible without the information technology. In an interesting comment, the Supreme Court considered that the services were *"largely automated"*.[150] Swiss VAT was therefore due from the foreign supplier, which also had to appoint a legal representative in Switzerland.

Some commentators have criticized the reasoning of the Supreme Court in the sense that too much importance seems to be given to the modality of the supply instead of the content (substance) of the service rendered.[151] Careful attention should also have been given to the rule applicable in the EU, in order to avoid double taxation. Indeed, under EU law, a distinction is made for digital services, between B2C and B2B transactions. It is also interesting to mention that, while referring to EU law, the Court rejected the opinion of the UK tax authorities, which, apparently came to a different conclusion and characterized those services as offering access to an online community, which are taxable at the place of suppliers. As one commentator has noted, should therefore X Inc. be sited in the United Kingdom, instead of the United States, a double effective VAT taxation would have occurred.[152]

A characterization issue also exists under Swiss law for import or supply of *software*. While, in general, software sold over the Internet corresponds to a supply of services, the question is more pertinent when the software is provided via physical means. In this case, a first distinction has to be made between data transmitted via telecommunication and software transmitted by data support items. In the latter case, an additional distinction exists between software with or without a market value. [153] According to the practice of the Federal Tax Administration (FTA) , all data transmitted via telecommunica-

---

[150] Swiss Supreme Court, ATF 139 II 366, 20 May 2013, para. 7.4.5; RDAF 2013 II p. 540.

[151] Candaux Nicolas, Cywie Arnaud and Morel Frédéric, Traitement TVA des prestations de services par Internet, L'Expert Comptable Suisse, 2014, p. 702.

[152] Sadik Alexandre, "Commentary" in: RDAF 2013 II p. 543.

[153] Federal Tax Administration, Federal Custom Authority, Publ. 52.21. "Software", Edition 2018, n. 2.

tion (software installation via telecom) are treated as services.[154] The same should apply to software transmitted on a data support item *with no market value* (Article 73 paragraph 3 VATL and 24 VATL). By contrast, software transmitted on a data support item with a market value should be regarded as a supply of goods. Consequently, in the absence of a market value of the support item, the supply of services is characterized as a supply of services. It follows that the recipient in Switzerland of such services transmitted from abroad are subject to the rules of acquisition of services (Article 45 paragraph 1 lit y VATL). The Federal Customs Authority provides for an exhaustive list of software supplied for data without any market value, which is defined in Article 111 paragraph 1 of the VAT Ordinance,[155] as a supply, independent from the type of support and the mode of storage, which, upon import: (a) cannot be acquired against consideration already fixed upon import and (b) cannot be used contractually against a unique license fee already fixed upon import. The data support may however entail software and computer data, sounds or images (Article 111 paragraph 2 VAT Ordinance).

B.   Swiss Reform Targeting Digital Platforms

Following the OECD report and the EU changes to VAT rules, Switzerland also plans to reform its VAT rules in order to better apprehend the intermediation activities offered by platforms.[156] Platforms would be defined broadly as any electronic interface which allows direct interactions online between various actors with a view to supplying goods or services (Article 3 lit. 1 of the draft federal law on VAT [L P-LTVA]). Following the EU model, the concept of the deemed supplier would also be introduced, for any platform that supplies goods, that is not outside the scope of VAT, according to Article 20a paragraph 2 P-LTVA. In case both the underlying supplier and the platform are resident in Switzerland, the supply between them will be treated as an export subject to a zero rate, which would thus allow the platform to credit any input VAT. Platforms subject to VAT would become liable to collect and pay the VAT (Article 24 paragraph 5bis P-LTVA). Their liability would however be limited to the correct processing of information provided by the supplier. There will also exist a secondary liability for the suppliers, notably in case of false information transmitted to the platform (Article 15 paragraph

---

[154]   Ibid.

[155]   Federal Ordinance on the VAT, 27 November 2009, Official Gazette, 641.201.

[156]   See, Federal Council, Message concernant la modification de la loi sur la TVA, 24 septembre 2021; Federal Tax Administration, Rapport explicatif à propos de la révision partielle de la loi sur la TVA (Développement futur de la TVA dans le cadre d'une économie numérisée), 19 juin 2020.

4bis P-LTVA). As a consequence, foreign platforms would have to register for VAT in Switzerland, notably if they reach a turnover of 100 000 CHF of low-value distance sales (Article 53 paragraph 1 lit. a LTVA).

C.   Application to Artificial Intelligence and Robots

It follows that comparable issues in EU VAT rules should apply in Switzerland on the tax treatment of the use by enterprises of AI and robots. The difference between supply and services appears to be rather similar to the EU. In addition, the definition of *digital* services, which will lead to taxation at the place of the recipient, is based on the same criteria as the EU Regulations. The case of the definition of taxation rules for a foreign "dating website" is interesting. It demonstrates the difficulties of applying proper characterization and localization rules for digital and automated activities. In this case, we see that the analogy with "comparable" human, face-to-face activities was rendered delicate due to the specific features and vast array of activities that only automation and digital services could offer. Following disputed reasoning, and contrary to the position of the UK HMRC, the Swiss Supreme Court disregarded a characterization of access to an online community, in favor of digital services. Hence, this case illustrates the potential risks of double taxation that difficulties of characterization of online automated activities could cause.

In addition, the Swiss position on the definition of the PE (or FE), for VAT purposes, seems to be broader than in the EU. Under the Swiss perspective, the concept of PE tends to correspond to the OECD definition of Article 5 of the OECD Model DTC. It follows that the presence of a PE could more easily be recognized under Swiss law. Indeed, the presence of human personnel at the place of business appears not to be required anymore, under OECD rules. Hence, AI systems and robots, to the extent that the other requirements are met, notably, a fixed place of business during a certain period, could fall into the definition of a PE for Swiss VAT purposes. In this situation, we see a coordination in the definition of PE, both for VAT and direct tax purposes.

V.   CONCLUSION

Many activities carried out by AI systems or robots are already subject to VAT at the level of the enterprises using them. At this stage, existing principles seem to solve most of the classical issues, such as the character of the transaction (supply of goods or services) and the corresponding place of supply. The existing technological complexities and the broad potential scope of functions that AI-autonomous systems or smart robots may cover could already trigger sensitive characterization issues. In general, a comparison with the economic functions of the activities of AI, from the perspective of the average consumer, offers an adequate solution to the precise character of most of the AI services. In particular, if the AI activities are treated as electronic services, a problematic issue would be to delimitate if AI or robots, as such, could fulfil the conditions of an FE at their place of location. Based on the recent case law of the ECJ, we do not exclude the possibility that this conclusion should be met, notably for smart robots.

As a result of the analysis of the VAT impact on AI activities, we may also conclude that VAT is indeed a very interesting and promising solution to better attract the added value resulting from AI. First, as the EU rules of taxation of cross-border electronic commerce have shown, the implementation of the localization of the supply, in accordance with the principle of destination, combined with an obligation to taxable non-EU suppliers to register and collect VAT on B2C transactions, allow the levying of VAT, even for supplies of a very low value. The implementation at the same time of the OSS, or the IOSS in case of import also offers a rule which alleviates compliance and administrative costs for taxable entities. Second, the advantage of VAT is that it focuses on the place of consumption, where the consumers or users are located. The criticism raised against taxation or AI, linked with competition or administrative difficulties in taxing the firms using AI, loses much weight in the VAT context. Indeed, the place of residence or location of the infrastructure does not matter so much anymore, notably in B2C transactions, since the foreign suppliers will have to register and collect VAT, to the extent there is a taxable transaction under EU law.

Over time, in a later stage, the complexities and extended technological capabilities of robots and AI may, however, require broader analysis. The scope of actions carried out by robots may indeed evolve in a way not comparable to human capabilities.[157] As already seen in some new forms of digital services, the comparison between physical or human activities might become arbitrary. In addition, to simply qualify such AI or robots' activities as electronic services may not correspond to the specific nature of their essential features. In this case, perhaps, new rules of localization could be adequate.

Finally, while we have focused in this chapter on the current VAT treatment of AI and robot activities within enterprises subject to VAT, we will analyze later, in Chapter 9: (1) whether the scope of the activities of AI subject to VAT could be broadened, and (2) the extent to which AI-autonomous systems and smart robots, as such, could in the future be required to charge VAT on their activities. This conclusion would require either that AI, under some conditions,

---

[157] Oberson Xavier, Taxing Robots? From the Emergence of an Electronic Ability to Pay to a Tax on Robots or the Use of Robots, 9 World Tax Journal, p. 256; same opinion, Beretta (2018), at 4.

would be recognized as legal entities, and therefore subject to tax or, even without a legal personality, would qualify as sufficiently autonomous and independent enough to become VAT taxpayers. In this respect, the platform rules described above may serve as a first attempt to grasp the activities of technology, mostly acting autonomously, and thus be a blueprint for a future model of an AI tax.

If we follow the reasoning of the Swiss Supreme Court, in the dating website case mentioned above, the minimal intervention criteria have been considered met, since the purpose of the platform was to improve the experience of the users. As a consequence, the connection of users by the platform through automation, without human intervention, should characterize it as electronic services. It follows that services rendered automatically by AI and robots should fall, already under current law, as electronic services rendered by platforms. In the future, should AI-autonomous systems and smart robots become entities subject to tax, the type of identification, collecting and payment obligations borne by platforms could also be applied to these new taxable AI entities. Thus, we see that, in the VAT context, the difficulties raised by the taxation of digital supplies may be reduced and even overcome, not only by involving the platforms, but also, more generally, AI systems and robots. We then might not be as far away as we think. After all, many platforms currently facilitate supplies using automated processing and AI systems.

9. The design of a tax on artificial intelligence

I. INTRODUCTION

Activities carried out with the use of AI, as we have seen, may not escape tax. First, AI or robots as part of the assets of corporations or enterprises, like any other production factors, contribute to the realization of sales, and therefore of profits.[1] The turnover attributable to robots' activities is reflected in the profit and loss account of corporations, or the income statement for entrepreneurs in non-corporate form, and taxable at the level of the entity owning and using robots. Furthermore, to stimulate innovation and notably investment in AI or robotics, many countries apply special incentives, such as accelerated depreciation rules, which should thus also result in taxable profits. Second, the consumption of goods and/or services supplied by enterprises using AI may also be subject to the VAT or sales tax.[2] When a consumer orders a book online, which is chosen in a warehouse by a robot, the price paid, potentially subject to VAT, also reflects the services rendered by automation.

We consider, however, that the current tax system should be reevaluated following the development of AI, its implementation into robotics and the resulting impact on the economy, notably on the labor market. To the extent that AI, as defined above,[3] might be able to replace human workers, eventually in most if not all sectors, the income tax base, represented by salaries, could drop drastically. As we have demonstrated above, this consequence could mean major revenue losses for the States, and the loss of one of their main financing resources, particularly for social security purposes. Consumption, and therefore VAT resources, could also drop as a consequence of a rise in unemployment and a loss of income from human workers. Finally, inequality would increase both between the workers and the entrepreneurs who own the knowledge (intellectual property and know-how) in AI and robotics or holding

---

[1]   See supra, p. 58 ff.
[2]   See supra, p. 105 ff.
[3]   See supra, p. 18 ff.

the relevant assets (automation), and between workers themselves, to the extent of their exposure to automation.

A taxation on AI or its use could address the issues identified above. First, by taxing AI *activities*, it would not only bring new and additional revenue to States but also logically replace the disappearing income tax base from human workers. In other words, a tax on AI would add an additional level of taxation, which still has to be defined, in order to consider the additional benefits granted to firms using AI systems instead of humans. In addition, taxation of AI activities could reintroduce neutrality between the use of humans or AI or robot workers. As the (human) labor tax base regressed, a new corresponding AI tax base would increase. Should labor and other human income disappear, the activities of AI would become the new global individual tax base. The owners and users of AI and robotics would also indirectly have to participate in the burden of this new system of taxation.

Second, at a later stage, we could also consider taxing not only the activities of AI, but an *AI system as such*. AI would then become subject to a new specific revenue tax, in parallel with other taxes levied at the level of the enterprises. This idea, however, requires recognition of an ability to pay of AI. In our view, by analogy with the legal status offered to companies, a possible solution to this issue is to develop from a legal standpoint an objective ability to pay for AI autonomous systems, in the form of a capacity of payment.[4] This solution also requests coordination within the tax system to consider potential double economic taxation between the taxation of the use of robots and robots themselves.

In any event, depending on the policy used by States, there are many different ways to elaborate a system of taxation of robots. In our view, from a tax standpoint, we should distinguish between a short and a long-term perspective. In the short-term, AI does not benefit from an ability to pay because it doesn't have financial means. It is not as such regarded as a legal entity or tax subject. Under this perspective, there are already many possibilities for designing taxes on the use of AI, as we will see below. In the longer term, the tax system might even evolve by recognizing AI autonomous systems as tax subjects and implementing specific new types of taxes on it.

---

[4]   See supra, p. 54 ff.

II.   TAXATION OF THE USE OF ARTIFICIAL INTELLIGENCE

A.   Artificial Intelligence Usage Tax

1.   Taxing the imputed salary of the use of artificial intelligence and robots

The solution to compensating the disappearing labor tax base is to bring it back into the system. Indeed, as automation replaces workers, it enters into an activity generating added value, which so far has been compensated by way of a salary paid in cash to humans. Hence, why not consider the economic value of activities rendered by AI as equivalent to the price the enterprise would have paid for similar activities carried out by humans? In other words, the solution that we recommend is to allocate an *"imputed salary"* to the use of AI, corresponding to the salary that the enterprise would have paid to hire the employee.[5] As such, from a tax standpoint, the hiring of a human or the use of an AI system would become neutral because the enterprise when using automation would need to account for a theoretical salary, subject to tax at the level of the enterprise.

As we have seen, such a system already exists, for instance, in Switzerland, which taxes homeowners on a so-called imputed rent.[6] Under Swiss law, homeowners are subject to income tax on a theoretical rent that corresponds to the rent that they should have paid in similar circumstances. While it may be difficult in practice to ascertain the amount of comparable rents, tax administrations have used various systems, such as a formula based on average rents in the area, which are adjusted according to relevant local information and a declaration from the taxpayer (value of the lodging, investments, localization, etc.).

2.   Defining the imputed salary

In the case of AI, the definition of the amount of imputed salary taxable at the level of the enterprise would be difficult, but not impossible, to ascertain. *Comparable salaries* already exist in traditional activities and professions. In addition, some methods have been implemented by the tax administration to calculate an estimated number of adequate salaries in the case of workers closely related to the corporation in which they work. For example, in practice,

---

[5]   See Oberson Xavier, Taxing Robots? From the Emergence of an Electronic Ability to Pay to a Tax on Robots or the Use of Robots, 9 World Tax Journal 2017, p. 254.

[6]   See supra, p. 53.

tax administrations have sometimes been confronted with cases of potential disputable deductions of so-called "excessive salaries" paid by some corporations to high-ranking executives, who also happen to hold company shares, to alleviate the burden of double economic taxation. Indeed, in order to mitigate the combined impact of both the profit tax at the level of the corporation and the income tax at the level of the shareholder receiving taxable dividends, some shareholders, working in a closely protected corporation, may try to exaggerate deductions of salary payments.[7] In such cases, courts and tax authorities have used various methodologies aimed at designing an objective salary, in accordance with the arm's length standard, namely, a salary that would be comparable to what a third-party worker (not closely linked with the paying corporation) would have earned in similar circumstances.[8]

However, with the development of automation, the situation might become more complex. AI implemented in robots might replace different or combined activities. Often, AI systems will work in collaboration with human workers or with other forms of automation. In such cases, the precise delimitation of the amount of theoretical salary attributable to centralized, combined or complex activities could be difficult. This issue, by analogy with transfer pricing methodology, could require a functional analysis, which would tend to allocate an adequate remuneration of the different activities exercised by automation in collaboration with humans. In other words, an objective amount of theoretical salary corresponding to the estimated value stemming from the use of automation would be attributable to the enterprise. Another solution would be to use lump-sum amounts based on an approximation of an adequate remuneration or average estimates of the value of theoretical work.[9]

3.   Impact of potential deductions from salaries paid to human workers

An important aspect of the taxation of workers should not be forgotten. Salaries paid to human workers are subject to income tax but are also deduct-

---

[7]   This issue has raised many controversies and case law, notably in Switzerland, see Meller Emily and Salom Jessica, Le salaire excessif en droit fiscal suisse, 67 Revue de droit Administratif et de droit Fiscal (RDAF) 2011, p. 106.

[8]   Supreme Court Decision, ATF/BGE 2C.188/2008, 19 August 2008. In practice, following the so-called method from Canton Wallis, the tax authorities may use, as a subsidiary method, a three-step methodology: (1) first the determination of an average salary based on statistics and the level of function and competence of the workers, (2) an adjustment of this salary based on a percentage in the turnovers (e.g. 1 percent) and from the profits of the company (e.g. 1/3), (3) a final comparison between the salary paid and the salary computed according to this method in order to determine if the disproportion is justified; see Meller and Salom (2011), p. 119.

[9]   See Oberson (2017), p. 255.

ible from the profit or income of the employer (corporation or enterprise), as the cost of conducting business. Hence, we could argue that the income tax losses attributable to the disappearance of salaries paid to human workers is at least partially compensated by a corresponding reduced deduction at the level of the employer, which triggers an equivalent increase in taxable profits. In other words, the amount of the disappearing deduction as salaries is automatically reflected in taxable profits. The author, however, believes that the impact of this disappearing deduction does not sufficiently compensate for the loss in taxable base. *First*, the rate of profit tax is usually, at least in most States, lower (sometimes significantly lower) than the rate of income tax. The disparity among rates is increasing and rates of corporate profit taxes tend to be further reduced.[10] It follows that the amount of tax attributable to the salary paid (income tax) does not necessarily correspond to the tax levied at the employer level (profit tax). Second, investments in AI systems are usually treated as depreciable assets. The use of automation is depreciated over time, with a corresponding tax deduction. Furthermore, the current trend of most States, in accordance with OECD recommendation, is to create an incentive in favor of automation with favorable accelerated depreciation policies or even expensing.[11] As a consequence, the impact of the deduction, from the profit tax, of salaries expenses for human workers is (at least partially) compensated by the deductible depreciation of investment in AI and robotics. In other words, a disappearing deduction of salaries paid to workers is potentially offset by the apparent deduction of amortization for the use of robots. This point may be demonstrated by the example in Table 9.1.

Thus, we argue that the replacement of human workers by AI systems could have a significant impact on the income revenue side. However, there is an *intrinsic link* between the salaries paid to the human workers and the corresponding deductions at the level of the enterprise that should be kept in mind while trying to design a tax on AI (or its use).

4.   Taxing outsourced payments, notably to independent persons

We could also consider, in addition to taxing the imputed salary of AI replacing humans, to include, in the tax base of the use of AI, the payments made by an enterprise to third-party AI systems acting as consultants or other types of independent robot advisers that have replaced human workers. Indeed,

---

[10]   Recently many countries have introduced new and lower rates of corporate profit taxes, including the United States, under the 2017 tax reform.

[11]   For an example of the impact of favorable depreciation rules in favor of automation in the US, see also Abbott Ryan and Bogenschneider Bret, Should Robots Pay Taxes? Tax Policy in the Age of Automation, 12 Harvard Law & Policy Review 2018, p. 20.

Table 9.1   Comparative table of the impact of the replacement of the employee by a robot

Scenario 1 (*with an employee*)			Scenario 2 (*with a robot*)				
In scenario 1, the company has only one employee to whom it pays a salary of 100 000. The company has a turnover of 150 000 and therefore its pre-tax profit is 50 000.			In scenario 2, the company fired its employee and replaced him with a robot. The investment cost of the robot is 500 000 and the depreciation period (lifetime) is 5 years, which corresponds to an annual charge of 100 000.				
The company pays taxes on its profits and the tax rate is 25% on pre-tax income.			The company pays taxes on its profits and the tax rate is 25% on pre-tax income.				
The employee pays taxes on his salary and the tax rate is 40% on his net salary.			The employee no longer has a salary and therefore no longer pays taxes on his salary.				
The social security contributions are due on the employee's salary. The social contributions rate is 30% on the gross salary, of which 15% is paid by the employee and 15% by the employer.			The employee no longer has a salary and therefore no longer pays social security contributions or his salary.				
I Hypotheses			**I Hypotheses**				
1). Company with an employee:			1). Company fired its employee and replaced him with a robot:				
a). Turnover of the company		150 000	a). Turnover of the company				150 000
b). Gross salary of the employee		100 000	b). Gross salary of the employee				0
			c). Robot investment cost				500 000
			d). Robot depreciation period (in years)				5
2). Social security contributions:	On gross salary	On net salary	2). Social security contributions:			On gross salary	On net salary
a). Employee's social security contributions	15%	17.65%	a). Employee's social security contributions			15%	17.65%
b). Employer's social security contributions	15%	17.65%	b). Employer's social security contributions			15%	17.65%

3). Tax rate:
a). The company (on pre-tax income)   25%
b). The employee (on net income)   40%

3). Tax rate:
a). The company (on pre-tax income)   25%
b). The employee (on net income)   40%

II Company

					Variations	
Turnover		150 000			150 000	
./. Net salary		-85 000			0	
./. Social security contributions (employee share)	17.65%	-15 000		17.65%	0	
./. Social security contributions (employer share)	17.65%	-15 000		17.65%	0	
./. Depreciation of the robot					-100 000	
Profit before tax		35 000			50 000	
./. Tax	25.00%	-8 750		25.00%	-12 500	
Net profit		26 250			37 500	11 250 43%

III Employee

					Variations	
Gross salary		100 000			0	
./. Social security contributions (employee share)	15.00%	-15 000		15.00%	0	
Net salary		85 000			0	
./. Tax	40.00%	-34 000		40.00%	0	
Salary available after tax		51 000			0	-51 000 -100%

IV Total taxes & social security contributions		IV' Total taxes & social security contributions		Variations	
Total taxes		Total taxes			
a). Income tax of the company	8 750	a). Income tax of the company	12 500	3 750	43%
b). Salary tax of the employee	34 000	b). Salary tax of the employee	0	-34 000	-100%
Total taxes	42 750	Total taxes	12 500	-30 250	-71%
Total social security contributions		Total social security contributions			
a). Social security contributions (employee share)	15 000	a). Social security contributions (employee share)	0	-15 000	-100%
b). Social security contributions (employer share)	15 000	b). Social security contributions (employer share)	0	-15 000	-100%
Total social security contributions	30 000	Total social security contributions	0	-30 000	-100%
Total taxes & social security contributions	72 750	Total taxes & social security contributions	12 500	-60 250	-83%

We can make the following conclusions in scenario 2 compared to scenario 1	V Conclusions		
	1. Increase in profit and margin of the company		
The company sees its expenses reduced by the replacement of its employee by a robot and therefore also sees its profit and margin increase. In our example, the net profit increases by 11 250 in Scenario 2, which is 43% compared to Scenario 1.	- In currency	11 250	
	- In percentage	43%	
	2. Decrease in the salary of the employee		
The employee who is replaced by a robot sees his available salary decrease. In our example, the available salary decreases by 51 000 in Scenario 2, which is 100% compared to Scenario 1.	- In currency	-51 000	
	- In percentage	-100%	
	3. Variation of taxes		
	a). Increase in taxes of the corporation		
The taxes paid by the company increase because of the increase of the profit. In our example, the taxes paid by the company increase by 3 750 in Scenario 2, which is 43% compared to Scenario 1.	- In currency	3 750	
	- In percentage	43%	
The taxes paid by the employee decrease because of the decrease of his salary. In our example, the taxes paid by the employee decrease by 34 000 in Scenario 2, which is 100% compared to Scenario 1.	b. Decrease in taxes of the employee		
	- In currency	-34 000	
	- In percentage	-100%	
Finally, the total taxes paid by the company and the employee decrease. In our example, the total taxes paid decrease by 30 250 (increase by 3 750 in the company, but decrease by 34 000 in the employee) in Scenario 2, which is 71% compared to Scenario 1. The decrease is due to the fact that the tax rate paid by the company (25%) is lower than the tax rate paid by the employee (40%). The lost tax on the employee is not fully recovered in the company.	c). Total decrease in taxes (corporation and employee)		
	- In currency	-30 250	
	- In percentage	-71%	
	4. Decrease in social security contributions		
The social security contributions on the employee's salary decrease because of the decrease of salary. In our example, the social security contributions paid decrease by 30 000 in Scenario 2, which is 100% compared to Scenario 1.	- In currency	-30 000	
	- In percentage	-100%	
Finally in our example, the total amount of taxes and social security contributions lost, amount to 60 250 in Scenario 2, which is 83% compared to Scenario 1.	5. Total decrease in taxes and social security contributions		
	- In currency	-60 250	
	- In percentage	-83%	

the income, which would otherwise have been paid to a human consultant, linked with those outsourced activities, will also disappear. In many States, and notably in Switzerland, income from independent activities is subject, not only to income tax (as income from independent activities), but also to social security contributions.

The legislator, in other words, when designing the tax on AI, could consider broadening the scope of the tax on all imputed activities carried out by AI systems and robots, which replace human labor, in the broad sense of the term, i.e. not only work stemming from a working contract, but also services activities effectuated by consultants and other third-party advisers.

B.   Automation Taxes

1.   Introduction

Another policy option is to introduce automation taxes. In a nutshell, these are taxes on the profits of corporations or enterprises that use automation instead of human workers, based on approximation of the profits generated from the use of automation. As we will see below, there are numerous possibilities when designing such taxes. First, a general automation tax may be introduced in an indirect way, based on the contributions of human workers to the revenues or profits of a company. Second, a tax on AI could be designed as a presumptive tax, in accordance with other indicators. Third, the tax may target the production factors stemming from the use of AI and robotics. Finally, special automation taxes could also be levied on particular autonomous processes.

2.   General taxes targeting the ratio of automation

This approach would try to tax automation indirectly, i.e. by reference to the contributions of human workers to the company's revenues. The more automation replaces human workers, the higher the rate would be.

As early as 2014, William Meisel, in particular, made an interesting proposal of an automation tax on *computers*, based on the following argument: "If software is to take over many jobs, why not have an income tax on software? We could perhaps think of it as a payroll tax on computers."[12] His proposal would help level the playing field and serve two purposes: (1) it would provide an incentive for a company to create jobs, notably investing in human-computer synergy, and (2) it would bring additional revenues, which could create more consumption and as a consequence, boost the economy.[13]

---

[12]   Meisel William, The Software Society, Trafford Publishing, United States 2014, p. 220.

[13]   Meisel (2014), p. 220.

According to his proposal, the *automation* tax would be based on the ratio of a company's revenues (total sales) to the number of employees. It should increase as a percentage as the revenue-per-employees (ratio) grows, making it more attractive to create jobs than to replace them with automation.[14] Meisel gives the following example:

> According to an Apple web site, Apple had about 47,000 employees in the US and 70,000 worldwide in 2012. The company was running at a revenue rate of about USD 40,000 per quarter. With about the same revenue, GM had about 70,000 employees in the US and about 200,000 worldwide. The ratio of worldwide revenues of employees at Apple is about USD 571,000 and at GM is about USD 200,000 per worldwide employee. Looking at the revenue ratio, Apple has 1.8 employee per million dollars of revenues worldwide and GM 5.0 employees per million dollars, almost three times as many.[15]

As such, this proposal is not a robot tax. The purpose of this tax is to tax the use of software. To achieve that purpose, this project uses an indirect method based on the percentage of human workers' contributions to the total revenue of a company. But the same logic could also apply to the use of AI or robots.

In the same vein, Abbott and Bogenschneider have outlined an automation tax system, suggesting a so-called *self-employment tax*. The tax would be calculated as a substitute for the employment taxes of the worker and employer if a human worker had continued to perform that work. The tax would follow the premises of Meisel's ratio approach but differ in the sense that it would be calculated based on a ratio of corporate *profits* to gross employee compensation expenses,[16] and not on gross sales. Meisel justifies the ratio on sales because profits "can be manipulated with deductions and other accounting complexities much more than revenue".[17] By contrast, Abbott and Bogenschneider favor a ratio based on profits because a sale ratio "may be unworkable in practice since the tax would prohibitively fall on firms with high sales and low profit margins, such as discounted retailers".[18] This system resembles the AI or robot usage tax that we have suggested but is not based on a theoretical salary corresponding to equivalent human work but to a predetermined ratio linked with the level of automation in a company.

In our view, the debate around the proper ratio demonstrates some of the technical difficulties that this solution could create. The tax, with its mechanical ratio approach, could have a different impact on various types of

---

[14] Meisel (2014), p. 221.
[15] Meisel (2014), p. 221.
[16] See Abbott and Bogenschneider (2018), p. 30.
[17] Meisel (2014), p. 221.
[18] Abbott and Bogenscheider (2018), p. 28.

industries, which could breach the principle of equality of treatment. In addition, the goal pursued by these types of tax is not always clear. According to Meisel, "In short the automation tax is a penalty for preferring automation to people when there is a fair tradeoff".[19] This approach seems to view the tax as designed to penalize companies using automation, which would characterize such tax more as a "Pigouvian" tax, which will be discussed further.[20] Abbott and Bogenschneider, however, seem to view an automation tax more as a tax policy tool focusing on a neutral tax treatment between human and robot workers.

The author is in favor of the solution of the AI usage tax on an imputed salary, despite certain practical difficulties of evaluating an adequate amount of the taxable base. First, it corresponds to the reality, i.e. taxing the activities of robots implementing AI and replacing humans. Second, this approach has the merits of offering an analysis based on comparable systems, which the tax system uses elsewhere, notably in transfer pricing situations. However, with the development of technology and complexities in the use of AI and robots, should the definition of an adequate imputed salary become unworkable or too difficult to implement, the tax system could use lump-sum amounts or, as an alternative, the ratio approach described above. In view of the different potential impacts on companies, taking into account particularly the principle of equality of treatment, the ratio approach should, however, serve as an approximation that would require further adjustments, in particular, to differentiate between the business models of the enterprises subject to the automation tax.

3.   Presumptive artificial intelligence taxes

The difficulty in defining AI for tax purposes and its effective contribution to the value creation of the profits of an enterprise could also justify the use of other indicators than the actual profits realized by this enterprise. Christina Dimitropoulo considers this and suggests a presumptive robot tax, the goal of which would be to consider the "hidden tax capacity" attached to the use of the "specific technological equipment qualifying as robots or AI and which cannot be accurately measured by the corporate income, or exceeds what the current taxation of corporate profits capture".[21] This approach also offers an interesting alternative to the imputed salary proposal mentioned above.

The approach based on presumptive taxation, as Dimitropoulo recognizes, relies more on the benefit principle, in the sense that the idea is to capture

---

[19]   Meisel (2014), p. 220.
[20]   See infra, p. 163 ff.
[21]   Dimitropoulou Christina, Robot Taxation: A Normative Tax Policy Analysis. Domestic and International Tax Considerations, PhD, University of Vienna, May 2023, p. 389.

the "rents" or "benefits" that would be approximated by reference to the use of certain assets.[22] She then examines two potential presumptive tax bases, namely: (1) an asset tax base, and (2) a turnover tax base.

The *asset* covered should be broadly defined in order to include total long-term technological assets that fall under the subjective scope of the tax.[23] Indeed, such a broad approach is justified by the fact that robots are difficult to identify from other technological assets and are operating in conjunction with other operating systems, using intangibles. The approach remains difficult according to Dimitropoulo, since the assets under the scope should produce a substitution effect, between labor and machine, to deal with the "robots-labor replacement" that the tax should address.[24] The difficulties of a presumptive robot tax on assets lies also in the valuation. As such, Dimitropoulo favors a cost method combined with a discounted cash method of all gross assets used in certain large businesses, but this solution still raises many difficulties.[25]

By contrast, a turnover tax that targets the earning capacity of the enterprise using robots could be simpler to administer. It would target the robot users' ability to escape taxation under the corporate income tax.[26] In order to alleviate double economic taxation, a deduction of such tax from the corporate income tax could be a solution.[27] Dimitropoulo however points out the inequities of a turnover tax, notably because it would affect very differently capital-intensive and labor-intensive businesses. These neutrality risks do not seem to make the tax overall proportional to its aim.[28]

However, having described these presumptive tax proposals, Dimitropoulo recognizes that she could not find "a sufficient convincing and normatively justified tax design for taxing robots in light of its goal, among the tax proposals that have been discussed".[29]

We tend to defend a different view, in the sense that we believe that tax policy reasons, based on the effect of AI systems and robots, would justify a tax on AI.[30] Among various possibilities, as defended here, a presumptive tax could also represent an interesting solution, either as a "lump-sum" approximation of an imputed salary or rent obtained by the firms using AI, or as an approach based on production factors (AI versus human workers). What

---

[22] Dimitropoulou (2023), p. 390.
[23] Id., p. 429.
[24] Id., p. 429 ff, 545.
[25] Id., p. 483, 546.
[26] Id., p. 507 ff, 511.
[27] Id., p. 512, 547.
[28] Id., p. 513, 548.
[29] Id., p. 550.
[30] See supra, p. 46 ff.

Dimitropoulo admits, however, is that the corporate profit tax system is incomplete and does not capture the "hidden" profits arising from the use of AI. In our view, a tax on AI systems remains, among others, a solution to tackle that additional margin.

In the same vein, Anton Korinek has also looked at a way to better include in the tax base the economic rents, such as information and notably intellectual property. He recognizes, from this perspective, that we should refrain from taxing the robots as a physical vessel and instead should focus on taxing "the design of the robot and the programs that are running on it because those are information goods that generate rent".[31] Thus, his view also is that hidden profits arising from the use of the intellectual property included in AI should be taxed. Our approach to a tax on AI has precisely this in mind.

In our view, the presumptive tax solution remains an interesting alternative. Such a tax would allow the inclusion in the tax base of the additional contributions to the profits of the enterprises that the use of AI would bring and which is not necessarily reflected in the profit tax base, if relying on the account books. This tax does not much depart from the imputed income proposal described above. Indeed, the imputed salary could also be based on a lump-sum approximation. As already discussed, this approximation would eventually evolve and disregard traditional approximations, since the activities carried out by AI systems and robots would in the future increasingly depart from typical workers' activities. The difficulty of a presumptive approach relies in the neutrality requirement and the risks of raising a disproportionate tax burden on some enterprises in comparison to others using less long-term capital. The design of the tax should remain as simple as possible and not rely on complex distinctions (such as AI systems with or without substitution effect). Over time, as technology evolves, AI systems could start with a positive complementing effect and develop into a negative labor substituting effect. In our view, the main criteria, like in the imputed salary proposal, should remain the comparison with a comparable "labor" activity that humans could have deployed instead of the AI systems or robots. By labor, we refer here either to work (meaning a relationship of worker) or services.

4. Automation taxes on production factors: an "artificial intelligence box"

Another way to introduce automation taxes is to try to design a system of taxing the use of AI as part of the production factors of the enterprise. Under this approach, specific revenues from AI or robotics could be extracted

---

[31] Korinek Anton, Taxation and the Vanishing Labor Market in the Age of AI, 16.1 The Ohio State Technology Law Journal, 2020, pp. 244, 256.

separately from the general revenues of a firm and taxed accordingly using a different rate.

This solution could resemble the so-called "*patent box*" system that is used widely internationally as a special favorable regime to promote innovation and R&D. There are different models of "patent box", but usually they apply special rules, typically a reduced profit tax rate, to qualifying income arising from eligible intellectual property assets. Following the OECD/BEPS Initiative, "patent boxes" are, however, subject to a requirement of substance (*nexus*), in order not to be characterized as harmful tax regimes.[32] In the EU "patent boxes" systems also have to comply with State Aid Rules.[33]

In compliance with our proposal, contrary to the "patent box", which creates a tax incentive in favor of innovation, the "AI box" would tax with a different, potentially additional, rate, qualifying income attributable to robots implementing AI. In other words, the box would here target margins arising from the use of automation and adopt a potentially higher rate of tax to profit from robotics.

This solution would of course be difficult to implement. It would notably require a proper definition of the "AI box". Should all activities generated by AI and robotics fall into the box? Would it be possible to separate these activities from other functions, notably in case of collaboration between humans and AI systems? In the case of the patent boxes, a solution has been found. It is, however, much easier to differentiate profits generated by the use of a patent than profits stemming from AI and robots. In a way, the ratio worker to revenues (or profits) described above may also be seen as an approximation of the determination of the contribution of AI and robots (or computers) to the overall profits of a firm.

---

[32] In the framework of the BEPS Initiative, the systems of IP boxes have been reviewed by the FHTP in accordance with the requirement of substance. In particular, following the nexus approach, which was finally adopted, the nexus criteria analyzes whether the IP benefits are conditional to R&D activities performed by the taxpayer requiring benefits; the proportion of expenditures directly related to the development activities "acts as a proxy for how much substantial activity" is undertaken by the taxpayer; see OECD/G20 BEPS, Action 5, Countering Harmful Tax Practices More Effectively, Taking into Account Transparency and Substance, Final Report, 2015, n. 28 and 29, p. 24.

[33] See Wittmann Johanna M., "'Patent Boxes' and Their Compatibility with European Union State Aid Rules" in: Kerschner I. and Somare M. (eds), Taxation in a Global Digital Economy, Linde Verlag, Vienna 2017, p. 427 ff.

5. Special automation taxes

Apart from general automation taxes, *special taxes* on the use of AI could also be envisioned. These taxes would be levied on a specific field of automation, notably in companies using robotics extensively, in comparison to humans.

In the Swiss canton of Geneva, for example, in mid-2017, the Socialist Party introduced a proposal for a special automation tax on supermarkets using "automated cashiers" that replace human workers. The tax would amount to 10 000 CHF per month. Revenues from the tax should serve to finance a fund designed for professional training and 30 percent of the tax should be repaid to shops without automated cashiers. The proposal has, however, raised strong opposition. First, it would be detrimental to innovation. Second, the compatibility of the draft with the principle of equality of treatment was challenged, notably due to its limited and "arbitrary" scope of application, leaving aside automation used in different and sometimes competing shops. The draft is currently being discussed in the Parliament of Canton Geneva. In our view, this proposal is interesting, but the scope is too narrow. In addition, as suggested here, a broad and coordinated approach is recommended in the area of robot tax. So far, the project has not been implemented.

On 21 September 2018, a Bill was passed in the City and County of San Francisco, which would authorize the City and County to impose a tax on each ride originating in the City and County of San Francisco provided by an *autonomous vehicle*.[34] This tax would cover all rides provided by an autonomous vehicle, facilitated by a transportation network company or any other person, or by a participating driver. The rate of the tax would not exceed 3.25 percent of net rider fares, for a ride, and 1.5 percent of net rider fares for a share ride. It is interesting to note that a lower tax could apply to net rider fares for a ride provided by zero-emission vehicles. The money collected would be dedicated to fund transportation operations and infrastructure within the City and County of San Francisco. This tax would correspond to some form of a *special robot usage tax*, in the sense that it would add a tax to the net fare of the ride.

C. Pigouvian Taxes

The tax system may also be used to encourage or discourage activities. In the first case, specific deductions or rules are implemented with the purpose of encouraging the desired behavior for public policy purposes (super R&D deductions, investments in environmentally friendly infrastructure or energy

---

[34] See, California Legislative Information, Assembly Bill No. 1184, Chapter 644, An act to add Section 5446 to the Public Utilities Code, relating to transportation, published 21 September 2018.

sparing policies). In the second case, taxes are used to discourage negative behavior by adding an additional burden to the taxpayer. For example, in the past, so-called "sin taxes" have been introduced to reduce consumption of tobacco, beer or wine. More recently, taxes have been implemented to incentivize the reduction of polluting behaviors (carbon emission taxes, taxes on composite organic compounds or sulfur) or at least to mitigate the costs caused by polluters. Sometimes described as "Pigouvian",[35] these taxes may pursue various policy goals. Their acceptance is sometimes politically sensitive, and their effect is notably dependent upon the elasticity of the demand of the price of the product involved, as the relative success of the tax on alcohol has demonstrated.

Another solution could be to levy an automation tax from a "Pigouvian" perspective, namely with a view to discouraging the use of AI over human workers. Here, the policy purpose would be different to the alternative of the AI usage tax, or the automation tax described above. Taxes on AI, designed as Pigouvian taxes, would serve as a corrective tax, designed to compensate the negative externalities linked with unemployment caused by automation. We have seen above that the robot tax proposal of R. J. Shiller goes in that direction, but as a transitory tool designed to help workers to adapt to the new economy.[36] Some commentators point out that such an automation tax would address the social costs, in case of mass unemployment, as a consequence of robotics and would in effect tax the surplus derived from the use of personal data and the disappearance of human work in favor of robotics.[37]

In our view, a Pigouvian tax is not an adequate solution, at least in the long term. The purpose of introducing a tax on AI, in the way we advocate it, is not to stop or limit innovation, AI or robotics. We cannot stop the progress of automation. As Yuval Noah Harari recently poignantly argued: "After all, what we ultimately ought to protect is humans – not jobs".[38]

In the short term, however, an alternative approach could be to levy such Pigouvian taxes in order to limit the path of automation, at least in some sectors, but only with the aim of allowing a transition period for the economy to adapt, should the path toward robotics accelerate dramatically without enough time for workers or the system to adjust. In the same vein, Shiller has argued in favor of a robot tax in order to mitigate the externality which is

---

[35] Abbott and Bogenschneider (2018), p. 8. The proper characterization of such taxes ("Lenkung Steuern" in German or "taxe d'incitation ou d'orientation" in French) has been subject to a vast debate.

[36] See supra, p. 3.

[37] Rosembuj Tuliom, Artificial Intelligence and Taxation, el Fisco, September 2018.

[38] Harari Yuval Noah, 21 Lessons for the 21st Century, London 2018, p. 24.

caused by workers losing their jobs. He wrote: "A moderate tax on robots, even as a temporary tax that merely slows the adoption of disruptive technology, seems a natural component of a policy to address rising inequality".[39] In any event, the implementation of a Pigouvian tax on AI would be difficult. It would require a different constitutional justification because of its non-financial purpose.[40] In addition, it should also consider that automation also gives rise to positive externalities, such as reducing or preventing damaging effects of routine tasks, fostering of innovation and helping education.

D.   Tax on the Global Value Added by the Use of Technology

In the past, some taxes have been introduced or planned, with a view to taxing the added value resulting from the use of new technologies, which tend to decrease the need for human workers.

For example, in Italy, there is a special tax on enterprises, the so-called IRAP ("imposta regionale sulle attività produttive"), which is levied by Italian regions to finance the health care system.[41] The tax is levied on traders (subject to certain exceptions, such as banks, other financial institutions and insurance companies) and is based on the difference between the value of production and production costs resulting from the company's financial account books. In a 2002 case, the ECJ admitted that the IRAP is not similar to the European VAT system and is thus not contrary to Article 33 of the EU VAT Directive.[42] Indeed, the IRAP is not proportional to the prices of goods and services provided by the enterprise subject to tax and is not intended to be passed on to the final consumer.[43]

The introduction of such taxes could represent another approach to the developments of technology, including AI and robotics, and its impact on human labor. As such, they are not taxes on AI because they do not specifically target AI or its use but broaden the base of the profit tax on the whole value added in order to include the profits arising from the use of technology.[44] The problems of these taxes are their potential different impacts in business sectors.

---

[39]   Shiller Robert J., Robotization Without Taxation? Project Syndicate, 2017, p. 3.

[40]   Oberson Xavier, Robot Taxes: The Rise of a New Taxpayer, Bulletin for International Taxation, 2021, p. 6.

[41]   Lexer Georgina Michaela and Scarcella Luisa, Artificial Intelligence and Labor Markets. A Critical Analysis of Solution Models from a Tax Law and Social Security Law Perspective, Rivista Italiana Di Informatica E Diritto, 2019, p. 53 ff, 67.

[42]   ECJ, C-475/03 (2006), *Banca Populare di Cremona Soc. Coop.a.r.l*, 3 October 2006.

[43]   Id, para. 30 ff.

[44]   Oberson (2021), p. 7.

In addition, they are difficult to administer since they require the computation of the global added value of the enterprise.

E.   Indirect Robot Tax by Limitation of Deductions

The system could also be adjusted in order to indirectly favor the use of human workers or at least not create too much incentive in favor of investment in automation. Another indirect way to achieve such a result is to disallow or reduce profit tax deductions for investment in AI and robotics. This strategy in fact goes in the opposition direction to current tax systems, which create an incentive towards automation by granting favorable depreciation and amortization rules on investment in AI or equipment in robotics.[45] The idea discussed here is to go in the opposite direction by reducing such an incentive with more restrictive amortization possibilities. In this respect, four different alternatives are feasible.

First, one approach is to simply disallow any tax deductions for investment in AI and robotics infrastructure. Second, another alternative, which has been introduced by South Korea, is to reduce the deduction for investment in automation.[46] This solution has indeed sometimes been described as the first "robot tax" in the tax system.

Third, the system could also be designed to include a "phase-out", related to the amount of a "reported level of automation".[47] In other words, the phase-out of amortization would be linked with a predetermined amount in accordance with a level of automation that the tax administration could define in regulations. As a consequence, after a certain threshold, firms with a high automation level would have their tax depreciation disallowed or reduced.

Fourth, more recently, Vincent Ooi and Glendon Goh, in the same line of thinking, have proposed a limitation on the rules of depreciation and capital allowances, designed to restrict the use of AI technologies.[48] Based on a Pigouvian perspective, they suggest distinguishing between the substituting and the complementing employment effects of automation. Employment substituting capital has the tendency to displace workers, while employment complementing capital leads to higher labor demand.[49] Therefore, they suggest restricting only the former with a mechanism of reverse depreciation. This

---

[45]   See OECD/G20 BEPS Project, Addressing the Tax Challenges of the Digital Economy, Action 1, 2015 Final Report, No. 92, p. 44.

[46]   See Abbott and Bogenschneider (2018), p. 25.

[47]   Abbott and Bogenschneider (2018), p. 25.

[48]   Ooi Vincent and Goh Glendon, Taxation of Automation and Artificial Intelligence as a Tool of Labour Policy, eJournal of Tax Research 2022, p. 273 ss.

[49]   Ooi and Goh (2022), p. 8.

approach is interesting but would in our view lead to complex characterization issues, in order to distinguish between the substituting and complementing effects of investments in capital.

The idea of restricting amortization in automation may be useful for levelling the playing field between AI and human workers. However, the idea of distinguishing between automation with substituting or with complementing employment effect would indeed create delicate administrative difficulties. Often, an AI system would not have such distinct features and could be combined with other intangible assets of a firm. In our view, another way to look at investments in an AI system would be to consider it as a special form of capital with the capability of interacting and autonomously deciding on its own. This type of capital would eventually become an "intelligent investment".[50] Thus, the concept of amortization should also be revisited. Investments in AI should therefore require new accounting rules since they cannot be compared with other ordinary forms of capital investments. The AI embodied in the systems or robots could eventually create more value in the company and make autonomous decisions, which could contribute to the realization of the profits of the company.

F.   Adjusting the Social Security Tax

1.   In general

As we have seen above, one of the main concerns over job disappearance is the impact on social security. Indeed, in most countries, labor income represents the main base of tax subject to social security levies.[51] As a rule, the burden of the social security contribution is shared equally among the employer and the employee (50 percent). Should human labor disappear, under the pessimist scenario previously described, the future of the world's social security systems is at risk. Indeed, the loss of human jobs, replaced by AI systems, affects the main taxable base (the payroll) of social security contributions, including health care contributions and unemployment insurance. To address this issue, many options may be contemplated.

First, should we introduce the tax on the use of AI, as suggested above, in the form of the "imputed salary" attributable to AI activities, the logical consequence would be to include such theoretical salary into the social security

---

[50]   We, however, do not go as far as De Lima Carvalho and Esteche to consider it "sentient" but at least AI is getting more and more autonomous with the capacity to interact and learn from experience, see De Lima Carvalho Lucas and Esteche Victor Guilherme, Sentience as a Prerequisite for Taxing AI, Tax Notes International, vol. 108, 5 December 2022, p. 1263.

[51]   See supra, p. 12.

contributions net.[52] In this case, the employer (or user of AI or robots) would have to contribute to social security on the attributable salaries imputed to robots' activities. In the same vein, a Spanish union, the Union General de Trabajadores (UGT), has suggested the introduction of a social security charge on enterprises using robots that replace workers, notably in industrial companies.[53] This approach would in our view fit perfectly into the current system of social security levies, the aim of which is to protect workers' disability and pension payouts. Since robots replace workers, it appears justified to ask the robots to contribute to these losses.

The social security tax on this imputed salary would increase the tax base for social security and would represent an *additional* tax burden for the firms using AI. In addition, in this case, the decrease of the social security tax base, represented by the disappearance of wages paid to human workers, is not alleviated by a corresponding disappearance of a tax deduction at the employer level. Indeed, social security contributions are usually not levied on the profits of corporations.

In some countries, like Switzerland, self-employed entities or enterprises in a non-corporate form are subject to social security tax on so-called income stemming from independent activities. If these non-corporate entities hired robots, the resulting loss in payroll subject to social security could be partially compensated by an increase of income from independent activities as a result of decreasing deductions (salaries). However, as mentioned above, an accurate estimation of the impact of such disappearing deduction should also consider the potential amortization of investments in AI. Finally, if we apply the characterization of "imputed" salary, the social security contributions should be deductible as business costs for the employer.

Second, to the extent that in the future there would probably exist more self-employed workers, the application of social security contributions to income from self-employed enterprise – including imputed salary attributable to robot workers – appears therefore to be an interesting option. In this context, a recent proposal made by *Avenir Suisse*, a think tank in Switzerland, to create a new legal concept of independent worker,[54] could represent an interesting path in the same direction.

Third, another approach could be to broaden the base of the social security contributions net, beyond income from dependent or independent enterprises,

---

[52]   Oberson (2017), p. 255.
[53]   Gomez Rosario, Tambien hay que cotizar por los robots, El Pais, 18 October 2016; Thibaud Cécile, Ça se passe en Europe: un grand syndicat espagnol veut faire payer des cotisations sociales aux robots, Les Echos, 21 October 2016.
[54]   Adler Tibère and Salvi Marco, Quand les robots arrivent, Avenir Suisse, 2017, p. 58 ff.

to include other types of income or transactions. In this respect, profits from corporations using automation could enter into the scope.

Historically, social security has been created to protect workers in case of unemployment, sickness or disability, and to prepare them for retirement. As human labor slowly disappears or changes drastically, so do the pillars of the social security system. New financing models need to be developed. It appears that the AI usage tax on imputed income is one alternative, as well as the extension of scope of social security contributions to independent workers or corporations using automation instead of workers.

2. Alternative methods: taxing the added value of the enterprise

In the context of robotization, an alternative method of financing social security has been described in a report of the Swiss Federal Council.[55] It consists of broadening employers' social security tax base to the global added value created by all enterprises. This tax, referred to as the tax on gross added value of the enterprise ("taxe sur la valeur ajoutée brute"), would subject to tax the global salaries paid, amortization charges on capital and the net profits of the enterprise. Thus, all production factors (capital and labor) would participate in the financing of social security so that the system would be neutral and at the same time alleviate the cost of labor.[56]

The Swiss proposal resembles the project "*Machinensteuer*", which was debated in Austria in 2016.[57] This tax was also designed to help finance social security. The tax would have been levied, unlike traditional social security levies, on the added value of the enterprise. This added value would have been based, not only on the sum of the wages paid to workers, but also on depreciations, profits, borrowed capital, rent and leases.[58]

This approach is similar, for social security levies, to the turnover taxes targeting the added value of the enterprises described above, for direct tax purposes.[59] It also raises many difficulties. The Swiss report, in particular, takes a critical position on this approach by mentioning that such reform would de facto tax more heavily the capital and its income, thus reducing the incentive in favor of most productive capital investments. In addition, this system would benefit labor-intensive enterprises and disadvantage capital-intensive sectors.[60]

---

[55] Swiss Federal Council, "Une étude prospective sur l'impact de la robotisation de l'économie sur la fiscalité et le financement des assurances sociales", Bern, 7 December 2019, p. 22.

[56] Id. p. 22.

[57] Lexer/Scarcella (2019), p. 66.

[58] Id. p. 66.

[59] See supra, p. 157 ff.

[60] Swiss Federal Council (2019), p. 23.

The "Machinensteuer", mentioned above, is also disputable for the same reasons, since it would impact differently some economic sectors.[61]

G.   Adjusting the VAT

Currently AI activities are already subject to VAT, to the extent that they are part of a supply against consideration by an enterprise using AI systems. Robots used in the industrial sector will mostly contribute to the realization of the supply of goods. Automation may also serve to supply services subject to VAT. In this context, as we have seen above,[62] the current taxation of activities performed by AI, notably in the digital economy, already raises many difficulties.

The EU, in this context, as seen,[63] has however introduced new interesting rules, which have notably allowed for better application of VAT for cross-border e-commerce transactions supplied by non-EU firms to EU customers or users. These rules have introduced, in particular: (1) requirements to register, identify and collect VAT on specific B2C digital supplies, (2) extended facilities to register in one portal with the OSS or IOS (in case of imports), and (3) new obligations for platforms facilitating specific transactions, with the introduction of the "deemed supplier" rules, which obliges the platform to levy and collect VAT on some e-commerce transactions by the underlying supplier. New proposals would further extend the implementation of the "deemed suppliers" model to new activities, such as rental and transport in all cases where the underlying supply is not subject to VAT.[64] The involvement of platforms facilitating transaction, within the scope of the VAT net, is an interesting development, which could be further broadened and which would in a way serve as a potential blueprint for future AI taxation. After all, most of the activities carried out by platforms are already widely automated.

VAT, as a consumption tax on goods and services, could also be adjusted in order to address the changes caused by automation, and notably the loss of human workers. The imputed salary proposal mentioned above is designed however for an income tax. This creates an imputed salary that is viewed as a deemed profit for enterprises using AI. This imputed salary would not be subject to VAT, just as salaries paid to human workers (with a working contract) are not considered to be subject to VAT. VAT, however, applies to all supplies by persons subject to tax against consideration, which already

---

[61]   Lexer/Scarcella (2019), p. 66.
[62]   See supra, p. 110 ff.
[63]   See supra, p. 120 ff.
[64]   See supra, p. 136 ff.

includes many activities carried out by AI systems or robots (assembly lines, facilitations by platforms based on algorithms, legal tech services, online games, etc.).

In view of the difficulties facing the financing of social security, Flückiger and Suarez have suggested a global reform of the VAT system.[65] Currently, only domestic consumption is subject to VAT. Private and public investments escape the tax burden because the enterprises can deduct the input VAT from their purchases. In addition, exports are zero rated, while imports are subject to tax, in accordance with the destination principle. In order to create a level playing field for all production factors (work and capital investment), these authors suggest a *gross* VAT ("taxe sur la valeur ajoutée brute de l'entreprise"), which would be levied on all supplies in the State of production, including investment supplies or exports.[66] As a consequence, the tax would be neutral towards production factors because it would cover wages, amortizations and other capital income.

At first glance, this solution appears interesting. However, as the authors themselves admit, it could have a negative impact on economic growth by penalizing some investments, which could suffer a double economic taxation: at the input (taxing investment cost at the level of production of equipment) and at the output side (taxing amortization).[67] In addition, it would require a complete recast of the global VAT system, including in the EU, which would appear difficult if not impossible to reach, bearing in mind, as an example, the difficulties of adapting the VAT rules to the digital economy. From an international standpoint, a move from the principle of destination, one of the guiding VAT principles, towards a production principle, appears problematic.

H.   An Object Tax on Artificial Intelligence Systems or Robots

Tax may not only be levied on streams of income (like wages or profits) or on consumption of goods or services (like VAT or sales tax) but also on goods. These taxes come from a very old tradition. For example, France has levied in the past a tax on the size of windows. These taxes may be justified for various public policy reasons, such as taxing a good which may be viewed as reflecting a specific affluence of the owner (tax on planes, motorcycle or cars) or because of the cost to society implied by these objects, like animals (tax on dogs or horses).

---

[65]   Flückiger Yves and Suarez Javier, "Propositions de réforme du financement de la sécurité sociale en Suisse" in: Pierre-Yves Greber (ed.), La sécurité sociale en Europe à l'aube du XXIe siècle, Helbing & Lichtenhahn, Basel 1996, p. 19.

[66]   Flückiger and Suarez (1996), p. 19.

[67]   Flückiger and Suarez (1996), p. 20.

An object tax on AI systems or robots, as a machine implementing AI, could be justified with a similar reasoning. The taxpayer would be the person owning or using the AI system or robot. The rate could be flat, as is usually the case with these types of taxes, or adjusted depending on different features of robots (for instance, use of environmental technology, impact on waste, etc.). This type of robot tax appears to have begun to be implemented in the State of California, where a so-called drone tax has been introduced.

It is submitted that this approach might be introduced by some States in search of a simple and practical solution, but in our view, it does not appear efficient.[68] Indeed, such an approach relies on an old vision of robots, regarded more like a machine or a piece of equipment and is not in line with the development of technology. In a way, we could draw a parallel between robots and animals. Robots are not humans but some of their capabilities make them resemble animals. But the comparison does not stand further analysis. Robots are evolving and, in many sectors, they are already more efficient than humans. While in the past, horses were replaced by cars, this time human drivers are replaced by robots (self-driving cars). An object tax on AI systems or robots remains enshrined in a static vision of robots as machines. Robots are potentially capable of learning from their experience (machine learning). They may be interconnected, and act and react in accordance with environmental changes. Finally, the idea of an object tax on robots would have to focus on robots in a physical form. This also confirms the "anthropomorphic" perspective of an object tax on robots. The modern approach that we defend is a more form-neutral definition of AI and robots focusing on the features of the capabilities of AI and their impact on the economy, notably on the labor market.

I.   A Fee as a Consideration for Using Artificial Intelligence

A tax may also be justified on the principle of equivalence. In this case, contrary to income tax or VAT, which are levied unconditionally by a State to finance its general needs, a tax, more precisely defined as a fee, may be introduced in order to compensate specific equivalent costs attributable to a taxpayer. There are numerous examples of these levies, such as toll fees for the use of state infrastructure (toll tax or airport use tax), administrative fees for state services (e.g. certification, authorization, permits), or recycling or collection installations for residents. Here, the tax is viewed as a price paid in exchange for a public service granted by the State to a taxpayer. To be justified, a sufficient link should exist between the levy of the fee and the counterpart granted by the State, in accordance with the principle of equivalence. In other

---

[68]   See Oberson (2017), p. 257.

words, the amount of the tax should basically correspond to the value, for the taxpayer, of the service or the advantage granted.

In accordance with this reasoning, an AI system or a robot fee could be introduced, based on the equivalence principle, as compensation for the service or economic advantage granted by the State to the users or owners of the AI system. The equivalent economic service or advantage granted by the State should represent an economic value, which is the counterpart of the payment of the fee. For example, a State could levy a robot fee as compensation for specific surveillance, certification requirement or public infrastructures installed for the use or control of robots.[69] This strategy would, however, have many limits. First, from a financial standpoint, it would not bring additional revenues to the States precisely because a fee, by definition, tends to cover costs generated by a State action. Second, it would not necessarily address the required public policy strategies to face the development of AI and robots. The link between job losses and a fee is too remote, and a fee cannot compensate for a global and general effect on the labor market.

In addition, the inequality impact mentioned above of the development of robotics is hardly covered by the levying of a fee. The owner of the AI technology would in fact only be required to cover, with a fee, specific costs that the State introduces in some limited aspect on the implementation of the robot industry (surveillance, control, or certification).

III.   A TAX ON ARTIFICIAL INTELLIGENCE SYSTEMS OR ROBOTS AS TAXPAYERS

A.   Introduction

We have seen above that discussions in favor of granting legal personality to AI or robots have emerged.[70] The EU Parliament has already suggested some typical features of a robot as a legal subject. This new potential form of legal personality was mainly designed for civil liability purposes in case robots caused damage to human beings. At this stage, following certain critical comments from experts from the political, scientific and academic worlds, the EU has not granted legal personality to robots. We cannot, however, assume that AI or robots could not also become tax subjects in the future. Such a definition, in our view, should not focus on the physical appearance of robots but adopt a form-neutral perspective, based on the impact of AI, notably implemented in

---

[69]   See also Oberson (2017), p. 258.
[70]   See supra, p. 23 ff.

robots in the labor market.[71] Thus, in our view, the tax policy issue is to focus on a potential tax capacity on AI autonomous systems, including smart robots.[72]

As demonstrated above, civil law recognition is an important element, which should also be considered from a tax standpoint, but such recognition is not sufficient. The introduction of a subjective AI tax liability also has to be justified from a tax standpoint. This implies that an AI entity should be regarded as benefiting from an economic ability to pay. Only under these conditions could we consider AI systems as taxpayers *per se.* Such a consequence would indisputably require sufficient autonomy from the AI system and the attribution of a financial capacity to pay the tax.[73] Similar to corporations, which have an objective ability to pay based on minimal equity requirement, robots should be able to access sufficient funds in order to be in a position to face tax liabilities themselves. In other words, the ability to pay of the AI entity would consist in a capacity to make payments. In a nutshell, we have suggested that a tax capacity could be designed by a legislator for an autonomous and identified AI system with a financial capacity, which would also include smart robots.[74] This new AI taxable unit, defined as an AITU, would benefit from the right to dispose of a financial capacity, but under limits designed by the law, and subject to the obligations to pay the relevant taxes, under a human control.

Currently, granting tax capacity to AI or robots appears to raise many legal and technical difficulties, but in the near future, the technological problems could be solved. An AI system could include processes designed to levy a tax on the flow of funds transferred via the AI activities. After all, direct electronic commerce is also held online, without any physical transfer of orders, goods or payments. We do not see why AI could not be designed to include a tax component for an AI or robot transaction occurring electronically. Should an AI system have sufficient autonomy in the decision-making process, it could be regarded as having an ability to automatically assess, compute and levy the tax on the activities subject to tax.

As another alternative, cryptocurrencies and Blockchain could also be used to levy a tax on AI. The transactions could be secured via Blockchain, and the tax could be levied not only on traditional currencies but on other forms of electronic or cryptocurrencies. In our view, it will be increasingly necessary to address this issue with the development of the autonomy of AI. Furthermore, with such developments, we might encounter significant difficulties in designing proper ownership, or simply attribution rules for AI and robotics. If the

---

[71]   See supra, p. 21 ff.
[72]   See supra, p. 29 ff.
[73]   See supra, p. 30 ff.
[74]   See supra, p. 31.

AI belongs to the assets of a company, the situation remains practicable. But what happens if the functionalities of AI are shared by various entities, closely related or not? Who would be the owner of such an AI system? Who should pay the tax attributable to the activities of AI? The idea to grant a tax liability to an AI system would at least offer a possibility of raising tax on the activities held by an entity recognized as a tax subject, to the extent it has sufficient control and autonomy as to the use of the funds generated from its activity.

Similar to the problems experienced with the emergence of corporations as new taxpayers, we would have to find viable solutions to multiple delicate questions. In particular, the type of tax which could be relevant (revenue tax, consumption tax, VAT or excise tax) should be determined. If we look at the tax system in general, various taxable transactions could be contemplated: (1) the acquisition of revenue (income aspect), (2) the ownership of funds (sparing aspects), and (3) the use of revenue (consumption aspect).

B. Artificial Intelligence Income or Revenue Tax

An AI taxable unit acquiring income (or revenue as the case may be) from its activity could be subject to a revenue tax. The design of such tax as a *profit* tax would correspond to legal entities such as corporations. In this case, similar to corporations, the taxable AI either use these profits for future investments or distribute them to its owners. In the latter case, double economic taxation should be avoided, and the potential income (profit) taxes levied on revenues distributed by the AI entity to its owners should be taken into account.

Another perspective, more in line with the principle of neutrality between human workers and the AI replacing them, could be to levy an *income* tax on AI. However, this solution has some limits. Indeed, the comparison to humans is limited to the impact of the market. As far as we are aware, AI or robots have no children to raise, no need for pensions, no healthcare problems and no rent to pay.

It would still need to be discussed whether the concept of income, as such, is a suitable indicator for the purposes of taxing an AI system. As the delicate analysis of a potential ability of AI to pay has shown, AI would only have an ability to pay to the extent that a financial capacity could be attributed to them. Companies, by contrast, have minimum capital and equity requirements, based on commercial law, with restricted possibility for dividend distribution before sufficient reserves are booked in the balance sheet. In addition, AI, in principle, would not be exposed to costs. Further, they would not be in a position to defer or modify the timing of realization of income.

The tax therefore should be based on the *gross revenue*, with no deduction allowed. In addition, AI could also be required to levy the AI usage tax described above, as a remuneration for work performed. In other words, we could design a specific algorithm to ensure that the revenue tax (on imputed salary) would be levied automatically by AI on a regular basis, during the activity period. In this case, the AI usage tax would be included in the AI revenue tax. Should we introduce an income tax on AI or robots as workers in a firm, the system should be coordinated with the tax already paid by the company. Indeed, a *double taxation* risk could exist. In particular, should we consider that the use of AI is taxable at the level of the enterprise (imputed salary) it would be inconsistent to tax this salary again at the AI level. This double taxation could be solved by traditional methods already in place under most systems of corporate taxation. For example, the salary attributable to AI and for which AI would have to pay a revenue tax should logically be considered as deductible at the level of the enterprise. In this case, the tax system would be neutral between a human and an AI system.

The new rules targeting *platforms* facilitating the intermediation of supplies of goods or services, developed so far in the VAT context, could also serve as a blueprint for future AI taxation for direct tax purposes.

C.   Artificial Intelligence Systems as Owner: An Artificial Intelligence Capital Tax

In case the implementation of a legal personality to AI entails recognition of the right to own or at least control assets, a taxation of *capital* could be introduced. In some States, such as Switzerland, resident individuals are subject to a cantonal wealth tax on the value of their net assets on 31 December of each year. In addition, a cantonal capital tax is also levied, under the same logic, on the net equity resulting from the balance sheet of corporations. Other countries levy a wealth tax, which is restricted to some specific assets. This is the case in France, following the 2017 reform, which abolished the global wealth tax (so-called "impôt de solidarité sur la fortune"; ISF), and replaced it with a tax on real estate. Following this approach, the net value of assets owned or controlled by a robot could be subject to a specific asset tax.

These types of taxes are in general subject to criticism. First, wealth taxes are problematic because they tax capital and not an increase of revenue resulting from a business activity. Certain commentators argue that a wealth tax could be an infringement to the constitutional right of ownership if they alter the substance of the net capital of an individual.[75] For example, in a landmark case, the German Constitutional Court held that the wealth tax was unconstitutional to the extent that it exceeds a burden of 50 percent of the total income

---

[75]   Tipke Klaus, Die Steuerrechtsordung, vol. 2, 2nd ed., 2003, p. 914 ff, 951.

of an individual.[76] However, some of the constitutional arguments against a wealth tax in general have a different flavor here. Indeed, while an AI autonomous system could become a legal entity, it appears problematic to grant them constitutional rights, conceived as rights of defense against state actions, as for humans. A limit on such a tax could be based on efficiency criteria, such as avoiding a prohibited burden based on sound economic practices.

D.   Artificial Intelligence Subject to VAT

1.   Artificial intelligence systems as taxable persons

We have seen above that activities carried out by AI are already subject to VAT, at least in countries that levy such a tax.[77] But in this case, entities subject to tax are the enterprises using AI to render taxable supplies of goods or services (e.g. factories building cars with industrial robots, online sellers using robot advisors or bots, etc.). With the introduction of a tax personality, at a later stage, an AI system *per se* could become VAT taxable persons.

The author considers that this consequence offers an interesting possibility for at least two reasons. First, contrary to income tax, the person subject to VAT does not necessarily need to have a legal personality. Indeed, for VAT purposes, entities subject to VAT may include enterprises without legal personality, such as partnerships or single enterprises, to the extent that they exercise a regular and independent activity and appear in the market as such. In other words, we would not need the recognition of an AI system as legal persons to treat them as VAT taxpayers. It is however necessary that they exercise their activity independently, which implies sufficient autonomy, the capacity to make decisions and to interact with others. In our view, the necessary control or supervision of the activities of AI should not represent an obstacle to such recognition. Second, the complexity raised by the principle of ability to pay, which we have discussed above for income tax, does not apply with the same intensity for VAT purposes. In the latter case, the ability to pay should be analyzed differently because an AI entity would receive a consideration in exchange for their taxable supplies. In other words, in most cases, AI would indeed "benefit" from a stream of funds as a counterpart for their supply of goods or services, which they may use for various purposes, following their autonomous decisions. An AI taxable entity would not, unlike the robot usage tax model, have to report income on a hypothetical revenue, such as an

---

[76]   Tipke (2003), p. 941; German Constitutional Court ("Verfassungsgericht"), judgment of 22 June 1995, BVerfGE 93, 1996, p. 121 ff.

[77]   See supra, p. 105 ff.

imputed salary or an income, corresponding to what would have been paid to a human.

In view of the above, with the introduction of a liability to collect VAT, an AI system could become subject to VAT and be required to charge the output VAT on their taxable supplies. The requirement of the AI autonomy, identity, financial capacity and human control, mentioned above, should also be met.[78] An AI taxable unit should thus have the right to credit the input VAT on its purchases. Technological developments could implement automated systems of tax collections (on the output and input sides) which could be secured by Blockchain or other technology.

In the EU, the recent obligations towards *platforms*, facilitating specific transactions, notably digital services or distant sales, could serve as a blueprint for a future taxation of AI or robots subject to VAT. So far, the obligations linked with the platforms are carried out by humans who control it. Eventually, with the development of technology, AI systems could be programmed to perform automatically these tasks, charge, collect and pay the net VAT to the competent tax authorities.

2.   Characterization and localization issues

Should an AI unit become a taxable person, the next issue would be to define the character of transactions performed by AI and their place of supply. In this context, the question is whether, following the neutrality principle mentioned above, supply of goods or services rendered by AI systems, as taxable persons, should be characterized in the same way as similar transactions carried out by humans or corporations. At first glance, we would tend to favor a solution based on the principle of neutrality. In addition, under VAT guiding principles,[79] an analysis of the features of the transaction should be based on the perspective of the average consumer.

We have already analyzed above the characteristics of transactions in AI, from the current VAT standpoint.[80] Similar considerations should apply here, subject however to the specific features of an AI system as a taxable entity. The guiding principle should remain the comparability of the supply with "traditional" supplies, from the standpoint of the customer. Hence, AI that provides medical services should be treated similarly to doctors, to the extent this characterization prevails under the perspective of the patient. An AI system

---

[78]   See supra, p. 29 ff.

[79]   Under VAT, according to the guiding principle of neutrality, similar goods or services, competing with each other, should not be treated differently, from the perspective of a "typical consumer", ECJ, C-219/13, *K Oy*, 11 September 2014, para. 25; C-479/13, *EU Commission v. French Republic*, 5 March 2013, para. 25.

[80]   See supra, p. 115 ff.

offering legal, accounting or banking services should therefore also fall under the respective categories. However, especially with the evolution of technology, the activities of AI will tend to differentiate more and more from human activities, and it would probably appear unsafe, if not hazardous, to compare AI activities with equivalent human tasks. Eventually, specific rules might become necessary. The various changes in the EU localization rules in digital transactions offer a good example of the difficulties of designing an adequate place of supply and implementing this rule with foreign online suppliers.[81]

E.   Artificial Intelligence System as Consumer

Eventually, AI, as taxable persons, might even become consumers. It would imply that an AI tax unit would have to pay, or account for, the supply of goods or services provided by enterprises or even other AI systems as VAT taxpayers. From an economic standpoint, and also taking account of the principle of neutrality, transactions offered to such AI should also entail VAT consequences. We could even imagine a world where most transactions occurred between robots. As Harari recently wrote: "It is far from certain that the future economy will need us even as consumers."[82] In this case, a global VAT system where AI, as a taxable person, would charge VAT on their supplies to other AI systems, acting as consumers appears possible.

F.   Artificial Intelligence Subject to Social Security

Finally, AI systems, as taxable entities, could also be required to charge social security contributions on revenue received, or attributed to them. AI would then be treated like independent self-employed individuals or any enterprise (in corporate form or not) entering into independent activities. It would appear appropriate – from a policy standpoint – that automation would thus contribute to financing social security which would then help unemployed workers.

G.   Summary

Various alternatives are possible for implementing a tax on AI.

If we try to summarize the evolution of the tax system, for direct tax purposes, we see that we could distinguish the following three phases: (1) taxation of the use of AI at the level of the enterprise, (2) taxation of an AI system as PE, and (3) taxation of an AI unit.

---

[81]   See supra, p. 118 ff.
[82]   Harari (2018), pp. 35, 36.

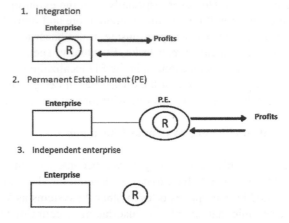

Figure 9.1   Direct tax – 3 phases

For VAT tax purposes, by contrast, we could distinguish the following four phases: (1) taxation of the use of AI at the level of the enterprise, (2) taxation of an AI system as PE, (3) taxation of an AI unit as independent enterprise (subject to tax, but without legal personality), and (4) taxation of an AI unit as an independent legal person.

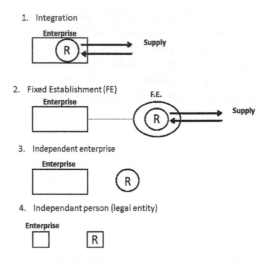

Figure 9.2   VAT – 4 phases

IV. OTHER STRATEGIES: CHANGING THE TAX SYSTEM

A. Increasing the Corporate Profit Tax Rate

It is indisputable that, by using AI technology, we foster innovation and productivity. Hence, some argue that AI should bring in more profits, which should compensate the income tax loss on the side of human workers. We have, however, demonstrated that this argument does not stand up to criticism since the system is not tax neutral between workers and AI. In addition, the share of the profit tax in comparison to the tax on workers or other taxes, notably VAT, is really not at all significant. It is highly disputable that the corporate tax might simply cover the loss. This is even more so because the current trend in corporate tax goes in the opposite direction. As already shown, there is a global trend to reduce the corporate profit tax rate. The most remarkable example is the 2017 US corporate tax reform, which has implemented a decrease of the rate from 35 percent to 21 percent.

It follows that another possibility for compensating the losses of taxation on labor could be to increase corporate tax. However, simply increasing corporate profit tax in order to address the impact of automation would in our view not be a proper solution. Indeed, it would impact all companies subject to tax, including those using human workers. Raising the rate could be in contradiction with the objective purpose of the increase, which is to compensate for the loss of human workers. In addition, corporate tax may be more easily impacted by amortization deductions in robotics. Indeed, the increase of the corporate tax rate, combined with accelerated deduction in favor of investment in automation, would give even more incentive in favor of such deduction.[83]

Finally, this position, as the development of the digital economy has shown, does not consider the high possibility of tax avoidance, aggressive tax planning and transfer pricing tactics in corporate taxation. As demonstrated by the recent initiatives and debate on the proper taxation of the digital economy,[84] a consensus is hard to find. The corporation profit tax rate, notably the marginal tax rate, hardly corresponds to the effective rate paid by MNEs engaged in digital economy. The increase of the corporate tax rate is easy to justify from a political standpoint, but the tax burden may be shifted abroad more easily than other types of taxes.

---

[83] Abbott and Bogenschneider (2018), p. 29.
[84] See supra, p. 75 ff.

B.   Increasing the Taxation of Capital Income

As demonstrated above, the development of AI and automation in general on the labor market may cause an important loss of revenue from labor in favor of capital owners. It may even occur that most of the profits from automation would go to the owners of AI or robots.[85]

To address that issue, another alternative would be to modify the taxation of capital income. It appears that most tax systems around the world tend either to discriminate against labor income in comparison to capital income, or at least entail favorable rules for capital income. For instance, in many countries, labor income is subject to progressive tax rates, while income from capital, notably capital gains, are either subject to a lower tax or, like in Switzerland, exempted from tax to the extent they belong to private wealth.[86] Labor income is also subject to social security contributions, or to payroll takes, like in the United States. By contrast, capital income, such as dividends, interests or capital gains usually do not contribute to social security. The same is true for corporate profit tax, which is in most cases exempted from any social security levies.

As a consequence, some commentators suggest – instead of taxing AI or robots – reforming the tax system in order to bring back parity between income from labor and capital.[87] Various solutions may be contemplated. *First*, the income tax on labor could be reduced. In particular, while in most systems, the social security contributions on labor are shared equally between employers and workers, a repeal of such a tax would arguably make sense because this administrative additional cost may create an incentive to use AI instead of human workers.[88] This solution would at the same time increase States' revenues accruing from labor income and the financing issues would thus remain unsolved. *Second*, income from capital could be subject to a comparable burden of tax than the one on labor, and also to social security contributions. *Third*, the preferential treatment of capital gains toward ordinary income could also be modified. *Finally*, the introduction of a wealth tax could also be contemplated.[89]

---

[85]   Brynjolfsson Erik and McAfee Andrew, Race Against the Machine: How the Digital Revolution is Accelerating Innovation, Driving Productivity, and Irreversibly Transforming Employment and the Economy, New York 2011, p. 33 f. Schwab Klaus, The Fourth Industrial Revolution, World Economic Forum, Crown, Digital Frontier Press, New York 2016, p. 92.

[86]   It should be noted, however, that Switzerland levies a cantonal wealth tax on worldwide assets of resident individuals.

[87]   Mazur Orly, Taxing the Robots, 46 Pepperdine Law Review 2018, p. 33 ff.

[88]   Mazur (2018), p. 27; Abbott and Bogenschneider (2018), p. 21.

[89]   Mazur (2018), p. 30.

In our view, the idea of finding a more appropriate balance between the taxation of labor and capital income is fully justified. Some suggestions, however, are not necessarily adequate. For instance, and following the German or the Swiss experience, levying a wealth tax on individuals creates many issues from a constitutional standpoint (confiscatory effects) and is highly delicate on a political side. Furthermore, this tax tends to exacerbate competition between States and may trigger avoidance strategies from high net worth individuals, such as a change of residence. The revenues arising from wealth tax should also not be overestimated. In our view, if changes to the tax system have to be implemented, they should focus on the revenue and the consumption side. However, these solutions do not specifically address the disruption caused by AI and robotics in the labor market and tend to offer a more global approach. Should the scenario of a massive disruption in labor occur, the new economy requires a new tax system. Partial changes and/or modifications to the existing system would indisputably not be sufficient. In view of the above, the solution consisting in taxing AI would represent a more adequate approach, given that such approach focuses on the core issue: the development of AI and its implementation into robotics.

C.   Taxing the Digital Economy

In Chapter 7, we analyzed various alternatives in relation to the taxation of the digital economy, either at the OECD, the UN, the EU or under the domestic laws of some States. In part, this taxation development may also be viewed as a solution to tax activities generated by AI and robotics. Indeed, most of these enterprises use AI for their activities, and algorithms are implemented to generate sales, advertising and digital services, or to adapt the business models in accordance with the data generated by users.

This approach, in a way, goes in the same direction as taxing the activities of AI but, as such, is not specifically designed for these. As we have demonstrated above it is more an indirect way of addressing automation. The purpose of these rules is to allocate differently the right to tax between the residence State of the enterprise in the digital economy and the source State, where the users and consumers also contribute to the realization of the turnover of the enterprise. The EU digital service tax, as a transitory solution, aims at taxing revenues generated from certain digital activities in which users in an EU State play a role in value creation. The digital PE would rely on a concept independent from a physical presence and be based instead on a digital presence in the source State. In addition, the digital service taxes introduced in some States would level the playing field between foreign and local domestic online sellers in order to create a similar taxation burden for both comparable situations. The UN new Article 12B represents, however, a closer approximation of a tax on automation since it would allocate more taxing rights to the source State for automated digital services.[90]

By contrast, recent developments seem to depart from the initial perspective of taxing the digital economy. Indeed, amount A of the OECD pillar-one solution now applies to large MNEs in all economic sectors (apart from extraction and financial activities) with a global turnover above 20 billion euros. Should the system be implemented globally, a multilateral convention would be adopted and would require all parties to remove all DST and "other relevant similar measures" with respect to all companies and to commit not to introduce such measures.[91]

D.   Taxing Data or Information

Another approach, which is gaining increasing attention, is to focus, not on the profits of MNEs, but on the data collected by them, which represent as such a value that the tax system fails properly to include. Indeed, new business models of the digital economy offer to MNEs the possibility of making wide use of data arising from users and consumers, either through advertising, marketing or other forms of profitable activities. Taxing data or information could also be seen as another system to attract activities of algorithms using these data, for the purpose of value creation.[92] In this context, we could also cite the suggestion, mentioned above, from Korinek which favors a taxation of the software that is running on robots because of the information embodied on them that generates rents.[93] It seems that some US States have proposed "data mining tax regimes" which would target businesses that extract and monetize data from users in their jurisdictions.[94]

In our view, a taxation of data could be designed to apprehend the added value generated by the use of big data by AI systems and robots as production factors.[95] The enhanced productivity resulting from the automated collection, analysis and treatment of big data in order to generate profits (machine learning, LLMs, etc.) could be subject to tax. As a result of the huge amount

---

[90]   See supra, p. 79 ff.

[91]   OECD/G20, Statement on a Two-Pillar Solution to Address the Tax Challenges Arising from the Digitalization of the Economy, 8 October 2021.

[92]   Brauner Yariv, Taxation of Information and the Data Revolution, SSRN paper, March 2023, p. 99 ff.

[93]   Korinek (2020), p. 256.

[94]   See Appleby Andrew, Subnational Digital Services Taxation, 81 Maryland Law Review 2021, p. 8.

[95]   For more details, see Oberson Xavier and Yacicioglou Efsun Alara, Taxation of Big Data, Springer, Cham, Switzerland, 2023.

of data received, an AI system could progress and adapt its behavior. Taxing data would thus allow taxation of the raw material required by AI to perform its tasks. From this perspective, some commentators have also suggested a "robot-data tax", which would correspond to a tax levied on the collection of data by algorithms and AI.[96] This approach focuses more on the *input side*, namely on data considered as raw material generating value for future profits of MNEs. It would, however, be different from the taxes on AI that we are suggesting here and would focus more on the *output* side. First, taxing the use of AI, as an imputed income for the enterprise using AI instead of human workers, generates an additional profit corresponding to a hypothetical salary (or service income). Second, a tax on AI systems would grant to the AI autonomous system and smart robots a tax capacity (as a new entity subject to tax) and thus apprehend the profits or income at the output side, for transactions carried out by those AI systems.

E.   An Education Tax

Vikram Chand *et al* have argued against the idea of a robot tax, favoring instead an education tax that could be used to train and help workers adapt to changes in the economy due to automation.[97] Under their proposal, government should monitor the impact of AI and robots on a regular basis and, should the trend indicate that jobs are disappearing, they should raise funds from an earmarked education tax. The revenues from such a tax would be used to finance and foster professional educational programs. This tax would be levied on all individuals and businesses that exceed a certain threshold.

This idea is not recommended here. In our view, this tax would go in the wrong direction. First, it would represent a shift from taxing automation (which is a form of capital) to taxing labor.[98] Second, it puts a burden on education as opposed to AI and robots which, as we argue, include a value creation and an ability to pay that the tax system should recognize.

---

[96]   Oberson and Yacicioglou (2023), p. 147 ff.

[97]   Chand Vikram, Kostic Svetislav and Reis Ariene, Taxing Artificial Intelligence and Robots: Critical Assessment of Potential Policy Solutions and Recommendation for Alternative Approaches, 12 World Tax Journal 2020, n. 4.

[98]   See also Shome Parthasarathi, Taxation of Robots, ADB The Governance Brief, Issue 44 2022, p. 3.

10. Taxing artificial intelligence from an international perspective

I.   TRENDS

As described above, automation is causing major changes in all economic sectors. From an international standpoint, as also analyzed under the OECD/G20 BEPS Action 1 Final Report, the increased productivity of automated factories makes it possible for MNEs to consider moving back manufacturing activities from offshore locations with lower labor costs to where most of the customers are.[1] In addition, the development of AI may reduce costs, notably by making factories less labor intensive, especially in small factories and workshops which will also be able to benefit from automation. As a consequence, further lowering the costs would also encourage the trend of bringing manufacturing activities closer to customers.[2]

Increased use of robotics would have a tremendous international impact. In Chapter 6, we already analyzed the application of international tax law rules to the *current* use of AI. The specificities of the digital economy and the difficulties of defining appropriate international tax rules were then discussed in Chapter 7. In this chapter, we will focus on the potential international tax consequences of introducing a taxation of AI, following the options described in Chapter 9. In this context, we will concentrate on two issues: (1) the application of DTT to an AI usage tax or a specific AI tax, and (2) the challenges raised by potential avoidance behaviors and the need for a global consensus on such new controversial taxes.

---

[1]   OECD/G20 BEPS Project, Addressing the Tax Challenges of the Digital Economy, Final Report, 2015, Action 1, n. 90, p. 44.

[2]   OECD/G20 BEPS Project, Addressing the Tax Challenges of the Digital Economy, Final Report, 2015, Action 1, n. 91.

II.   TREATY ASPECTS

A.   Introduction

Under current law, the use of AI, notably in the framework of the digital economy, already raises many issues, which are currently being discussed at the OECD level, under Action Plan 1. In addition, the EU and many States have introduced or proposed unilateral measures in order either to level the playing fields between foreign and local online suppliers or to design new attribution rules between the residence and the source State for profits stemming from online activities, including those of robotics.[3] Delicate international issues, such as the definition of the PE concept, characterization, allocation or transfer pricing rules are currently being discussed.

Should, however, new types of taxes be introduced, such as taxes on the use of AI or on AI as such, specific and new treaty issues would come into play. These taxes would in most cases apply to complex cross-border situations, where robots implementing AI and the companies owning or using them could be sited in different States. In order to analyze the application of DTT to AI taxes, we will distinguish between the two phases described above, namely (1) the introduction of a tax on the use of AI and (2) the tax on AI as such.

B.   AI Users' Taxes

1.   Introduction

AI taxes may be levied on the use of AI. The introduction of such taxes does not require recognition of a tax personality for AI. Such taxes, as we have seen, will be applied to the enterprises (corporations or partnerships) that use them. In such context, the persons benefitting from treaty protection would not be AI – which lacks a tax personality – but the enterprises (corporations, partnerships, single entity) that qualify as persons within the meaning of Article 1 OECD Model, to which income covered by the treaty may be attributable.

2.   Artificial intelligence usage taxes covered by a DTT

a.   Treaty definition

To determine which of the various models of AI taxes fall under the scope of DTT, we first need to clarify the concept of *tax* which is relevant for the purpose of a DTT.

---

[3]   See supra, p. 86 ff.

According to Article 2 OECD Model, the Convention applies to taxes on income and on capital. The taxes under the scope are "all taxes imposed on total income, on total capital, or on elements of income or of capital, including tax on gains from the alienation of movable or immovable property, taxes on the total amounts of wages or salaries paid by enterprises, as well as taxes on capital appreciations" (Article 2 paragraph 2 OECD Model). However, "social security charges, or any other charges paid where there is a direct connection between the levy and the individual benefits to be received, shall not be regarded as taxes on the total amount of wages".[4] The convention also applies to "any identical or substantially similar taxes that are imposed after the date of signature of the Convention in addition to, or in place of, the existing taxes" (Article 2 paragraph 4 OECD Model).

It follows that the DTT applies to income and capital (wealth) tax. The word *tax* is, however, not defined in the DTT. It is not disputed that this term applies to tax ("impôt", "Steuer"), in a traditional sense, which does not include fees ("taxe causale", "Abgabe") that are levied as a consideration for services rendered by a State.[5] In other words, taxes are compulsory levies, paid unconditionally, i.e. without any counterpart or specific advantages granted by the State to the taxpayer. The specific method of levying the tax is also irrelevant. It may be levied by direct assessment, at source, in the form of surcharges, or as an additional tax.[6]

Income and *capital taxes* are defined in broad terms. In general, the use of the revenues stemming from income or capital (wealth) tax is without importance for the characterization.[7] Indeed, the DTT applies to taxes on income and on capital imposed not only on behalf of a State, but also of its political subdivisions or local authorities, irrespective of the manner in which they are levied (Article 2 paragraph 1 *in fine* OECD Model). Taxes on total or elements of income and capital are also within the scope. Therefore, individual income tax, payroll taxes, profit taxes on companies and capital gains taxes on movable or immovable property are all included.

By contrast, indirect taxes, such as turnover taxes, GST, VAT, customs duties or excise taxes are excluded. The same applies to social security contributions, or similar charges, to the extent there is a "direct connection between the levy and the individual benefits to be received".[8] This condition is also

---

[4]   OECD Commentary, n. 3 at Art. 2.
[5]   Dubut Thomas, Chapter 2 Impôts visés, in: Danon Robert et al. (eds), Modèle de Convention fiscal, OCDE concernant le revenu et la fortune, 2014, p. 85 ff., n. 25 at Art. 2 OECD Model.
[6]   OECD Commentary, n. 2 at Art. 2.
[7]   Dubut (2014), n. 32 at Art. 2 OECD Model.
[8]   OECD Commentary, n. 3 at Art. 2.

a confirmation of the traditional concept of tax used under DTT. A connection between the levy and the individual benefits demonstrates a link between the contributions and a specific advantage from the State, a feature which goes against the nature of a tax.

The concept of "income" or "capital" is, however, not defined in the treaty. In general, income taxes are based on flows, while capital taxes are levied on stock figures.[9] As a rule, *income* will refer to the *Haig-Simons-Schanz* definition and correspond to the net accretion of wealth during a taxable period.[10] By contrast, *capital* reflects the net amount of wealth of a taxpayer at a precise moment in time, typically 31 December. In particular, it should be noted that income tax is usually based on the ability to pay of the recipient of the payment.[11] The purpose of an income tax is indeed to charge part of the economic capacity of an income earner. By contrast, consumption taxes, which in our view are also based on the principle of ability to pay, are levied on the economic capacity of the consumer.[12] Hence, consumption taxes, including turnover taxes, seek to "capture the spending power of the payer".[13] It follows that the analysis of the purpose of the tax is crucial in order to determine the precise scope of Article 2 OECD Model DTC. Since consumption and turn-over taxes are outside the scope of DTT, the relevant question will notably consist of analyzing whether the purpose of the tax is to address the economic capacity of the recipient, and not of the payor.[14]

It is interesting to note that the issue of whether "fictious income", namely taxable revenue arising from imputed benefits, where there is not a net accretion of wealth, qualifies as income for tax treaty purposes, has also been discussed.[15] The main example, as we have seen, is the imputed theoretical rent for homeowners, which is considered by some countries as a taxable income. In our view, there is little doubt that such income, which is levied for example under the Swiss federal and cantonal harmonization tax law, falls under the scope of treaties. The imputed rent represents an income, which economically corresponds to the amount of rent that the owner of a house or apartment would

---

[9] Ismer Roland and Jescheck Christoph, The Substantive Scope of Tax Treaties in a Post-BEPS World: Article 2 OECD MC (Taxes Covered and the Rise of New Taxes), Intertax The Netherlands, 2017, p. 384.

[10] Ismer Roland and Blank Alexander, Article 2 Taxes covered in: Ekkehart Reimer and Alexander Rust, Klaus Vogel on Double Taxation Conventions, 5th ed, Wolters Kluwer, the Netherlands, 2022, n. 34 at Art. 3.

[11] Ismer and Jescheck (2017), p. 384.

[12] Oberson Xavier, Droit fiscal Suisse, 5th ed., Helbing & Lichtenhan, Basel 2021, p. 42.

[13] Ismer and Jescheck (2017), p. 384.

[14] Ismer and Jescheck (2017), p. 384.

[15] Ismer and Blank (2022), n. 37 at Art. 2.

have been required to pay in similar circumstances. In the same vein, some commentators concur with the position and argue that leaving the taxation of imputed rent outside the scope of DTT would appear "doubtful", since the consumption potential may well increase the economic power of the owner.[16]

Based on these premises, we may now try to ascertain the extent to which AI usages taxes fall under the scope of a DTT.

b.   *Application to artificial intelligence usage taxes*

A treaty will apply to any new taxes which are identical or "substantially" similar to existing taxes covered by a DTT (Article 2 paragraph 4 OECD Model).

Therefore, arguably, some of the models of AI usage tax described above could indeed fall under the scope of double taxation treaties. This is particularly true for the alternative of taxation on the *imputed salary* arising from using AI instead of human workers that we recommend. In our view, the tax would be levied on income or profits generated by the enterprise from using AI and thus avoiding salary expenses for human workers. Like a homeowner being spared the necessary payment of the rent in order to live in his or her home, the enterprise would derive an economic benefit by avoiding salary payments. In addition, if we apply the purpose test described above, it seems clear that the goal of the tax is to capture the economic capacity of the *recipient* of the imputed income. By taxing the use of AI, part of the increased economic capacity of an enterprise is charged. Therefore, such imputed income (profit) tax would in our view still fall under the category of income tax for treaty purposes.

The application of a DTT is more questionable for the model of *automation* taxes that we have discussed above. In this case, the tax would at first glance follow the same purpose as the tax on imputed salary. In addition, in at least one of the alternatives described above, it would be levied on profits arising from the use of automation instead of workers. The method of computation would however be different from traditional profit taxes and rely on a ratio of automation in comparison to human workers. As such this particularity would not necessarily be detrimental because, according to the OECD Model, the method of levying the tax is immaterial. It follows that these automation taxes, to the extent that they are levied on profits of companies, could also fall under the scope of the DTT. Under this perspective, the model proposed by Abbot and Bogenschneider, of a so-called self-employment tax, could be regarded as a special tax on profits, covered by a DTT because the ratio is still based on the profits in comparison to the gross employee compensation expenses. By

---

[16]   Ismer and Blank (2022), n. 37 at Art. 2.

contrast, William Meisel's proposal, which relies on a ratio based on gross revenues, in comparison to the number of employees, seems to adopt a different perspective. His approach, described as a "payroll tax on computers", tends not to levy the tax on the profits of the company but more on turnover stemming from the use of automation instead of human workers.[17] Depending on their design, the presumptive taxes, also described by Dimitropoulo, could also be regarded as being covered by a DTT. Turnover taxes would notably not escape treaty coverage, and would be regarded as income tax if they still have some connection with corporation tax as such and have the possibility of being credited against the corporate profit tax for avoiding double taxation.[18] An asset tax could also be regarded as a capital tax, pursuant to Article 22 OECD Model DTC.[19] In most cases, in fact, for the application of a DTC, the issue would not focus on the character of such a tax, as an income or a capital tax, but on the applicable distribution rule.[20]

The *social security* contributions paid on the imputed salary due by using AI is also a special case. At first glance, it could be argued that, as a social security contribution, this tax should not fall under the scope of DTT. However, there is no effective link between the payment and the benefits to be received. On the contrary, to the best of our knowledge, robots will not benefit from social security pensions or future payments. By using AI systems in place of workers, the employer would contribute to social security for the benefits of human workers or persons having lost their jobs. As a consequence, the characterization of such social security payments is much closer to an income tax, falling under the scope of a DTT than social security contributions in the traditional sense of the term.

Finally, the *object* tax on robots, as well as the *fee* in consideration for the use or supervision of robots would clearly not be covered by a DTT.

3.   Allocation rules

We have seen that some possible models of AI usage taxes could fall under the scope of a DTT. The next issue would then be to define the appropriate

---

[17]   Meisel William, The Software Society, Trafford Publishing, United States 2014, p. 220; see also supra, p. 157 ff.

[18]   Dimitropoulou Christina, Robot Taxation: A Normative Tax Policy Analysis. Domestic and International Tax Considerations, PhD, University of Vienna 2023, p. 533.

[19]   Id., p. 530.

[20]   Dimitropoulo (2023), p. 529; in the same vein, Wattel Peter and Marres Ottmar, Characterization of Fictitious Income under OECD-Patterned Tax Treaties, European Taxation, the Netherlands, 2003, p. 67; with a different perspective, Lang Michael, "Fictitious Income and Tax Treaties" in: A Tax Globalist, Essays in Honor of Maarten J. Ellis, IBFD, the Netherlands, 2005, p. 34 ff.

allocation rule. For example, should we introduce the AI usage tax on imputed income, we might consider that the income subject to tax would be based on the amount of salary that should have been paid to human workers. Could we then consider this payment as income from employment, governed by Article 15 OECD Model? Under this system, however, it is the enterprise that would be subject to tax. Indeed, at this stage, the AI system would not be recognized as a legal person, or at least a taxable "person". The income would correspond to the economic advantage obtained by using automation, instead of human workers. In our view, under current law, such tax should be governed by Article 7 OECD Model.[21] It would qualify either as an additional profit tax on companies using AI, or income tax from independent activities performed within an enterprise, such as a partnership, a single enterprise or any independent enterprise without legal personality using AI.

The same conclusion would apply to some types of automation or presumptive taxes described above, to the extent that they may be regarded as income (profit) taxes, within the meaning of Article 2 OECD Model.

C.   A Tax on Artificial Intelligence Systems

1.   Introduction

The potential application of DTT to a tax on AI requires a different analysis. In this case, we would be faced with a recognition of an AI taxable unit or smart robot as a legal entity, or at least taxable persons. We have seen above that this issue has already been discussed at the EU level and in some States, such as Estonia. While so far this idea has been rejected, it is still carefully analyzed. We have argued above that this development could also lead to recognition of a tax capacity of AI.[22] In order for DTT to apply to those new types of AI taxes, the following conditions would have to be met. As we will see, first, it would require that AI and robots as such are recognized as persons under the scope of the DTT. Second, the question of the residence of AI would have to be determined. Third, the specific taxes into which AI should fall under the scope of DTT would have to be determined. Finally, the allocation rules would also have to be discussed.

2.   Artificial intelligence as "persons" under the scope of DTT

Should we introduce a tax on AI systems, as such, the AI taxable unit would thus become a taxpayer. For a DTT to apply to an AI entity, they would need

---

[21]   Same opinion, Dimitropoulo (2023), p. 530.
[22]   See supra, p. 29.

to be recognized as "persons", within the meaning of Article 1 paragraph 1 OECD Model.

Under a treaty following the OECD Model, the term *person* includes an individual, a company and any "other body of persons" (Article 3 paragraph 1 lit. a OECD Model). The definition is not exhaustive and is used in a wide sense.[23] This conclusion may also be drawn from the definition of a company, which, according to the Model is any body corporate or any entity that is treated as body corporate for tax purposes (Article 3 paragraph 1 lit. b OECD Model). It follows from these definitions that, as a whole, the term person includes "any entity that, although not incorporated, is treated as a body corporate for tax purposes".[24] As a consequence, a foundation or a partnership is regarded as a person. In addition, a body corporate is an entity which is: (1) incorporated and (2) to which the tax system attributes a legal capacity in a similar way to individuals, taking into account legal relationships which by nature belong to individuals.[25] What is relevant is not the legal capacity for private or public law purposes but "it is essential that the entity has legal capacity for tax purposes".[26] While it is sometimes disputed, it appears that the relevant law for the purpose of granting the legal tax capacity is the law of the place in which the body corporate is resident.[27] In addition, the entity – created as a body corporate – should be subject to a separate profit (income) tax.[28]

Enterprises, by contrast, are not regarded as persons. The term enterprise applies to the carrying on of any business (Article 3 paragraph 1 lit. c OECD Model). This term, which is not really defined in the Model, is not congruent to the term "person" as listed in Article 3 paragraph 1 lit. c OECD Model.[29] The person is the tax subject, and the enterprise is the object. In other words, it is not the enterprise which carries on the business but the person behind it.[30]

It follows that in order to be recognized as persons for tax treaty purposes, AI systems, to the extent they may be properly defined under the legal system,[31] should at least be granted some sort of *tax capacity* from the State of resi-

---

[23]   OECD Commentary, n. 2 at Art. 3.
[24]   OECD Commentary, n. 2 at Art. 3.
[25]   Rust Alexander, Article 3 General definitions, in: Ekkehart Reimer and Alexander Rust (eds), Klaus Vogel on Double Taxation Conventions, 5th ed., Wolters Kluwer, The Netherlands 2022, n. 27 at Art. 3.
[26]   Rust (2022), n. 27 at Art. 3.
[27]   OECD Commentary, n. 3 at Art. 3; Rust (2015), n. 27 at Art. 3.
[28]   Rust (2022), n. 29 at Art. 3.
[29]   Reimer Ekkehart, Article 3 General definitions, in: Ekkehart Reimer and Alexander Rust (eds), Klaus Vogel on Double Taxation Conventions, 5th ed., Wolters Kluwer, The Netherlands 2022, n. 41 at Art. 3.
[30]   Reimer (2022), n. 41 at Art. 3.
[31]   See supra, pp. 15, 18 ff.

dence. More precisely, they would have to be recognized as tax subjects for corporate, or income tax, and taxed separately from their owners, controllers or shareholders.

3.   Residence of artificial intelligence for DTT purposes

Should AI autonomous systems benefit from a tax capacity, and hence become persons for treaty purposes, they should also be regarded as residents from a contracting State to be able to claim treaty benefits.

Residence of a contracting State, according to Article 4 paragraph 1 OECD Model is the place where a person is liable to tax, under the law of that State, "by reason of his domicile, residence, place of management or any other criterion of a similar nature". Until recently, for persons other than an individual, such as a company, in case of conflict of residence between two States, the State in which the effective management resides would prevail (Article 4 paragraph 3 OECD Model). Under the BEPS Project, notably in Action 2 on hybrid arrangements, the issue of dual resident companies was addressed.[32] It appears that potential tax avoidance schemes of dual resident companies should be addressed on a case-by-case basis.[33] As a consequence, a change of Article 4 paragraph 3 OECD Model was suggested, in order to reflect this approach.[34] Such solution was endorsed by the Committee on Fiscal Affairs of the OECD.[35]

Hence the following new version of Article 4 paragraph 3 was adopted:

> Where by reason of the provisions of the paragraph 1 a person other than an individual is resident of both contracting states, the competent authorities of both Contracting States shall endeavor to determine by mutual agreement the Contracting State of which such person shall be deemed to be a resident for tax purposes of the Convention, having regards to the place of effective management, the place where it is incorporated or otherwise constituted and any other relevant factors. In the absence of such agreement, such person shall not be entitled to any relief or exemption from tax provided by the Convention expert to the extent and in such manner, as may be agreed upon by the competent authorities of the Contracting States (Article 4 paragraph 3 OECD Model).

---

[32]   OECD/G20, Neutralizing the Effects of Hybrid Mismatch Arrangements, Action 2, Final Report, 2015.

[33]   See Sakuth Konstantin, "The Concept of Corporate Tax Residence in Light of the Digital Economy" in: Ina Kerschner and Maryte Somare (eds), Taxation in a Global Digital Economy, Linde Verlag, Vienna 2017, p. 94; OECD/G20, Neutralising the Effects of Hybrid Mismatch Arrangements, Action 2, Final Report, 2015, p. 73.

[34]   See also OECD/G20, Preventing the Granting of Treaty Benefits in Inappropriate Circumstances, Action 6, Final Report (2015) p. 74.

[35]   OECD Commentary, n. 23 at Art. 4.

The determination of the place of residence for an AI autonomous system is a delicate issue, which requires careful analysis, based on all facts and circumstances. It appears however that the place of residence would depend greatly on the legal definition of AI applicable for tax purposes. We may, however, draw some analogies with companies, which are usually regarded as resident in the place of incorporation or the place of effective management. The latter concept usually refers to the place where the day-to-day business decisions are taken.[36] In case of residence conflicts for companies, the competent authorities would have to consider a series of factors,

> such as where the meetings of the person's board of directors or equivalent body are usually held, where the chief executive officer and directors or equivalent body are usually held, where the chief executive officer and other senior executives usually carry on their activities, where the senior day-to-day management of the person is carried on, where the person's headquarters are located, which country's laws govern the legal status of the person, where its accounting records are kept, whether determining that the legal person is a resident of one of the Contracting States but not of the other for the purpose of the Convention would carry the risk of an improper use of the provisions of the Convention, etc.[37]

It appears from this analysis that the relevant criteria, at least for companies, is the place where *humans* (directors, executives, accountants, etc.) manage the company. From that perspective, we could consider that for an AI system, we should also take into consideration the place where humans effectively control and supervise its activities. In the same vein, Daniel Smit argues that for the determination of the place of effective management, legal responsibility for any automated decision will ultimately still have to be allocated to human beings, as the ultimate owners of the automated entity.[38] This perspective, however, requires a differentiated analysis. In the case of companies, the presence of a board of directors is required by law. These directors have a legal responsibility to manage the company in accordance with corporate governance rules. Their names are usually recorded in public official gazettes. For AI, in some cases, it would often be extremely difficult to ascertain who is controlling the robots. Sometimes, even AI could be controlled by another AI or

---

[36] See for instance, Swiss Supreme Court, 4 December 2003 ("*BVI*" case), published in Swiss Tax Revue ("Steuer Revue" 2004, p. 524), in which a BVI offshore entity, active in oil trading, but effectively managed from Switzerland was treated as a Swiss resident entity for profit tax purposes, and taxed accordingly.

[37] OECD Commentary, n. 24.1 at Art. 4.

[38] Smit Daniel, "Flexibility, Mobility and Automation of Labour under Article 7 of the OECD Model? A First Conceptual Exploration" in: Weber Dennis (ed.), The Implications of Online Platforms and Technology for Taxation, IBFD Amsterdam 2023, p. 167.

robot resident in another State. We have mentioned above that eventually, AI could be completely autonomous and controlled by another AI.[39] It seems that the peculiarities of the technology involved probably require specific rules of determination of the residence of robots for treaty purposes. The principal test could rely on the place of effective use of the robots, but it should be adjusted in accordance with other factors, such as the presence of a register of robots, the place of supervision, or of the technological infrastructure, in particular.

De Lima Carvalho suggests adopting a different perspective. As a general rule, his policy prescription is to tax the income of autonomous AI (AAI) as though it were an individual.[40] Based on that premise, robots should not only have a taxable personality but a taxable residence. To define residence, De Lima Carvalho recommends a two-tier analysis. Following his approach, an AAI should first be considered as a resident of a given jurisdiction if, in a first-tier analysis, its primary place of business (PPB) is physically located in that jurisdiction.[41] If the PPB cannot be reasonably associated with such AAI, then, under the second-tier analysis, it would be regarded as a resident of a single virtual jurisdiction, which would require: (1) a blanket source taxation and (2) a harmonized approach for taxing income of that single virtual jurisdiction worldwide.[42] In other words, if there is no PPB, it would mean that no residence has been recognized and that the source jurisdiction would be allowed to tax at source.

This proposal has some merits. It demonstrates the difficulty of defining a proper place of residence for AI and robots. However, the analogy with the regime of individuals seems to go too far, at least at this stage. We prefer to keep the analogy with entities such as corporations and, based on that premise, define a proper rule of residence in accordance with the role of humans controlling or supervising AI. After all, AI and robots remain a technology embodied in software and machines, which remain mostly under human control. Our proposed definition of an autonomous AI taxable unit indeed includes a requirement of human control (which as such does not exclude autonomy). Should AAI, without human control, become the norm, other criteria focusing on the place of supervision or effective management could be put in place. But it remains true, after all, that autonomous AI could be placed anywhere. Focusing on the place of use of AI would become a solution, which would then lead us more towards taxation at source. The new provision of Article 12B UN

---

[39] See supra, p. 30 ff. See also, De Lima Carvalho Lucas, Spiritus Ex Machina: Ad-dressing the Unique BEPS Issues of Autonomous Artificial Intelligence by Using "Personality" and "Residence", 47 Intertax 2019, p. 430, 441.

[40] De Lima Carvalho (2019), p. 441.

[41] Id.

[42] Id.

Model already goes in this direction. The difficulty of defining the residence of AI should, however, not serve as a reason to simply reject the taxation of AI autonomous systems or robots for direct tax purposes.

4.   Artificial intelligence taxes covered by the treaty

As we have seen above, only income and capital taxes, including similar taxes, would fall under the scope of a DTT. The application of Article 2 DTT would clearly depend upon the types of taxes levied on AI.

Income is not defined under the treaty.[43] In general, as we have seen, most States tend to follow, sometimes in approximate ways, the so-called *Haig-Simons-Schanz* definition of income, as the net accretion of one's economic power during a certain period of time. This definition is recognized globally as a leading concept. While domestic law may offer differentiated views on the definition of income, it would usually correspond to its core elements. It is, however, debated among commentators whether the concept of income has to be defined in accordance with the laws of the contracting States or should be given an autonomous interpretation.[44] It seems that the latter interpretation should prevail, following leading commentators.[45]

In summary, for *individuals*, most States consider income as the net accretion of wealth during the taxable period, subject however to a requirement of realization. For *corporations*, usually, profit tax is generally assessed on the net profit arising from the profit and loss accounts, following tax or commercial accounting rules (subject to specific derogatory rules).

AI revenue taxes, depending on their design, could be regarded as income taxes for treaty purposes. Under the purpose test, income tax would tend to capture some of the economic capacity of robots replacing human workers. We have seen above that the concept of income could fit with difficulty for robots, based on a limited ability to pay. To try to capture some of the economic capacity of robots, like that of a corporation, for tax purposes, AI would be required to hold or control some financial means, in forms of equity or access to a fund. In any event, it seems that specific rules should be designed to take into account the peculiarities of a robot income tax.

Capital taxes are typically levied on wealth. Again, commentators are divided on whether the concept of capital has to be defined in accordance with the laws of the contracting States or should be given an autonomous meaning.[46] In addition, the concept of capital, for treaty purposes, is broad and

---

43   Dubut (2014), n. 39 at Art. 2.
44   Ismer and Blank (2022), n. 35 at Art. 2.
45   Ismer and Blank (2022), n. 35 at Art. 2.
46   Ismer and Blank (2022), n. 40 at Art. 2.

applies both to gross and net (taking into account deduction of debts) capital.[47] Following the majority view, we tend also to favor an autonomous interpretation. Under this line of thinking, a tax on the capital of an AI system could fall into the scope of the treaty.

5.   Allocation rules

Characterization of income derived from robots would raise new and delicate issues. The difficulties in defining proper characterization rules for income derived from the digital economy may serve as an illustration of the problems to come.[48] However, in our case, the situation will be exacerbated by the fact that AI or robots may interact physically with the environment in a physical form or electronically, including online.

In a first step, we may consider, to the extent that AI activities still bear some similarities to human actions (robot workers, sellers, advisors, etc.), that the application of allocation rules on robot taxes could be analyzed in accordance with the principle of *neutrality*. In other words, a comparison could be made between the revenue attributable to robots, with a tax capacity, and income received by humans for similar activities. To the extent that such a comparison appears practical and adequate, we could argue in favor of using comparable allocation rules. Hence, income attributable to robot workers on an assembly line of cars could be regarded as a salary, within the meaning of Article 15 OECD Model, should a similar characterization prevail for human workers. By contrast, payment to robot advisors, or consultant-providing services would, under the same line of reasoning, be governed by Article 7 OECD Model. In extreme cases, already discussed among commentators, under which some kind of legal intellectual property rights could be granted to AI or smart robots,[49] we might even consider applying Article 12 OECD Model. Indeed, this provision governs the allocation of royalty payments, which refers to

> "payments of any kind received as a compensation for the use of, or the right to use any copyright of literary, artistic or scientific work including cinematograph films, any patent, trade mark, design or model, plan, secret formula or process, or for information concerning industrial, commercial or scientific experience" (Article 12 paragraph 2 OECD Model).

---

[47]   Ismer and Blank (2022), n. 41 at Art. 2.

[48]   See Ohm Lenker, "Issues Regarding the Characterization of Income Derived by Digital Enterprises" in: Kerschner I./Somare M. (eds), Taxation in a Global Digital Economy, Linde Verlag, Vienna 2017, p. 212.

[49]   In this sense, Groffe Julie, "Robot et droit d'auteur" in: Les robots, objets scientifiques, objets de droits, Mare & Martin, Presses Universitaires de Sceaux, Paris, 2016, p. 205 ff.

Should AI replace humans or develop the capabilities of doing similar or at least comparable activities to humans, this solution would make sense.

Over time, however, this methodology may not be adequate. First, the specific nature of AI activities will render the comparison more and more problematic. Second, with the development of AI technologies, the features of activities might bear unique characteristics, so that the situation would have to be properly determined on a case-by-case-basis. Perhaps, in the long term, a new and specific allocation rule designed for AI activities would have to be designed.

In addition, challenging issues would have to be analyzed in the future, in case of cross-border transactions between AI and robots. Let's assume that a robot, regarded as a legal person in one State, enters into activities with another robot in another state. We have seen above that, already under current law, robots' infrastructure may fulfill the conditions of a PE. The evolution of this concept in the digital economy may even lead to the recognition of a significant digital presence as a new type of digital PE.

In these situations, we could be faced with the need to allocate profits between AI or robots, characterized as taxable persons, and robots as PE in other States. Not to mention transfer pricing issues between associated AI in different States. Going into these fascinating issues would go beyond the scope of our contribution and would require further research. Some guidance may, however, be found in the analysis of new suggested methods of allocations between head office and PE, in the digital economy.[50]

III.   THE NEED FOR AN INTERNATIONAL COORDINATION OF RULES

A.   Introduction

Introducing taxes on AI systems or the use of AI may exacerbate competition. This point has already been widely raised and belongs to one of the classical arguments against robot taxes.[51] On the one hand, countries with many human workers faced with job losses could be hard hit by automation and have to implement new tax policies to address this issue. On the other hand, some States could try to take advantage of these changes. In our view, it serves no purpose to try to hold back technological progress and innovation in the tax system. However, the potential massive revenue losses and the shift from labor to capital have to find an adequate and equitable solution.

---

[50]   See supra, p. 81 ff.
[51]   See supra, p. 45.

In the past, we have seen that, when faced with problematic and urgent international issues, notably in the field of taxation, the States, either at the UN, the OECD or the EU level, have been able to act rapidly and reach a level playing field. Two recent examples, namely the development of international exchange of information in tax matters, on the one hand, and the BEPS action plans, on the other hand, are good demonstrations of such successes. In view of the huge issues that the developments of automation raise in the design of a tax system in the future, it seems to us that some coordination and global analysis are necessary. Current works at the UN, the OECD and the EU level, on the taxation of digital economy, both for indirect and direct tax purposes, may offer a good example of potential global approaches.[52] In the past, the issues related to the taxation of cross-border electronic commerce also raised new and delicate characterization issues and have required the definition of a suitable rule of allocation of profits.[53] Eventually, some guidance and a consensus could be reached on a guiding principle. In particular, for VAT purposes, the so-called 1998 Ottawa framework on e-commerce transactions was finally endorsed by the EU, which was later implemented in a Directive on certain electronic supplied services, effective as of 1 July 2003.[54] On the taxation of profits of large MNEs, a consensus was reached, in 2021, within the IF with the two-pillar solution designed by the OECD. Its implementation, as far as the first pillar is concerned, remains subject to discussion, but the outcome reached, at least for the introduction of pillar two, already represents a landmark achievement.

These discussions should in our view focus on a coordinated perspective, both to design taxation of AI and robots from a domestic standpoint and to develop coordinated rules at the international level.

B.   Domestic Coordination

With the development of technologies, AI and robots will develop new models of activities and work in collaboration with humans or between AI systems. At the first stage, AI actions may be comparable with human activities of a similar

---

[52]   See in particular G20/OECD BEPS, Action 1, Final Report (2015), and Intermediary Report (2018); see also Zichittella Carlo, International Initiative in Addressing Challenges Posed by the Digital Economy in: Kerschner I./Somare M. (eds), Taxation in a Global Digital Economy, Linde Verlag, Vienna 2017, p. 3 ff.; Da Luz De Souza Jacqueline, Tax Treaty Policy in Addressing Challenges Posed by the Digital Economy in: Kerschner I./Somare M. (eds), Taxation in a Global Digital Economy, Linde Verlag, Vienna 2017, p. 25 ff.

[53]   See OECD, Treaty Characterization Issues Arising from e-commerce, July 2005.

[54]   Pathiyil Rathish, "e-Books and VAT" in: Kerschner I./Somare M. (eds), Taxation in a Global Digital Economy, Linde Verlag, Vienna 2017, p. 330.

nature. After all, a self-driving car replaces a chauffeur. The actions of industrial robots in assembly lines building cars or in warehouses packing books or toys ordered by customers still may be compared with human workers in factories.

Later, however, AI actions may become more complex and difficult to compare with existing models. First, AI systems are going to collaborate with each other, and with humans. In that case, the precise determination of their respective role in the value chain might become unfeasible, if not arbitrary. Second, the specific nature of "income" received by AI still requires some further clarification. As described above, the ability to pay of an AI entity is an objective concept, referring to its capacity of payment, which may not be compared with the subjective ability to pay of a human, which should also consider his or her personal situations and needs. Comparison between humans and AI, for tax purposes, in the future, may become inappropriate. It follows that States need to address those issues. A coordinated approach should take place, taking into account the global impact of automation on business models, corporations, enterprises and individuals, in order to design rules at the domestic level.

There are various *models* of AI taxes. Coordination between States on the most appropriate model could also be useful. The first stage, notably the AI usage tax model, appears to be an interesting solution, which still requires various policy choices, notably in the design and the framework of taxation (base and applicable rates). Some recommendations could also address whether the AI usage tax should be based, among other possibilities, on imputed income, follow the automation model or be based on production factors. The second stage, namely the introduction of a tax on AI, still requires further analysis. First, States should decide whether or not they agree to grant a tax capacity, and perhaps also a legal personality to an AI autonomous system, which should be clearly defined for that purpose. Second, the definition of the appropriate tax model of tax on AI would require careful analysis. Finally, the adequate use of the funds arising from the tax should also be determined.[55]

C.   International Coordination

AI and robots' activities, which are global by nature, will also require the design of coordinated rules on the application of double taxation treaties. We have seen above that the development of technology intensifies the complexity of characterization issues. The recognition of AI as taxpayers would further underline these difficulties. As a consequence, the application of allocation and transfer pricing rules might become quite controversial with, as a conse-

---

[55]   See infra, p. 203 ff.

quence, risks of double international taxation or double non-taxation, not to mention tax avoidance risks.

First, it should be recognized that existing treaty rules may offer an appropriate solution. After all, income arising from the use of AI may very well fall under Article 7 OECD Model and existing rules, like in e-commerce, might offer an adequate solution.

In the future, we might however need to reconsider existing rules; notably, should we introduce taxes on AI? Like the introduction more than a century ago of a legal personality for companies, the introduction of a taxation of AI, to the extent it may be properly defined, would represent a major change in the tax policy of all States. Such change would require balanced and coordinated solutions to ensure that treaty rules are met, notably of attribution of income or profits and international allocation rules between the new form of taxpayers, AI, on the one hand, and the other persons subject to tax, on the other hand, namely companies and humans. For instance, should one State recognize AI systems as persons subject to tax for treaty purposes, and another State treat them as transparent, we might be confronted with traditional international conflict of allocation issues, which could result in double or non-taxation.

It seems therefore necessary to define an international level playing field for the design of appropriate treaty rules. The recent difficulties in reaching a consensus on the delimitation of the taxing rights between domestic and source State in the area of the digital economy is a perfect example of the potential risks of failure in finding a consensus. Indeed, there is currently a dangerous trend of countries adopting unilateral rules, trying to avoid the application of treaties, to address domestic problems of a level playing field between foreign and local online suppliers, or in order to address urgent base erosion issues.[56]

Perhaps, in the future, a multilateral instrument, similar to the MLI designed to implement treaty rules of the BEPS Program, could also offer a proper framework to implement new rules on the taxation of AI.

---

[56]   OECD/G20 BEPS Project, Tax Challenges Arising from Digitalization, Interim Report, 2018, p. 134 ff.; Danon Robert, "Can Tax Treaty Policy Save Us? The Case of the Digital Economy" in: Arnold Brian (ed.), Tax Treaties after the BEPS Project. A Tribute to Jacques Sasseville, Canadian Tax Foundation, Toronto 2018, p. 83.

11. Financing the disruption and automation costs (notably universal basic income)

I. INTRODUCTION

Automation is likely to have a tremendous impact on the job market. While it is not disputed that AI and robotics will create new jobs, it is not clear whether sufficient new jobs would be created to replace the disappearing ones. In addition, in the long term, it is even foreseeable that many, if not most, activities traditionally carried out by humans could be performed by robots. In Chapter 9, we discussed in detail how the tax system could be modified in order to adapt to the changes caused by AI, either by taxing the use of AI, or AI autonomous systems, and/or create a level playing field between humans and robot workers. This new system would reintegrate in the tax base labor income attributable to AI activities, revenues allocated to AI and robots and consumption increasing therefrom.

Taxation of AI would also raise additional revenue for the State for financing the emerging and increasing cost of disruption. This chapter will examine how revenues stemming from the tax changes analyzed above (AI tax, reform of the tax system towards more capital income taxation, VAT) could be used to help human workers adapt to the new economy. Among various suggestions, two ideas require careful consideration. First, revenues could be used to help finance education, training and reconversion. Second, a universal basic income (UBI) could also be introduced.

II. FINANCING EDUCATION, TRAINING AND RECONVERSION

The impact of automation on the labor market is a matter of controversy. At least, it appears not to be in dispute that many routine and low-skilled jobs will disappear. Industrial robots have already replaced human workers in cars computer and shoe factories. Self-driving cars may soon create unemployment for truck or taxi drivers. Replacement of some activities by AI systems is not necessarily a bad development, since sometimes boring, routine, toxic or even dangerous tasks could now be carried out by machines. However, many workers will lose their jobs and need training and help to find new and more suitable jobs. Today, the precise impact of robotization on the labor market is difficult to determine. It is probable that many low-skilled jobs would still be necessary, either in collaboration with AI or robots, or as activities which require contact with a human (nurse, social assistant, trainers). Recent studies suggest that routine work is mostly at risk.[1] By contrast, some highly skilled jobs also face the risk of disruption. In the mid/long term, accountants, tax filers or radiologists, to name a few, might also be replaced by highly effective robots.[2] These workers will also have to adapt and train in other professions. In other words, both low- and high-skilled workers could be affected by automation, but for different reasons.

The tax system could therefore be designed to favor such educational, retraining and reconversion costs. Revenues from tax and social security contributions should provide sufficient funds to help finance education and training costs. This would for instance be in line with the Swedish policy which, following the principle "focus on workers not on jobs" has funded a council helping to find jobs for displaced workers.[3] Chand et al also focus on the need for the government to be proactive and focus on "reskilling workers by providing appropriate education instead of funding support schemes that entail handing out minimum wages".[4] We, however, tend not to follow their recommendation for financing such measures, which would consist of introducing an education tax for enterprises and individuals above a certain threshold.[5]

However, the idea that all affected workers would have enough time, opportunity and skill to adjust to the new economy does not seem realistic. Not everybody may become a computer programmer, a childminder or a life coach within a few months![6] In addition, with the evolution of technology, as more and more jobs are replaced by AI and robotics, additional and parallel solutions would have to be implemented.

---

[1]   In this sense, among others, Damijan Joze P., Damijian Sandra and Vrh Natasa, Tax on Robots: Whether and How Much, Working Paper, Growinpro, March, 39/2021; see also Thuemmel Oscar, Optimal Taxation of Robots, University of Zurich, October 2020.

[2]   Susskind Richard and Susskind Daniel, The Future of the Professions, Oxford University Press, 2015, p. 46 ff.

[3]   See also Mann Roberta, Should We Tax Robots? Policy Forum, 4 May 2018, p. 4.

[4]   Chand Vikram, Kostic Svetislav and Reis Ariene, Taxing Artificial Intelligence and Robots: Critical Assessment of Potential Policy Solutions and Recommendation for Alternative Approaches, 12 World Tax Journal 2020, n. 4, p. 25.

[5]   See supra, p. 185.

[6]   Harari Yuval Noah, 21 Lessons for the 21st Century, Vintage, London 2018, p. 30.

III.   UNIVERSAL BASIC INCOME (UBI)

A.   The Concept

One very popular and widely discussed solution to unemployment due to auto-mation is the introduction of a UBI. Under this system, each resident citizen in a State would receive a basic uniform amount of income. This system should ensure a basic standard of living and would not be subject to any condition or requirement. It would replace all other types of benefits which require condi-tions and are usually means-tested. The growing interest in this idea can be justified due to concerns associated with disruption, growing inequality and the risk of job losses due to automation.[7] The COVID-19 pandemic has also reinforced the interest in such a system. The impact of the pandemic has in fact led various States to offer direct payments to their residents, which could be described as a type of "informal" UBI.

The key elements of this system may be summarized as follows. First, it is *unconditional*. The UBI is automatically distributed to all the resident persons in one State, without any test related to their personal situations (sufficient means, poverty, disability, etc.). This aspect differentiates UBI from the guar-anteed minimum income (GMI), which tends to be subject to specific condi-tions. Second it is *basic*. The amount received should cover all the basic needs of a person. Finally, it is *universal*. This means that the basic income should be distributed to all residents of one country (or State, canton, province) without any additional requirement. Finally, the UBI is *individual*. Each person should receive the income, independently of their marital or household status.

B.   Historical Development

The idea of a UBI has a long history. Some elements of this concept may be traced back to Thomas More, who, in 1516, described in *Utopia* a society where wealth is shared, all things are common to everyone and under which everybody has enough means to live, without the link between work and sub-sistence.[8] Thomas Paine is often described as one of the first to have suggested the idea of an unconditional attribution of a lump-sum of money to everyone,

---

[7]   OECD, Basic Income as a Policy Option: Can it Add Up? Policy brief on the future of work, May 2017, p. 1.

[8]   More Thomas, Utopia, English translation, 1516, Penguin Books, London 2012, pp. 30, 60, 119.

as compensation for the fact that some people own lands and others don't. He wrote:

> Having thus, in a few words, opened the merits of the case, I proceed to the plan I have to propose, which is, to create a National Fund, out of which there shall be paid to every person, when arrived at the age of twenty-one years, the sum of Fifteen pounds sterling, as a compensation in part for the loss of his or her natural inheritance by the introduction of the system of landed property.[9]

During the industrial revolution, Charles Fourier declared his support for a guaranteed minimum income, along with John Stuart Mill.[10]

Other prominent economists from all sides of the political spectrum, both right and left, have also advocated such a system. For instance, Friedrich Hayek, clearly on the conservative side, was a strong proponent of a minimum income, which he developed in his work *Law, Legislation and Liberty*, published between 1973 and 1979.[11] On the other side, recently, in France, during the 2017 French presidency campaign, Benoît Hamon, representing the Socialist Party, also advocated a system of unconditional minimum income. Mark Zuckerberg, in his Harvard commencement speech to the class of 2017, recommended "explor[ing] ideas like universal basic income to give everyone a cushion to try new things".[12]

C.   Concrete Examples

Many countries, notably the United States, Canada, Holland, Finland and Brazil, have debated or introduced some – in general limited – forms of guaranteed income.[13] But in its theoretical form, UBI as such has not yet been properly tested.

Finland in particular implemented in January 2017 a two-year pilot program, targeting 2000 citizens between 25 and 58 years old. Critics, however, argue that the result of the program is not convincing as it was "poorly designed".[14]

---

9   Paine Thomas, Agrarian Justice opposed to Agrarian Law, and to Agrarian Monopoly, London 1797, p. 6.
10   Abott Ryan and Bogenschneider Bret, Should Robots Pay Taxes? Tax Policy in the Age of Automation, 12 Harvard Law & Policy Review 2018, p. 5, n. 16.
11   See Hayek Friedrich, Law, Legislation and Liberty, vol. III, 1979, p. 155; Ford Martin, Rise of the Robots, Basic Books, New York 2015, p. 258.
12   See, The Harvard Gazette, 25 May 2017.
13   For a summary, OECD, Basic Income as a Policy Option: Can it Add Up? Policy brief on the future of work, May 2017, p. 2, Box 1.
14   See The New York Times, "Why Finland's Basic Income Experiment Isn't Working", 20 July 2017.

Its implementation was also linked with a high administrative burden and, according to some commentators, its concrete design may hardly be characterized as a "real UBI".[15]

On 5 June 2016, the Swiss people rejected a proposal to introduce in the Federal Constitution a guaranteed minimum income.[16] The proposal was limited to the basic principles of a UBI, leaving it to the authorities to implement its essential elements. The proponents, however, suggested a minimum unconditional amount of 2500 CHF per month. According to some studies, this proposal would have cost about 208 billion CHF. However, after coordination with existing programs, the net cost would amount to approximately 25 billion CHF. To finance the UBI, a new tax on electronic transactions, at a rate of 0.2 percent, was suggested. According to the committee proposing the UBI, such a tax would raise about 200 billion CHF. In the end, this concept was rejected by the Swiss people, with a 76.9 percent negative vote. The debate was, however, open and interesting. It was a rare occasion to debate in public the pros and cons of the UBI. This idea, new at such a political level, could indeed come back in a different form.

D. Argument Pros and Cons

Recently many voices have favored the UBI system. As Daniel Ford puts it:

> The conservative argument for basic income centers on the fact that it provides a safety net coupled with individual freedom of choice. Rather than having governments intrude into personal economic decisions, or get into the business of directly providing product and services, the idea is to give everyone the means to go out and participate in the market.[17]

In addition, this system should not be too complicated to implement and should preserve the key aspect of a market economy, in the sense that everybody would be free to increase their standard of living by working or investing more, but if they don't, they would still have enough money to live and act as consumers.[18]

---

[15] See in this sense, Lexer Georgina Michaela and Scarcella Luisa, Artificial Intelligence and Labor Markets. A Critical Analysis of Solution Models from a Tax Law and Social Security Law Perspective, Rivista Italiana Di Informatica E Diritto, 2019, p. 53 ff., with a broad description of the system.

[16] See Le Monde, "Le revenu de base inconditionnel proposé en Suisse en 4 questions", 5 June 2016.

[17] Ford (2015), p. 259.

[18] Brynjolfsson Erik and McAfee Andrew, The Second Machine Age, W.W Norton, New York 2014, p. 232.

There are, however, many arguments against such a system. First, and obviously, many people argue that a UBI would encourage people to favor leisure and laziness. This argument is controversial. It could indeed be argued that what motivates people is the activity itself and the fulfillment in doing something meaningful than the money in consideration. In the same vein, adverse incentive effects on benefits linked with the existing social protection system also appear to be a concern.[19] This could occur in the case where some benefits disappear when workers start a job or increase the level of their salaries.[20] This consequence appears more an implementation issue that requires coordination of the various benefits granted by the system.

Second, the important costs required to implement the UBI is viewed as a major obstacle. Again, there are contradicting views on financing costs. The figures depend upon the possibility of coordinating and consolidating the UBI with existing social security programs. Should the UBI effectively replace the partial benefits programs that require specific conditions to be met, the effective net cost of UBI could appear less than it seems. This is demonstrated notably by the variation in figures on the Swiss UBI proposal mentioned above. In the same vein, some critics wonder whether a UBI would not require excessive funding, since the government would lose a "significant sum of money" to pay people who in fact do not need to receive those benefits.[21] In other words, the suitability of this system may be challenged because instead of distributing the same amount of money to everybody, such money could be better used by targeting people in need.[22]

Third, contrary to what its name could imply, UBI is not universal, in the sense that it applies to a State or a specific area (such as a canton or a province). To make it truly universal would require its introduction globally, recommended by major institutions such as the UN, the OECD or at least the EU.

Fourth, practical implementation difficulties should not be underestimated. A UBI should cover at least an individual's "basic needs" for which the required amounts should be evaluated. As various proposals around the world suggest, great variations exist between countries. In addition, as the Swiss discussion around the referendum has shown, sensitive political issues are at stake. People have markedly different views on what the term "basic" encompasses. In any event, like the robot tax mentioned above, it seems that the practical aspects – which are clearly sensitive – are not as such strong enough to

---

[19]   OECD, Basic Income as a Policy Option: Can it Add Up? Policy brief on the future of work, May 2017, p. 7.
[20]   OECD, Basic Income as a Policy Option: Can it Add Up? Policy brief on the future of work, May 2017, p. 7.
[21]   Lexer and Scarcella (2019), p. 61.
[22]   Lexer and Scarcella (2019), p. 61.

discount per se the concept of a UBI. Most of the technical issues exist also in general in social security funding or pensions systems and could be overcome.

Some authors, after analyzing various options to face the shift from labor to capital, offer a more balanced view, by recognizing that the idea of a basic income would perhaps need to be revisited, but that it is "not [their] first choice".[23]

In our view, despite many drawbacks, the idea of a UBI is worth analyzing further. Should, in the future, employment disappear, slowly but inexorably, this system should remain on the agenda of policymakers. If automation takes over, there will not be enough new jobs to replace the disappearing ones. Many people will not have enough time or opportunity to retrain, adapt and find new jobs created by the new economy. A system of UBI would appear to represent a promising solution. Should this happen, the development of new creative, artistic, philanthropic or simply human caring activities, could blossom.

E.   Variations

There are some variations on the UBI. We have already mentioned the GMI, which represents a minimum amount paid to a citizen but is usually means-tested. Another idea is the *negative income tax*, which was notably suggested by Milton Friedman.[24] Under this system, should income remain under a certain threshold or "break-even" point, a fraction (negative tax) of the income would be refunded by the State to the taxpayer. The advantage of that model is that it combines a guaranteed minimum income with an incentive to work,[25] hence why Friedman prefers the system of negative income tax to the UBI.

---

[23]   Brynjolfsson and McAfee (2014), p. 234.
[24]   See Friedman Milton, Capitalism and Freedom, University of Chicago Press, 1964.
[25]   Brynjolfsson and McAfee (2014), p. 238.

12. Main findings and final recommendation

I. SUMMARY OF FINDINGS

For the past few years, some people have been calling for the introduction of a robot tax. In Chapter 1, we tried to describe how and when the idea of taxing robots emerged. What could appear at first as a superficial or "anthropomorphist" view of robots is now taken much more seriously and is the object of careful and detailed analysis.

The development of AI and its implementation into robotics raises new and fascinating questions for the tax systems of each country, as demonstrated in Chapter 2. The so-called disruption of the economy has just started. AI and robots are entering into all aspects of our lives. So far, robots have been used mainly in the industrial economy (notably in factories and warehouses), but AI and robots nowadays are increasingly active in the service sector. We see AI helping or providing services usually attributable to lawyers (such as "Ross"), doctors (notably for diagnosis), journalists, bankers, brokers, insurance advisers, entertainers and nurses, just to name a few examples. With the progress of broad AI, smart robots are nowadays capable of autonomous behavior, able to learn from experience (deep learning) and to evolve and interact with the outside environment.

It follows that the widespread use of AI and robots in numerous spheres of the economy raises some concerns. First, the effective impact on the labor market and notably on the number of human jobs available in the future is a matter of controversy. In short, there are two schools of thought. The optimists, on the one hand, rely on scientific studies and believe that, like the previous industrial revolutions, the so-called fourth revolution would indeed destroy many jobs, but at the same time create sufficient if not more new jobs for everybody. On the other hand, the pessimists consider that "this time is different" and that the emerging skills of new robots and of AI more generally could eventually affect most if not all human jobs.

The author is not able to look at his crystal ball and define who is right and who is wrong in this debate. However, it appears doubtful that sufficient new jobs, appropriate for human workers left behind by automation, would be created in sufficient time to allow for an adaptation of human skills. On a long-term basis, the chances are high that an insufficient number of new jobs would exist, given that technology and automation is constantly evolving. Recently, the important development of AI, including collaborative forms of AI, using large language models, have increased concerns over the impact of AI in all sectors of the economy. In the author's opinion, this situation is highly problematic because, under the pessimist scenario, a triple negative consequence could occur. First, with the disappearance of human labor, the taxable base of most States would shrink drastically. In this context, it should be mentioned that the social security system of most States is highly dependent upon taxes and social security contributions, which are levied on labor income. Second, the State would face additional needs for financing of social security programs for human workers without jobs. Third, by losing their revenues, human workers would also reduce their consumption, causing a general threat to the economic system as a whole.

From another more global perspective, automation is also likely to raise inequality among citizens. AI and robots may first replace on a large scale low-skilled or eventually medium-skilled jobs, thus widening the disparities. Recent studies tend to demonstrate that routine jobs are most at risk, at least in the short term. Therefore, discrimination could occur from two different perspectives. First, among the workers themselves, between low and high-skilled jobs, affected differently by the impact of AI. Second, more generally, between labor and the owners of capital. The owners of AI, robot technology or intellectual property rights may increase their position of control over a growing concentration of wealth among a shrinking and limited group of persons.

We do not know with certitude today what will be the consequences of the growing automation and use of AI. But, in the author's opinion, we cannot wait to see who, in the future, proves to be right or wrong on these crucial issues, such as the impact of the use of AI and robots on the labor market or on the distribution of income and wealth among citizens. We should urgently find and analyze potential alternatives to prevent the negative consequences arising from the pessimist's scenario. The taxation of AI and robots, or their use, offers an interesting solution. Should the optimists turn out to be right, it would always be possible to adapt, modify or not apply these rules.

The purpose of this book is to demonstrate that the idea of taxing AI, which includes robots, even though it seems controversial, is both justified, and feasible, under different alternatives that need to be carefully balanced and coordinated with the general tax system.

In Chapter 3, we have tried to provide a practical and realistic definition of AI and robots that could also be suitable for tax purposes. To date there is no precise legal definition of both AI and robots. In general, AI is a broader concept covering all approaches and designs of machines capable of rendering similar functions to the human brain. By contrast, robots are usually regarded more as a "physical" implementation of some forms of AI. From a tax standpoint, we should focus on the economic impacts of automation. Robots are the implementation of AI. In our view, the tax should therefore concentrate on the effect of AI. What is essential is more the impact of AI, including robotics, on the economy than a formalistic view of robots in a "physical" form, which could easily be circumvented. In this book, we have suggested focusing more generally on AI autonomous systems and "smart robots", i.e. robots which implement AI and are capable of autonomous behavior. In other words, the decisive criteria is the autonomy of AI and robots. What should be relevant is the degree of intelligence of AI and its implementation in robots.

The legal system could then consider, under specific conditions, that AI and robots could eventually be regarded as a new form of a legal person. In the past, corporations underwent a similar experience until the law granted them legal personality. As a consequence, these new legal entities became subject to a new type of income tax, specially designed for them: the profit tax. In Chapter 4, we discussed to what extent some form of legal personality could be attributed to AI and robots. Indeed, like corporations, such recognition could lead to a tax capacity and trigger a tax on AI systems, subject however to additional conditions such as the ability to pay. After all, most legal systems have tended to grant some types of legal personality, or rights, not only to companies but to other things, such as a human fetus or animals. Such recognition would have to be adopted by the legislator. The features of this new type of legal entity should however correspond to the characteristics of AI and robots and not necessarily be based on elements taken from humans or corporations. In summary, in order to recognize an AI system as a taxable person, the legislator could choose, either (1) to grant legal personality to it, which, as a consequence, would also entail the duty to pay a tax, or (2) design a new type of entity subject to tax, which does not necessary require the granting of a legal personality. We have nevertheless shown that the idea of granting a legal personality or a tax capacity is not a necessary precondition to introduce a taxation of AI and robots. At the first stage, a tax could already be justified by taxation at the level of the companies or enterprises *using* them. However, at a later stage, a tax capacity could be designed by a legislator for an AI system *as such* that meets four essential elements: autonomy, a distinct patrimony, identification as such and control by humans. In other words, the legislator could choose to create a new taxable unit in the form of an AI autonomous and identified system with a financial capacity and proper human control. This would include smart robots. This new AI taxable unit, which we could define as an AITU, would then be granted some rights, such as the right to dispose of a financial capacity, under the limits designed by the law, and obligations, namely, to pay taxes and follow the applicable control rules.

Introducing a taxation of AI systems or robots, like any new tax, should rely on justified reasons. It is not easy to plead in favor of taxation of AI, as explained in Chapter 5. There are serious objections that have been raised by some commentators and that need careful consideration. First, AI and robots are difficult to define and any distinction between these concepts relies on significant subjective judgement. Chapter 3, however, has demonstrated that a definition of AI, suitable for tax purposes, is reachable. Second, a frequent objection is that the taxation of AI would restrict innovation and productivity and thus could cause harm to the economy. This objection requires both: (1) an analysis of the impact of such taxes on enterprises in order not to hamper productivity and (2) a coordination of any new tax within the existing system. However, it doesn't disqualify as such a tax on AI. After all, royalties, copyright and other intellectual property income have been taxed for decades. This does not appear to have jeopardized innovation in the past. Third, the tax on AI would be difficult to collect and implement. This objection, however, applies to any new taxes, such as an ecological tax, a tax on carbon or a tax on the digital economy, which are dependent on the evolution of technology. The same is true for a fourth criticism pertaining to the possibility of tax avoidance in planning with the activities of AI potentially subject to tax. Finally, recent analysis has shown that the developments of AI could even lead to some cases of non-taxation of profits, should the AI have sufficient autonomy not to distribute anything to the entities or humans controlling it. In this case, introducing a tax on the AI system and "smart" robots could even reinforce the integrity of the tax system as a whole.

After having gone through these various objections, we tried to justify a tax on AI and robots or the use of them, both from an economic and constitutional standpoint. It appears notably to the author that this analysis should distinguish between a tax on the use of AI and on AI as such. Indeed, as of now, AI and robots are not regarded as legal or tax persons. First, a tax on the use of AI would be compatible in our view with the principle of ability to pay. This ability to pay would be based on the imputed income that the enterprise would obtain by using automation instead of human workers. By using automation, enterprises would spare salaries that they should have paid to the human workers. Second, should we later recognize a tax capacity of autonomous AI or smart robots per se, an ability to pay of AI and robots could be recognized to the extent that, like corporations, they would benefit from an economic capacity to pay such tax. This would require the attribution of some financial means that could be used for tax purposes. As we have demonstrated, an *objective* ability to pay of AI and robots would, like corporations, correspond to an effective capacity of payment.

AI systems and robots are, however, part of the assets and investments of any enterprise or persons that use them as production factors. As such, profit or income emerging from the use of AI and robots is already subject to tax but at the level of global profits of the enterprise owning or controlling them. Chapter 6 describes, both from a domestic and international standpoint, how the profits or income derived from the activities of enterprises using AI and robots are currently apprehended by the tax system. Domestically, AI and robots are generally regarded as investments that benefit from generous amortization rules, which, in accordance with the current OECD recommendations, tend to incentivize the use of automation. In the author's view, the rules applied to capital investments cannot simply be transposed to investments in AI. The "labor component" embodied in it should also be considered. As such, different amortization rules should apply which include the "intelligent" part of this investment. From an international standpoint, the use of automation abroad may trigger the presence of a PE in the source State. In particular, AI providing automated services, embodied in servers, as well as in robots, could be characterized as a PE, within the meaning of Article 5 paragraph 1 OECD Model DTC. Indeed, the business of an enterprise may be carried out without any "on-site" human intervention. Current double taxation treaties already define the features of automation as a PE and also address the allocation of profits between the head office and the PE.

Chapter 7 is devoted to the analysis of the vast discussion on the existing and potential future rules of taxation of the digital economy and on their impact on the taxation of AI and robots or the use of automation. The current international system is based on a distribution of power to tax between residence and source countries that was developed in the early twentieth century, starting with the work of the League of Nations and then further developed at the OECD or the UN level. The consensus reached at the time was based on a brick-and-mortar economy. The PE concept, defined as a fixed place of business through which the activity of the enterprise is carried on, fundamentally relies on a physical presence of the enterprise in the source State. The digital economy does not need such a physical presence and non-resident companies, through the Internet or other communication technologies, are able to reach customers all over the world online. This led the OECD, under Action 1 of the BEPS Initiative, and other institutions, such as the UN or the EU, to try and design new alternatives to address the challenges of the digital economy. Solutions, such as a new PE threshold based on digital presence, specific digital taxes or withholding taxes, have been analyzed. A consensus seems difficult to reach. Interestingly, the UN, in the meantime, has introduced a new Article 12B Model DTC, which provides for a taxation at source on "automated digital services". Furthermore, the EU has proposed an interim measure in the form of a digital services tax and a long-term proposal of a new digital presence threshold as a more comprehensive solution to better take into consideration the impact of users and consumers on the business models of digital enterprises. In parallel, some

States have entered into unilateral measures against foreign digital enterprises, in the form of a so-called diverted profit tax, digital service taxes or withholding taxes. In particular, the concept of a digital PE would raise the issue of the adequate attribution of profits. In the context of automation, and notably with the potential use of AI, the concept of "significant people functions" would require a different analysis. Some functions, and therefore value, could be attributed to intelligent machines replacing humans. Finally, in 2019, the OECD suggested a compromise with the two-pillars solution. The main elements of this proposal have been accepted as a matter of principle by more than 140 jurisdiction members of the OECD Inclusive Framework. The first pillar, still under discussion, would notably introduce a new regime of international allocation of profits for large MNEs, with a formulaic apportionment rule in favor of the States of sales (so-called amount A).

All these measures are briefly discussed in this chapter with a view to ascertaining how they might also be considered as one of the ways to address the taxation of automation. Indeed, most of the digital enterprises make abundant use of AI, robots and automation in their business models to choose and sell goods online or to process, analyze and sell, with the help of algorithms and data obtained from users.

Currently, AI and robot activities are not only subject to profit or income tax, as part of the assets of enterprises, but may also enter into the scope of VAT. As demonstrated in Chapter 8, automation is already present in many taxable supplies of goods or services. An industrial robot, used for instance in an assembly line of a car factory, contributes to the supply of vehicles to the final consumers. The same applies, for example, to services rendered by robots participating in medical diagnosis or surgeries. The precise VAT consequences of the activities provided by AI systems raise however delicate and challenging issues, such as the characterization of the transaction, the delimitation of the place of supply, the existence of an FE (fixed establishment) or the possibility to claim input VAT credit. In this respect, based on the case law of the ECJ, we have notably seen that the FE concept tends to be stricter than the PE OECD definition, in the sense that it requires at least some presence of human personnel at the place of business. Recent case law, however, seems to broaden the scope of the FE concept for VAT purposes. By contrast, Swiss law has coordinated the VAT PE notion with Article 5 of the OECD Model DTT. Eventually, the development of AI could require a broader definition of the concept of FE, which would focus less on the presence of humans, and more on the technical capabilities of AI implemented in robots, which, like humans, would render autonomous decisions, interact and evolve with experience through *e-learning*. Recent developments of the digital economy bring interesting perspectives that are also relevant for the VAT taxation of AI. VAT, as a consumption tax, will also address the use of automation by taxable enterprises, which will charge VAT on supplies of goods or services to the final consumer. The author believes that VAT will remain crucial in the future since, contrary to profit tax which today still relies heavily on the physical presence of an enterprise or a PE, notably for digital services, it is based on the destination principle and therefore focuses on the place of the consumers. In this context, the recent rules in EU legislation, requiring digital *platforms* to register, assess, levy and collect VAT on some digital transactions, can be viewed as a blueprint for some form of taxation of AI systems. Indeed, platforms mainly use algorithms and software to collect, analyze and use data obtained from various users worldwide.

At this stage, existing principles seem to solve most of the typical VAT issues (characterization and definition of the place of supply). As a rule, a comparison with the economic functions of AI activities, from the perspective of the average consumer, offers a potential solution to the precise character of most robot services. At a later stage, the complexities and extended technological capabilities of AI or robots may, however, require a different perspective. Indeed, the activities carried out by AI and robots could evolve in a way not comparable to human actions. In addition, to simply characterize such activities as electronic services may not correspond to the specific nature of their essential features. In this case, perhaps the introduction of new rules of localization could be adequate.

Having analyzed the current tax consequences of using automation in an enterprise, both from a direct and VAT perspective, we focused, in Chapter 9 on the design of a potential new form of taxation of the use of AI systems, or on autonomous AI (including smart robots). Based on the previous analysis, we have seen that under current law, neither AI nor robots benefit from a legal or tax capacity. As such, they are not regarded as having some form of ability to pay, from a tax standpoint. Hence, we may develop taxation on AI or robots in two different stages.

In a first stage, a tax could focus on the *use* of AI and robots, which, as demonstrated in Chapters 4 and 5, could be justified both from an economic and legal standpoint as representing an ability to pay on enterprises in the form of an imputed income. We call this tax an *AI usage tax*, which corresponds to a profit tax levied at the level of the enterprise on the imputed salary or income corresponding to the hypothetical income that the enterprise using AI would have paid for equivalent human activities. In addition, a State could implement such a tax with a broad definition of the imputed salary and also include imputed services and other outsourced activities which have been replaced by automation. We have also explored other alternatives, such as *automation* taxes, which could be either general or special, i.e. focusing on limited or specific areas. Automation taxes could be based either: (1) on a ratio of automation in comparison to human workers, or (2) related to the production factors linked with automation. In this context, the use of presumptive taxes, which try to attract profits arising from the use of AI, which are not reflected in the books of the enterprise, represent another interesting alternative. A tax on production factors could also correspond to an "AI box". We have shown that the use of AI may also be subject to other types of specific taxes following different perspectives or policies, such as a *Pigouvian* tax designed to internalize the externalities caused by automation, an *object* tax on the detention of robots or a *fee* for the costs attributable to the supervision or registration of AI. In our view, the most suitable solution, should the pessimists be right, and labor drastically shrink in favor of automation, would however be the AI usage tax on the imputed income from the activities performed by AI systems. It contributes both to including in the profits of enterprise the imputed income, which human labor represented, and to level the playing field between capital (automation) and human-oriented enterprises. In addition, and logically, this imputed income could be subject to social security contributions.

In a second stage, should the legal system recognize, under specific conditions, that AI become legal and taxable entities as such, we could even consider introducing a tax on the AI system. This development would, however, require that some form of ability to pay be attributed to them. This ability to pay would be defined, in the same way as corporations in the past, as an objective ability to pay corresponding to a capacity of payment. With the development of technology, an allocation of financial means could become reality. Based on those premises, a tax *on AI autonomous systems and smart robots* could be implemented in various forms. First, we could introduce an AI and robot revenue tax on income (imputed or not) that is attributable to AI and robot activities. Second, a capital tax on AI and robots could be levied on assets that AI and robots own or control. Third, AI and robots could become subject to VAT and would be required to charge VAT on their output supplies to other human persons, or other robots, and could credit input VAT on VAT charged on the transactions they received. Recent EU VAT rules requiring platforms to register and collect tax on some transactions (digital services or distant sales) represent, according to the author, a first step towards a potential recognition of AI as an entity subject to VAT and required to register for VAT purposes. Logically, an AI system, as a legal or tax person, could then also become consumers of VAT transactions.

Chapter 9 takes into consideration a perspective other than introducing new taxes on AI, which is to modify the tax system. The current tax system tends to rely too heavily on taxation of labor and creates an incentive in favor of capital. A more balancing system of taxation between labor and capital income could therefore be implemented. In addition, the recognition of the importance of data as a value creation element could also lead to the introduction of various forms of data tax, on which an "AI data tax" could be levied at the stage of data collection, similarly to turnover taxes on oil or other forms of raw material for the enterprises acquiring them.

The introduction of new AI and robot taxes, either as AI and robot usage taxes or taxes on AI and robots per se, would have to comply with existing international tax rules. Chapter 10 analyses how these new taxes could apply in cross-border situations and the potential impact of DTT in this framework. First, some of the models of *AI usage taxes*, discussed previously, notably the tax on the imputed salary from AI used in corporations, would fall under the scope of a DTT. Under current law, this tax should also be governed by the allocation rules of Article 7 OECD Model DTC (income from enterprise). Second, should the applicable law introduce a tax on AI as such, the analysis would be quite different. For DTT to apply, some AI autonomous systems, including smart robots, should be recognized as persons and be resident in one of the contracting States. This would require that the residence State attributes to them a tax capacity. The definition of the residence of an AI system would also raise delicate issues. In our view, the main test could rely on the place of effective use of AI, which could be adjusted with other factors, such as the presence of a register of AI or robots, the place of supervision or of the technical infrastructure. In short, it appears that these new taxes could indeed be designed in compliance with existing international tax rules, but subject to adjustments based on the specific nature of AI. Comparison between humans and AI in the future may, however, become inappropriate. Recent works in the digital economy show that reaching a consensus on those issues would be extremely difficult. This is the reason why new taxes on the use of AI or on AI *per se* need to be discussed and analyzed in depth today, from a coordinated and global perspective.

Finally, Chapter 11 addressed another controversial issue, which is the use of the revenues from taxation of AI systems or of their use. At the beginning of the book, we saw that one of the main concerns in the development of automation is the potential disappearance, or at least drastic decrease (transitory or not), of human labor. This fear is not new but is exacerbated by the development of technology where AI and robots are now slowly replacing not only the physical functions of human beings (such as arms and legs), but their cognitive and intelligence capabilities. To address this major concern, the new financial means resulting from a taxation of AI or its use could first be allocated to education, apprenticeship opportunities, retraining or agencies devoted to promoting more adequate skills for human workers who have lost their jobs or are in transition.

In this context, the old idea of a minimum income allocated to humans has also emerged. The concept of a universal basic income (UBI) is now discussed by politicians and experts as a potential solution to ensuring that many human workers without jobs still find, unconditionally, sufficient resources to finance their basic needs. The author considers that the UBI is indeed an interesting solution that needs careful consideration and should be analyzed further. A recent Swiss vote on this issue has shown that the concept needs to be adequately designed and requires a coordinated and global approach. Should labor disappear in the long term, humans will have to adapt and develop their own ways of living a meaningful life.

II. MAIN RECOMMENDATION IN SUMMARY

The main findings and recommendations of this book may be summarized as follows. For tax purposes, the distinction between AI and robots no longer makes sense. What is relevant, independent of the form, is the impact of AI (including robots) on the economy as a whole and the labor market in particular. With this concept in mind, should human labor continue to deteriorate due to the development of automation, a taxation of AI would represent a solution. This new approach could also help to alleviate the rising inequality between labor and capital. In the absence of an AI tax capacity, we could introduce this new tax system in two phases.

In a first phase, the legislator should focus on the *use* of AI (including robots) by enterprises. To implement this solution, taxes (including social security levies) on the imputed salaries (or services) that enterprises spare by using AI systems instead of human workers seem the most appropriate solution. Alternatively, so-called automation taxes or presumptive taxes, focusing on the added value that the use of AI contributes to the results of enterprises could be introduced. Transactions realized by enterprises using AI systems should also be subject to VAT.

In a second phase, a tax capacity could be introduced by law for AI systems with sufficient autonomy to act independently. As a consequence, this new taxpayer, similar to a corporation, could be liable to income tax, eventually a capital tax, and become subject to VAT. This consequence would require that the AI, as defined by law, should: (1) be *autonomous*, (2) be attributed the right to the benefit and use of a *separate patrimony* which could serve for the purpose of tax payments, (3) be *identified* as such, and (4) be under a system of human *control*. This rule would include "smart" robots. The introduction of a tax capacity could, but does not necessarily, also entail a legal personality to autonomous AI systems. The introduction of an AI tax capacity would include legal and technological limits and safeguards. From a tax standpoint, this could also include some ethical limits to the possibility of "planning" the system. The human control would at the same time serve to ensure the respect of legal requirements.

The recent development, notably in the EU, of introducing a tax liability for digital platforms for registration, assessment, collection and payment of VAT on some specific transactions (notably, accommodation and transport services), seems to us a blueprint of a potential future taxation of AI. This liability could indeed further be broadened to other VAT transactions, and later even include a tax liability for other types of taxes, such as direct taxes.

A final thought. Perhaps one day, the whole tax system will rely on AI systems, as taxpayers and consumers, which would pay all the taxes, collect them and finance the various infrastructure required for humans. It is hoped when that day comes that we have implemented sufficient mechanisms of human control because otherwise AI and robots could either refuse to pay their taxes or force us to pay them! When this happens, we might in fact have become robots ourselves without realizing it. When we have found out about it, it could be too late. We would ourselves have become the taxpayers of the tax on AI ...

Bibliography

I. BOOKS

Asimov Isaac, I, Robot, New York 1950.

Asimov Isaac, Robots and Empire, Doubleday, New York 1985.

Ault Hugh J. and Arnold Brian J., Comparative Income Taxation: A Structural Analysis, 3rd ed., Wolters Kluwer, The Netherlands 2010.

Barfield Woodrow and Pagallo Ugo, Law and Artificial Intelligence, Edward Elgar Publishing, Cheltenham, UK and Northampton, MA, USA 2020.

Batti Gabriel Bez, "Cloud Computing Services and VAT" in: Kerschner Ina and Somare Maryte (eds), Taxation in a Global Digital Economy, Linde Verlag, Vienna 2017, p. 351.

Bekey Georges A., Autonomous Robots. From Biological Inspiration to Implementation and Control, MIT Press, Cambridge, Massachusetts 2005.

Beretta Giorgio, "Fixed Establishment in the 21st Century" in: EU Value Added Tax and Beyond, Essays in Honour of Ben Terra, IBFD, Amsterdam, 2023 p. 167.

Bensamoun Alexandra (ed.), Les robots. Objets scientifiques, Objets de droits, Collection des Presses Universitaires de Sceaux 2016.

Bensoussan Alain and Bensoussan Jérémy, Droit des robots, Larcier, Bruxelles 2015.

Brynjolfsson Erik and McAtee Andrew, Race Against the Machine: How the Digital Revolution is Accelerating Innovation, Driving Productivity, and Irreversibly Transforming Employment and the Economy, New York 2011.

Brynjolfsson Erik and McAfee Andrew, The Second Machine Age, W.W Norton, New York 2014.

Calo Ryan, Froomkin Michael A. and Kerr I., Robot Law, Edward Elgar Publishing, Cheltenham, UK and Northampton, MA, USA 2016.

Cataldi Matteo, "The Attribution of Income to a Digital Permanent Establishment" in: Kerschner Ina and Somare Maryte (eds), Taxation in a Global Digital Economy, Linde Verlag, Vienna 2017, p. 143.

Da Luz De Souza Jacqueline, "Tax Treaty Policy in Addressing Challenges Posed by the Digital Economy" in: Kerschner Ina and Somare Maryte (eds), Taxation in a Global Digital Economy, Linde Verlag, Vienna 2017, p. 393.

Danon Robert, "Can Tax Treaty Policy Save Us? The Case of the Digital Economy" in: Arnold Brian (ed.), Tax Treaties after the BEPS Project: A Tribute to Jacques Sasseville, Canadian Tax Foundation, Toronto 2018, p. 75.

Danon Robert, Gutmann Daniel, Oberson Xavier and Pistone Pasquale (eds), Modèle de Convention OCDE concernant le revenu et la fortune, Commentaire, Helbing & Lichtenhahn/Editions Francis Lefebvre, Lausanne/Paris/Geneva/Vienna 2014.

Dimitropoulou Christina, Robot Taxation: A Normative Tax Policy Analysis. Domestic and International Tax Considerations, PhD, University of Vienna 2023 (on file with the author).

Dubut Thomas, in: Danon Robert et al. (eds), Modèle de Convention fiscal, OCDE concernant le revenu et la fortune, 2014, p. 85 ff.

Endo Tsutomu, "Modification of a Taxable Nexus to Address the Tax Challenges of the Digital Economy" in: Kerschner Ina and Somare Maryte (eds), Taxation in a Global Digital Economy, Linde Verlag, Vienna 2017, p. 105.

Englisch Joachim, "Digitalization and the Future of National Tax Systems: Taxing Robots?" in: Haslehner Werner, Kofler Georg, Pantazou Katerina and Rust Alexander (eds), Tax and the Digital Economy, Series on International Taxation, Wolters Kluwer, The Netherlands 2019, p. 261.

Fanti Sébastien, "Switzerland" in: Bensoussan Alain et al. (eds), Comparative Handbook: Robotics Technologies Law, Larcier Bruxelles 2016, p. 297.

Ford Martin, The Rise of the Robots, New York 2015.

Friedman Milton, Capitalism and Freedom, University of Chicago Press, 1962.

Grinbaum Alexei, Parole de machines, Humensciences, Paris, 2023.

Groffe Julie, "Robot et droit d'auteur" in: Les robots, objets scientifiques, objets de droits, Mare & Martin, Presses Universitaires de Sceaux, Paris 2016.

Gunkel David J., Robot Rights, MIT Press, Massachusetts 2019.

Gunkel David J., The Machine Question, MIT Press, Massachusetts 2012.

Harari Yuval Noah, 21 Lessons for the 21st Century, Vintage, London 2018.

Hawkins Jeff, A Thousand Brains: A New Theory of Intelligence, Basic Books, New York 2021.

Hayek Friedrich, Law, Legislation and Liberty, vol. I, 1973, vol., II, 1976, vol. III, 1979, reprinted in one volume by Routledge, London 1982.

Ismer Roland and Blank Alexander, in: Ekkehart Reimer and Alexander Rust, Klaus Vogel on Double Taxation Conventions, 5th ed, Wolters Kluwer, The Netherlands 2022.

Jain Arpith Prakash, "Challenges Posed by Permanent Establishment-Exemptions in the Context of the Digital Economy" in: Kerschner Ina and Somare Maryte (eds), Taxation in a Global Digital Economy, Linde Verlag, Vienna 2017, p. 161.

Kerschner Ina and Somare Maryte (eds), Taxation in a Global Digital Economy, Linde Verlag, Vienna 2017.

Kofler G., Poiares Maduro M. and Pistone P. (eds), Human Rights and Taxation in Europe and the World, IBFD, Amsterdam 2011.

Kothari Vipul Mangesh, "The Treatment of Bitcoin Transactions for Indirect Tax Purposes" in: Kerschner Ina and Somare Maryte (eds), Taxation in a Global Digital Economy, Linde Verlag, Vienna 2017, p. 373.

Lamensch Marie, European Value Added Tax in the Digital Era, IBFD Doctoral Series, Amsterdam 2015.

Lang Joachim and Englisch Joachim, "A European Legal Tax Order Based on Ability to Pay" in: Amatucci Andrea (ed.), International Tax Law, Kluwer Law International, The Netherlands 2006.

Lang Michael, "Fictitious Income and Tax Treaties" in: A Tax Globalist, Essays in Honor of Maarten J. Ellis, 2005, p. 34. Lang Michael, Pistone Pasquale, Schuch J. and Staringer C. (eds), Introduction to European Tax Law on Direct Taxation, 3rd ed., Vienna 2013.

Meisel William, The Software Society, United States 2014.

Michielse Geerten M.M. and Thuronyi Victor (eds), Tax Design Issues Worldwide, Wolters Kluwer, The Netherlands 2015.

More Thomas, Utopia, 1516 (original version), Penguin Books, London 2012.

Musgrave Richard A. and Musgrave Peggy B., Public Finance in Theory and Practice, 5th ed., McGraw-Hill, United States 1989.

Nevejans Nathalie, "Les robots: tentative de définition" in: Bensamoun Alexandra (ed.), Les robots : objets scientifiques, objets de droits, Collection des Presses Universitaires de Sceaux, 2016, p. 81.

Nolan Alistair, "The Next Production Revolution: Key Issues and Policy Proposals" in: The Next Production Revolution, OECD, Paris 2018, p. 25.

Oberson Xavier, Droit fiscal Suisse, 5th ed., Helbing & Lichtenhan, Basel 2021.

Oberson Xavier, Précis de droit fiscal international, 5th ed., Stämpfli, Bern 2022.

Oberson Xavier and Yacicioglou Efsun Alara, Taxation of Big Data, Springer, Cham, Switzerland 2023.

Ohm Lenka, "Issues Regarding the Characterization of Income derived by Digital Enterprises" in: Kerschner Ina and Somare Maryte (eds), Taxation in a Global Digital Economy, Linde Verlag, Vienna 2017, p. 211.

Paine Thomas, Agrarian Justice opposed to Agrarian Law, and to Agrarian Monopoly, London 1797.

Pantazou Katerina, "The Taxation of the Sharing Economy" in: Haslehner Werner, Kofler Georg, Pantazou Katerina and Rust Alexander (eds), Tax and the Digital Economy, Series on International Taxation, Wolters Kluwer, The Netherlands 2019, p. 215.

Pathiyil Rathish, "E-Books and VAT" in: Kerschner Ina and Somare Maryte (eds), Taxation in a Global Digital Economy, Linde Verlag, Vienna 2017, p. 329.

Reimer Ekkehart and Rust Alexander, Klaus Vogel on Double Taxation Conventions, 5th ed., Wolters Kluwer, The Netherlands 2022.

Ricardo David, On the Principles of Political Economy and Taxation, 1st ed., London, 1817; 3rd ed., 1821, Batoche Books, Canada 2001.

Rochel Johan, Les robots parmi nous, Savoir suisse, Switzerland 2022.

Schumpeter Joseph, Capitalism, Socialism and Democracy, Harper & Brothers, United States 1942.

Schwab Klaus, The Fourth Industrial Revolution, World Economic Forum, Crown, Digital Frontier Press, New York 2016.

Searle John, Minds, Brains and Science, Harvard University Press, Cambridge, Massachusetts 1984.

Simons Henry C., Personal Income Taxation, University of Chicago Press, Chicago & London 1929.

Smit Daniel, "Flexibility, Mobility and Automation of Labour under Article 7 of the OECD Model? A First Conceptual Exploration" in: Weber Dennis (ed.), The Implications of Online Platforms and Technology for Taxation, IBFD, Amsterdam 2023, p. 159.

Susskind Richard and Susskind Daniel, The Future of the Professions, Oxford University Press, Oxford 2015.

Taipalus Päivi, "The Fixed Establishment and the Principle of Legal (Un)certainty" in: EU Value Added Tax and Beyond, Essays in Honour of Ben Terra, IBFD, Amsterdam 2023, p. 241.

Tegmark Max, Life 3.0, Being Human in the Age of Artificial Intelligence, Deckle Edge, New York 2017.

Terra Ben and Kajus Julie, A Guide to the European Directives, IBFD, Amsterdam 2022.

Terra Ben J.M. and Wattel Peter J., European Tax Law, 6th ed., Wolters Kluwer, The Netherlands 2012.

Tipke Klaus, Die Steuerrechtsordung, vol. I, 2nd ed. 2000, vol. II, 2nd ed. 2003, vol. III, 2nd ed. 2012, Dr. Otto Schmidt Verlag, Cologne 2000–2012.

Tipke Klaus and Lang Joachim, Steuerrecht, 24th ed, Dr. Otto Schmid Verlag, Cologne 2021.

Türker Hazal Isinsu, "The Concept of a Server in the Digital Economy" in: Kerschner Ina and Somare Maryte (eds), Taxation in a Global Digital Economy, Linde Verlag, Vienna 2017, p. 123.

Van Norden Gert-Jan, "The Allocation of Taxing Rights to Fixed Establishments in European VAT Legislation" in: VAT in an EU and International Perspective, Essays in Honor of Han Kogels, IBFD, The Netherlands 2011, p. 36.

Vàzquez Juan Manuel and Čičin-Sain Nevia, "Tax Reporting by Online Platforms: Operational and Fundamental Implications of DAC7 and the OECD Model Rules" in: Weber Dennis (ed.), The Implications of Online Platforms and Technology for Taxation, IBFD, Amsterdam 2023, p. 9.

Vogel K., Klaus Vogel on Double Taxation Conventions, 3rd ed., Wolters Kluwer, The Netherlands 1997.

Vogel K. and Lehner M., Doppelbesteuerungs-abkommen Kommentar, 5th ed., Verlag Beck, Munich 2008.

Wittman Johanna M., "'Patent Boxes' and Their Compatibility with European Union State Aid Rules" in: Kerschner Ina and Somare Maryte (eds), Taxation in a Global Digital Economy, Linde Verlag, Vienna 2017, p. 423.

Zichittella Carlo, "International Initiative in Addressing Challenges Posed by the Digital Economy" in: Kerschner Ina and Somare Maryte (eds), Taxation in a Global Digital Economy, Linde Verlag, Vienna 2017, p. 393.

II.   ARTICLES

Abbott Ryan and Bogenschneider Bret, Should Robots Pay Taxes? Tax Policy in the Age of Automation, 12 Harvard Law & Policy Review 2018, p. 1.

Acemoglu Daron, Manera Andrea and Restrepo Pascual, Taxes, Automation and the Future of Labor, MIT Research Brief 2020.

Ahmed Sami, Cryptocurrency & Robots: How to Tax and Pay Tax on Them, South Carolina Law Review 2018, p. 699.

Alvadaro Mery., Digital Services Taxes across Europe in the Midst and Aftermath of the COVID-19 Pandemic: A Plausible Option to Raise Tax Revenues?, 61 European Taxation 2021, n. 9, p. 4.

Appelby Andrew, Subnational Digital Services Taxation, 81 Maryland Law Review 2021, p. 8.

Aslam Aqib/Shah Alpa, Tec(h)tonic Shifts: Taxing the "Digital Economy", IMF Working Paper, Volume 2020, Issue 076, 29 May 2020.

Atkinson Robert D., The Case against Taxing Robots, ITIF – Information Technology & Innovation Foundation, 8 April 2019, p. 16.

Avi-Yonah Reuven, Globalization, Tax Competition, and the Fiscal Crisis of the Welfare State, 113 Harvard Law Review 2000, p. 1575.

Avi-Yonah Reuven, The International Implications of Wayfair, Tax Notes International, 9 July 2018, p. 161.

Avi-Yonah Reuven, The Structure of International Taxation: A Proposal for Simplification, 74 Texas Law Review 1996, p. 1303.

Avi-Yonah Reuven S. and Halabi Oz, A Model Treaty for the Age of BEPS, University of Michigan Law School, Law and Economics Working Papers, 2014, p. 1 ff, 15.

Bal Aleksandra, Online Marketplaces and EU VAT: Global Reach but Compliance Still Local, Kluwertax blog, Com/2020/02/26.

Bal Aleksandra, VAT and the Metaverse, Taxing Virtual Events (Correct), Daly Tax Report, 30 March 2022.

Balkin Jack, 2016 Sidley Austin Distinguished Lecture on Big Data Law and Policy; The Three Laws of Robotics in the Age of Big Data, 78 Ohio State Law Journal 2017, p. 1217.

Bayern S., The Implications of Modern Business-Entity Law for the Regulation of Autonomous Systems, 19 Stanford Technology Law Review 93 2015, p. 93.

Beck Suzanne, Der Rechtliche Status autonomer Maschinen, AJP/PJA (Pratique Juridique Actuelle) 2017, p. 183.

Beretta Giorgio, VAT on Financial and Insurance Services at the Dawn of the Fourth Industrial Revolution, 29 International VAT Monitor 4 2018.

Blanchard Kimberly, The Tax Significance of Legal Personality: A U.S. View, Colloquium on Tax Policy, 3 February 2015, p. 6.

Brauner Yariv, Taxation of Information and the Data Revolution, SSRN paper, March 2023.

Brauner Yariv and Pistone Pasquale, Some Comments on the Attribution of Profits to the Digital Permanent Establishment, Bulletin for International Taxation, 26 March 2018.

Brauner Yariv and Baez Andres, Withholding Taxes in the Service of BEPS Action 1: Address the Tax Challenge of the Digital Economy, IBFD, 2 February 2015.

Bogenschneider Bret N., Will Robots Agree to Pay Taxes? Further Tax Implications of Advanced AI, 22 North Carolina Journal of Law & Technology 2020, p. 1.

Burri Thomas, The Politics of Robot Autonomy, European Journal of Risk Regulation 2016, p. 341

Calo Ryan, Robotics and the Lessons of Cyberlaw, 103 California Law Review 513, 2015, p. 529.

Calo Ryan, Robots as Legal Metaphors, 30 Harvard Journal of Law & Technology 2016, p. 209.

Candaux Nicolas, Cywie Arnaud and Morel Frédéric, Traitement TVA des prestations de services par Internet, L'Expert Comptable Suisse 2014, p. 698.

Cannas Francesco, The VAT Treatment of Cloud Computing: Legal Issues and Practical Difficulties, World Journal of VAT/GST 2016, p. 92.

Chand Vikram, Kostic Svetislav and Reis Ariene, Taxing Artificial Intelligence and Robots: Critical Assessment of Potential Policy Solutions and Recommendation for Alternative Approaches, 12 World Tax Journal 2020, n. 4.

Damijan Joze P., Damijian Sandra and Vrh Natasa, Tax on Robots: Whether and How Much, Working Paper, Growinpro, March, 39/2021.

Daurer Veronika, Kofler Georg and Mayr Gunter, "Austrian Report" in: IFA, Berlin Congress, Big Data and Tax-Domestic and International Taxation of Data Driven Business, IFA CDFI 2022, vol. 106B, Rotterdam 2022, p. 141.

De la Feria Rita, On the Evolving VAT Concept of Fixed Establishment, EC Tax Review 2021, p. 201.

De la Feria Rita and Grau Amparo Ruiz, "Taxing Robots" in: Grau A. (ed.), Interactive Robotics: Legal, Ethical, Social and Economic Aspects, Springer Nature 2022, Chapter 17.

De la Feria Rita and Schofield M., Towards an (Unlawful) Modernized EU VAT Rate Policy, EC Tax Review 2017, p. 89.

De Lima Carvalho Lucas, Spiritus Ex Machina: Addressing the Unique BEPS Issues of Autonomous Artificial Intelligence by Using "Personality" and "Residence", 47 Intertax 2019, p. 430 ss.

De Lima Carvalho Lucas and Esteche Victor Guilherme, Sentience as a Prerequisite for Taxing AI, 108 Tax Notes International, 5 December 2022, p. 1263.

Dhuldhoya Vishesh, The Future of the Permanent Establishment Concept, 72 Bulletin for International Taxation No. 4a (special issue) 2018.

Ehrke-Rabel Tina and Pfeiffer Sebastian, Umsatzsteuerbarer Leistungsaustausch durch "entgeltlose" digital Dienstleistungen, SWK 2017, p. 533.

Elkins David, Horizontal Equity as a Principle of Tax Theory, 24 Yale Law & Policy Review 2006, p. 43.

Erdogdu M. M. and Karaca C., "The Fourth Industrial Revolution and a Possible Robot Tax" in: Institutions & Economic Policies: Effects on Social Justice, Employment, Environmental Protection & Growth, Ludond 2017, p. 103 ff.

Finley Ryan, Wayfair Decision Echoes Case for Digital PE Standard, Tax Notes International, 2 July 2018, p. 14.

Flückiger Yves and Suarez Javier, "Propositions de réforme du financement de la sécurité sociale en Suisse" in: Greber Pierre-Yves (ed.), La sécurité sociale en Europe à l'aube du XXIe siècle, Helbing & Lichtenhahn, Basel 1996.

Frey Carl Benedict and Osborne Michael A., The Future of Employment: How Susceptible are Jobs to Computerization, 114 Technological Forecasting & Social Changes 2017, p. 254.

Hemel Daniel, Does the Tax Code Favor Robots? 16 The Ohio State Technology Law Journal 2020, p. 220 ff.

Hoke William, Taxing Automations, Tax Notes International, 2 October 2017, p. 11.

Hongler Peter and Pistone Pasquale, IBFD Blueprints for a New PE Nexus to Tax Business Income in the Era of Digital Economy, Working Paper, 20 January 2015.

Hufbauer Gary Clyde and Lu Zhiyao (Lucy), The European Union's Proposed Digital Services Tax: A De Facto Tariff, Policy Brief 18–15, Peterson Institute for International Economics, June 2018.

Hug Thomas, Daten als mehrwertsteuerliches Entgelt? zsis.ch, 2020, p. 7.

Ismer Roland and Jescheck Christoph, The Substantive Scope of Tax Treaties in a Post-BEPS World: Article 2 OECD MC (Taxes Covered and the Rise of New Taxes), Intertax, 2017, p. 382.

Kofler Georg, Mayr Gunter and Schlager Christoph, Taxation of the Digital Economy; "Quick Fixes" or Long-Term Solutions? European Taxation 2017, p. 523.

Korinek Anton, Taxation and the Vanishing Labor Market in the Age of AI, 16.1 The Ohio State Technology Law Journal, 2020, p. 244.

Kornprobst Emmanuel, La notion de services fournis par voie électronique en matière de TVA, Droit fiscal, 21 avril 2016, p. 288.

Kovacev Rob, A Taxing Dilemma: Robot Taxes and the Challenges of Effective Taxation of AI, Automation and Robotics in the Fourth Industrial Revolution, The Ohio State Technology Law Journal 2020, p. 182 ff.

Kudkepp A., Online Platforms are in the VAT Spotlight in the European Union, Bloomberg Daily Tax Report: International, 1 December 2022.

Lafrance Adrienne, What is a Robot? The Atlantic Daily, 22 March 2016.

Lamensch Marie, Adoption of the E-Commerce VAT Package: The Road Ahead is Still a Rocky One, EC Tax Review 2018, p. 186 ff.

Lamensch Marige, "Taxing Digital Supplies" in: Haslehner Werner, Kofler Georg, Pantazou Katerina and Rust Alexander (eds), Tax and the Digital Economy, Series on International Taxation, Wolters Kluwer, The Netherlands 2019, p. 189.

Lexer Georgina Michaela and Scarcella Luisa, Artificial Intelligence and Labor Markets: A Critical Analysis of Solution Models from a Tax Law and Social Security Law Perspective, Rivista Italiana Di Informatica E Diritto, 2019, p. 53 ff.

Li jinyan, Choi Arjin and Smith Cameron, Automation and Workers: Re-Imagining the Income Tax for the Digital Age, Canadian Tax Journal 2020, p. 99.

Lips Wouter, The EU Commission's Digital Tax Proposals and its Cross-platform Impact in the EU and the OECD, Journal of European Integration, 23 December 2019.

Lopucki Lynn, Algorithmic Entities, 95 Washington University Law Review 4, 2018, p. 887 ff.

Mann Roberta F., I Robot: U Tax? Considering the Tax Policy Implications of Automation, 64 McGill Law Journal, June 2019, p. 763.

Mazur Orly, Taxing the Robots, 46 Pepperdine Law Review 2018, p. 1.

Melan Nevada and Wecke Bertram, Umsatzsteuerpflicht von "kostenlosen" Internetdiensten und Smartphone-Apps, Deutsches Steuerrecht 2015, p. 2267, 2811.

Meller Emily and Salom Jessica, Le salaire excessif en droit fiscal suisse, 67 RDAF 2011, p. 105.

Million David, Theories of the Corporation, Duke Law Journal 1990, p. 201 ff.

Müller Melinda F., Roboter und Recht, Pratique Juridique Actuelle (PJA) 2014, p. 597.

Oberson Xavier, How Taxing Robots Could Help Bridge Future Revenue Gap, OECD Yearbook 2017.

Oberson Xavier, Taxing Robots? From the Emergence of an Electronic Ability to Pay to a Tax on Robots or the Use of Robots, 9 World Tax Journal 2017, p. 247.

Oberson Xavier, Taxer les robots? Pratique Juridique Actuelle (PJA/AJP) 2017, p. 232.

Oberson Xavier, Robot Taxes: The Rise of a New Taxpayer, IBFD Bulletin for International Taxation, August 2021, p. 370.

Ooi Vincent, Automation Tax: Adopt with Caution, Austaxpolicy: Tax and Transfer Policy Blog, 27 June 2022, Available at www.austaxpolicy.com/automation-tax-adopt-with-caution/.

Ooi Vincent & Goh Glendon, Taxation of Automation and Artificial Intelligence as a Tool of Labour Policy, eJournal of Tax Research 2022, p. 273.

Owens Jeffrey and Costa Oliveira Nathalia, The Tax Treatment of the Metaverse Economy and the Potential for a New Offshore Tax Haven, Tax Notes International 2022, p. 544.

Pfeiffer Sebastian, VAT on "Free" Electronic Services? International VAT Monitor 2016, p. 158 ff, 161.

Petruzzi Raffaele and Buriak Svitlana, Addressing the Tax Challenges of the Digitalization of the Economy: A Possible Answer in the Proper Application of the Transfer Pricing Rules? 72 Bulletin for International Taxation, No. 4a (special issue) 2018.

Pinkernell Reimar, "Germany Report" in: IFA, Berlin Congress, Big Data and Tax-Domestic and International Taxation of Data Driven Business, IFA CDFI 2022, vol. 106B, Rotterdam 2022, p. 381.

Rosembuj Tuliom, Artificial Intelligence and Taxation, el Fisco, September 2018.

Rosenblatt Gideon, The Robot Tax Fallacy; Anthropomorphizing Automation, Automation, 5 June 2017.

Rosenbloom David H., International Aspects of US Tax Reform: Is This Really Where we Want to Go? International Tax Report, 2 January 2018.

Sakuth Konstantin, "The Concept of Corporate Tax Residence in Light of the Digital Economy" in: Kerschner Ina and Somare Maryte (eds), Taxation in a Global Digital Economy, Linde Verlag, Vienna 2017, p. 83.

Sapirie Marie, Permanent Establishment and the Digital Economy, 72 Bulletin for International Taxation, No. 4a (special issue) 2018.

Schmalenbach-Gesellschaft, Transfer Pricing "Working Group", European Taxation 2020, p. 495.

Sheppard Lee A., Digital Permanent Establishment and Digital Equalization Taxes, 72 Bulletin for International Taxation, No 4a (special issue) 2018.

Shiller Robert J., Robotization without Taxation? Project Syndicate, 22 March 2017, p. 1.

Shome Parthasarathi, Taxation of Robots, ADB The Governance Brief, Issue 44, 2022.

Solum Lawrence B., Legal Personhood for Artificial Intelligences 70 North Carolina Law Review 1992, p. 1231.

Tavani Herman T., Can Social Robots Qualify for Moral Consideration? Reframing the Question about Robot Rights, Information 2018, MDPI, 29 March 2018, Information 9, 73.

Tavares Romero and Owens Jeffrey, Human Capital in Value Creation and Post-BEPS Tax Policy: An Outlook, Bulletin for International Taxation, 2015, p. 590.

Thliveros P., EU OSS & MOSS: A Solution to the Challenges of the Digital Economy? in: Kerschner I. and Somare M. (eds), Taxation in a Global Digital Economy, Linde Verlag, Vienna 2017, p. 393.

Thuemmel Oscar, Optimal Taxation of Robots, University of Zurich, October 2020.

Turing Alan M., Computing Machinery and Intelligence, 59 Mind, New Series, 1950, p. 433.

Uslu Yasin, An Analysis of "Google Taxes" in the Context of Action 7 of the OECD/ G20 Base Erosion and Profit Shifting Initiative, 72 Bulletin for International Taxation, No. 4a, 2018.

Vàzquez Juan Manuel, Digital Services Taxes in the European Union: What Can We Expect? Kluwer International Tax Blog, 14 February 2023.

Wattel Peter and Marres Ottmar, Characterization of Fictitious Income under OECD-Patterned Tax Treaties, European Taxation 2003, p. 67.

Wildhaber Isabelle, Robotik am Arbeitsplatz: Robot-Kollegen und Robot-Bosse, AJP/ PJA (Pratique Juridique Actuelle), 2017, p. 213.

White Josh, The Case against the Robot Tax, International Tax Review, 20 April 2018, p. 1.

Zawodsky Florian, Value Added Taxation in the Digital Economy, British Tax Review 2018, p. 606 ff.

III.   REPORTS, OFFICIAL DOCUMENTS, ETC.

Adler Tibère and Salvi Marco, Quand les robots arrivent, Avenir Suisse, October 2017.

EU Commission, Directorate General Taxation and Custom Union, Explanatory Notes on VAT e-commerce rules, September 2020.

EU Parliament, Commission on Legal Affairs, Draft Report with Recommendations to the Commission on Civil Law rules on Robotics, No 2015/2193(INL), 27 May 2016.

EU Parliament, Report with Recommendations to the Commission on Civil Law Rules on Robotics, No 2015/2193(INL), 27 January 2017.

Gouvernement français, ChatGPT ou la percée des modèles d'IA conversationels, Eclairage sur …, April 2029 #06.

OECD, An Introduction to the Role of Platforms and Their role in the Digital Transformation, May 2019.

OECD, Basic Income as a Policy Option: Can It Add Up? Policy brief on the future of work, May 2017.

OECD/G20 BEPS Project, Addressing the Tax Challenges of the Digital Economy, Action 1, 2015, Final Report.

OECD/G20 BEPS Project, Countering Harmful Tax Practices More Effectively, Taking into Account Transparency and Substance, Action 5, 2015, Final Report.

OECD/G20 BEPS Project, Tax Challenges Arising from Digitalization, Interim Report, 2018.

OECD/G20, Developing a Multilateral Instrument to Modify Bilateral Tax Treaties, Action 15, 2015, Final Report.

OECD, International VAT/GST Guidelines, 2017.

OECD, Model Tax Convention on Income and on Capital, 2017.

OECD/G20, Neutralizing the Effects of Hybrid Mismatch Arrangements, Action 2, 2015, Final Report.

OECD/G20, Preventing the Artificial Avoidance of Permanent Establishment Status, Action 7, 2015, Final Report.

OECD/G20, Preventing the Granting of Treaty Benefits in Inappropriate Circumstances, Action 6, 2015, Final Report.

OECD, Taxation and Employment, Tax Policy Studies No 21, 2011.

OECD/G20, Statement on a Two-Pillar Solution to Address the Tax Challenges Arising from the Digitalization of the Economy, 8 October 2021.

OECD, The Next Production Revolution, Implications for Governments and Business, 2018.

OECD, The Role of Digital Platforms in the Collection of VAT/GST on Online Sales, March 2019.

OECD, Treaty Characterization Issues Arising from e-commerce, July 2005.

OECD, Outcome Statement on the Two-Pillar Solution to Address the Tax Challenges Arising from the Digitalization of the Economy, 11 July 2023.

UN Committee of Experts on International Cooperation in Tax Matters, Tax Challenges in the Digitalized Economy: Selected Issues for Possible Committee Consideration, UN 2017.

UN, Model Double Taxation Convention between Developed and Developing Countries, 2011.

WEF, The Future of Jobs: Employment, Skills and Workforce Strategy for the Fourth Industrial Revolution, Geneva, January 2016.

WEF, The Future of Jobs Report, Centre for the New Economy and Society, Geneva, 2018.

WEF, Future of Jobs Report, May 2023.

Index

Printed and bound by CPI Group (UK) Ltd, Croydon, CR0 4YY